W9-CYF-945

Puppetry In Early Childhood Education

by Tamara Hunt and Nancy Renfro

Nancy Renfro Studios

Other books published by Nancy Renfro Studios
Puppetry in Education Series

A PUPPET CORNER IN EVERY LIBRARY

PUPPETRY AND THE ART OF STORY CREATION

PUPPETRY AND CREATIVE DRAMATICS IN STORYTELLING

MAKE AMAZING PUPPETS (Learning Works)

Copyright © 1982 Tamara Hunt and Nancy Renfro
all rights reserved

The authors, however, grant permission for patterns and drawings shown in this book to be reproduced for use in **non-profit** puppet activities in the classroom, church, library, theater or recreational areas. No part of this publication may be reproduced or transmitted in any form or means (electronic, mechanical, photocopying, recording or by any information storage or retrieval system) for any other purposes without the written permission from Nancy Renfro Studios

Published in the United States of America by
Nancy Renfro Studios   1117 W. 9th Street, Austin Texas 78703

Library of Congress
PN1979.E4H8   372.1´3078   81-85786

All photographs by Tamara Hunt unless otherwise noted
All puppets by Nancy Renfro Studios unless otherwise noted
All illustrations by Nancy Renfro

Cover Credit
Front: paper plate "Rainbow" puppet, paper "Family" glove puppet and "Sue Snake" puppet by Nancy Renfro Studios
Back: Tamara Hunt with Nerf Ball Pumpkin

For My Parents

Max and Jeannette Miller

This book is a search into a single art form—puppetry, and how that art form can be integrated into the entire spectrum of a multi-sensory learning experience on a day to day basis. We believe, also, that it can serve as a model, both in its conceptualization and spirit for similar searches into other forms of art.

Tamara Hunt and Nancy Renfro

Foreword

My students in the early childhood teacher education program at the University of Hawaii are very lucky to have the opportunity to take a course in puppetry for young children from Tamara Hunt. I have been impressed by the students' enthusiasm for the subject, by the charming and original puppets and creative story aprons they make, and the skill and exuberance with which they share their creations in my classes. The joyful spirit of their involvement has been captured in this collaboration between Tamara Hunt and Nancy Renfro in their book *Puppetry in Early Childhood Education*. As an early childhood educator, I especially appreciate the emphasis on process rather than product, the concern for the development of creativity in children and in teachers, and the deep respect for children as people in the process of development.

Children love puppets. My college students love puppets. And I think many more teachers will learn to love puppets when they discover their natural and joyful contribution in working with children through the simple and effective approaches presented in this book.

Stephanie Feeney
Associate Professor
Department of Curriculum and Instruction
University of Hawaii

Editor's Note:

Every child, male or female, has an enormous potential which begs to be realized. Therefore, in an effort to make the text, as well as the content, completely non-sexist, the dominant gender is switched from masculine to feminine, so as to avoid reading what "he" does on every page.

It did not seem quite right, however, to feminize all the personal pronouns, thereby committing the same injustice to men as has been committed to women by the exclusive use of the single-gender pronoun, whether that pronoun be "he" or "she." Therefore, until a good neutral term is developed in English to replace the cumbersome "he/she" combination, I have chosen to use the rather inconsistent but certainly well-intentioned method of switching genders throughout the text in order to achieve a note of balance. The reader's tolerance, and/or suggestions, are hereby requested.

Ann Weiss Schwalb
Chief Editor

The Schools
Capital Area Rehabilitation Center, Austin, Texas
The Children's Montessori School, Austin, Texas
Clara Barton Pre-School, Fullerton, California
The Early School, Honolulu, Hawaii
The Family Learning Center, Honolulu, Hawaii
Hale Pua Lei, Honolulu, Hawaii
Hokulani Elementary School, Honolulu, Hawaii
Leny Kam's Family Day Care, Honolulu, Hawaii
North Slope Borough School, Barrow, Alaska
Parent Participation Nursery School, Kaneohe, Hawaii

The Teachers
Mary Craven
Michelle Coleman
Tamara Hunt
Anna Fleming
Joy Kouts
Marcus Pottinger
Iris Shimizu
Grace Schmitt
Ellen Turner Scott
Debbie Sullivan
Sherri Wallin
Marie Wilson
Helen Winberg
Janie Wright
Kathryn Wright
George Yokoyama
Sharon Tyau
Joan Yonemitsu

The Photographers
Robert W. Bethune
Arman Kitapci
John Hunt
Tamara Hunt
Robert Renfro
Ann Weiss Schwalb

Additional Participants
Matthew Cardenas
Jeany Coleman
Eleanor Click
Baxter A. Kootchook
Julia Schwalb
Rebecca Schwalb

Acknowledgments

What began as a casual communication between two puppet "enthusiasts" working in disparate parts of the world—Hawaii and Texas—soon resulted in an accumulation of material enough for several books. Our similar interest in education for the very young and the potential of puppetry for achieving that goal, triggered an avalanche of creative output and a smooth melding of ideas that, to me, has been a rarity in my many collaborations.

Becoming acquainted with Tamara Hunt's extraordinary sensitivity to young children and their processes for learning has been a richly rewarding experience. Most of the written material is hers. Whatever role I serve as designer, illustrator and co-author grew from her initial structure and terminology.

I sincerely thank the teachers and librarians in all my workshops who continue to inspire me and know how to "share" generously!

I would also like to thank Robert T. Renfro, my husband, and Helen Winberg and Lala Renfro, my mother and mother-in-law for their continual faith in my work; Ann Weiss Schwalb, an enduring friend, consultant and chief editor for supporting my aspirations and helping me to launch my publications; Irma Goldbloom who shared my first puppetry experiences and whose gifts as a creative teacher of young children continue to inspire me; Joanne Click, my associate, for her editorial assistance and graphic arts design and help in our entire Studios; Anne Bustard for her talents in compiling and organizing the various final bibliographies throughout this book; also all the very capable, enthusiastic members of our puppetmaking team who have carried on business as usual with diligence and dedication.

Nancy Renfro

At the University of Hawaii I would like to thank all my students for sharing their ideas and motivating me to be a more creative teacher.

Especially appreciated are Maxine Nu'uhiwa, Naomi Okuma and Cheryl Willoughby for their assistance in compiling the bibliographies of children's books. Also my department chairperson, Dr. Edward Langhans for his advice and support and our secretary Nancy Takei who has assisted me in so many little ways along the way.

I am indebted to my dear friend Mary Craven who opened the doors of her school for my very first puppetry experiences with young children and has continued to give me encouragement throughout the writing of this book; the staff at The Early School for providing me with space to set up a Puppet Corner and try out new ideas, and to Joan Yonemitsu and Marjorie Doi for inviting me into their kindergarten classes at Hokulani Elementary School to photograph the children.

My deepest appreciation goes to my husband, John Hunt, whose continued love and support enables me to fulfill so many dreams, both professional and personal; my children, Ian and Tara, who inspired me to write the book and helped me to discover the real value of puppetry in the lives of young children; my parents, Max and Jeannette Miller, to whom this book is dedicated. They gave me a childhood rich in the kind of freedom that encourages personal growth and creative expression; And, of course to my collaborator, Nancy Renfro, who saw the potential in my ideas and so graciously invited me into her "family" of authors.

Dr. Tamara Hunt
Associate Professor of Theatre
University of Hawaii
Honolulu, Hawaii

Table of Contents

Part I

This "friend" is privy to the child's inner world

INTRODUCTION

"Each second we live is a new and unique moment of the universe, a moment that never was before and never will be again. And what do we teach our children? When will we teach them what they are: You are a marvel. You are unique. In all the world there is no other child exactly like you."

Pablo Casals

The inexpungeable stamp of individuality begins at an early age; at the moment of birth it emerges, to be formulated by a lifetime's turbulent processes. The process of education plays a key role in the shaping of the child and takes liberties in either fostering or inhibiting the sense of "uniqueness" inherent to every individual. The early years are perhaps the most crucial period in the development of any child; it is here that patterning begins and the personality is at its most malleable, a stage at which the tools of learning can make their greatest impact. The young child's mind is a "magic window" through which beauty, ideas and concepts can be enjoyed simply by opening the eyes. Children are explorers of many languages involving color and texture, forms and shapes, pattern and body movements, speech and sound. These "languages" are the basic raw materials for shaping the child into a unique human being. Puppetry offers a magnificent opportunity to serve the teacher as a tool in broadening these dimensions, offering a great degree of flexibility in meeting the requirements of the class-

room as well as discovering the sense of uniquity in both child and teacher.

For the child, the introduction of puppets can create a fresh and creative learning environment. Young children can generally accept the puppet as a non-threatening, sympathetic friend to whom they can entrust their thoughts and feelings without fear of ridicule or reprimand. This "friend" is privy to the child's inner world and is able also to communicate with the outer world as an intermediary. It is perhaps here that the teacher finds in puppetry its most valuable asset for contributing to the process of education. A skillful teacher can take advantage of special moments of puppet-inspired communication to tune into the child's thinking and to open up new avenues for learning. On an informal play level, the child can use puppets to discover ideas and concepts in an unstructured, free manner; while in a more structured and directed teaching situation, the educator can employ puppets to accomplish specific goals such as reinforcing colors, numbers, words and such. Incorporation of both methods will lead to a balance of teaching procedures for which this book offers supporting material.

For the teacher, the adaptation of puppets in the curriculum offers a creative approach to soften the constraints of a purely academic program. The puppet, in pursuit of this goal, is a legitimate tool that is at once visual, audio and tactile. Sesame Street has proven that children learn faster and better through the reinforcement of additional sensory impressions. The young child is at a developmental level which exploration of the senses is at an apex. Puppetry offers a means by which maximum educational benefits may be derived by heightening a child's sensorial receptiveness.

If the child thinks it looks like a lion, then let us call it so!

18

CREATIVE PUPPETRY
The Puppet as a Process

In education today, a great deal of emphasis is placed upon the finished product rather than the process of creation. For the artist and for the child the activity itself, whether it is the creation of a drawing, a dance or a puppet, is one of the highest joys to be achieved. It is here that the most valuable learning occurs. The completed project is simply the conclusion of this creation process: it is anticlimactic to the total scheme of things insofar as the child is concerned. Moreover as an artifact, capable of being compared, it opens the child up for possible criticism. How often in many well-intentioned ways, are remarks offered that imply judgment, for example: "That lion does not look like a lion, dear," or "Grass isn't blue, is it?" Thus as the child grows older, little by little, the artist within her shrinks and the joyful experience of creation gives way to the production of standardized objects that more nearly conform to society's expectations. By the time the child reaches adulthood, her ability to be creative has been squashed—literally undone. Hence, it is extremely important in working with young children to approach puppetry *as a process* in which the making and using of puppets assumes preeminence over the puppet as a finished product. If the child thinks it looks like a lion, then let us call it so!

Definition of Terms

Creative puppetry, like its counterpart in the other arts, espouses a definite philosophy and a variety of techniques for use with children. The following definition of terms were designed specifically for the early childhood teacher and offer a new vocabulary for which to structure and integrate classroom material:

● **Puppet Play** (i.e. playing with puppets) is the simplest form of puppetry which, like dramatic play, occurs spontaneously and without adult intervention. A child may talk freely to a puppet, two children may interact with each other's puppets or several children may experiment with puppets in front of a mirror or behind a make-shift stage.

● **Puppetizing** is closely supervised by one or more adults who apply creative dramatic techniques to direct children in the use of puppets for acting out stories, poems, songs and such. With puppetization there is neither audience or stage; the children merely perform informally for one another.

● **Puppetelling** involves the use of puppets by the teacher to make music and literature visually exciting, to enrich storyhours and to stimulate an appreciation of literature. A monkey puppet can mischievously turn the pages of H.A. Rey's *Curious George* or a Santa puppet can merrily direct Christmas carol singalongs with the children.

● **Puppetalking** employs puppets on a one-to-one basis to encourage conversations related to social and emotional growth. A classroom "mascot" puppet might welcome new children on the first day of school while a nurse puppet can entice a child to talk about a forthcoming surgery.

● **Puppeteaching** uses puppets to facilitate the acquisition of knowledge and skills. Rainbow puppets aid in color identification while inchworm-metric fingerpuppets reinforce concepts of measurement.

Regardless of the kinds of puppets created or the ways in which they are used, there are several factors in creative puppetry that remain constant. There must always be (1) a child or group of children, (2) a teacher or leader who participates directly or indirectly in the puppetry activities, (3) puppets that are child-made, adult-made or store-bought, (4) a physical space such as a Puppet Corner for making and using puppets and (5) an environment that reflects a process-oriented approach to puppetry.

The Child

There is a place for puppets in every child's life. Children are naturally drawn to puppets and never tire of playing with them or watching them perform. In creative puppetry the role of the child is simply to be there. Few expectations should be placed on the child other than to be sincere in his or her own creative output and to respect others' ideas and creations. Since children need latitude to develop their potential through puppetry, we must constantly remind ourselves that the child is a participant, not a performer, and that it is the creative process, not the product, that counts.

It is important also that children be sincerely acknowledged for their individual efforts and contributions. Remember there is no *norm* in creativity. Every child is an individual and should be encouraged to make puppets and create characterizations in her own special way.

Among the many values attributed to creative puppetry, the following stand out as being especially significant for the child.

● **Enhances positive self-concept.** Children involved in creative puppetry quickly learn to perceive of themselves as people and artists whose creations are unique. Helping a child to feel good about what she thinks and does fosters a sense of inner-confidence and self-worth.

● **Encourages language development through verbal expression.** As soon as a child physically picks up a puppet, he wants to make it talk. By giving it a voice, he also gives it life. In the Puppet Corner children will experiment without inhibition using different vocal sounds and character voices (high, low, cackly, husky, old, silly, stern, royal, etc.). No other form of expression, except creative dramatics, offers such a broad range of opportunities for verbal experimentation. Language development follows logically as the children encounter new and challenging situations in which their puppets can talk and interact with one another.

● **Provides acceptable avenues for releasing emotions.** The many, diverse feelings a young child experiences daily (e.g., anger, joy, sadness, fear, etc.) need healthy outlets for release. With a puppet on hand, a child can practice saying what he feels. "Don't do that" can replace a punch "Move, please" can supplant a shove. Children can also redirect their feelings through puppets. An angry or sad child can "talk out" his innermost concerns through the puppet without ever claiming personal responsibility for what the puppet says. Just being a character in a make-believe conflict can release antagonisms that a child is unconsciously experiencing in her life. Loud, boisterous "wild thing" puppets can substitute for aggressive actions toward other people.

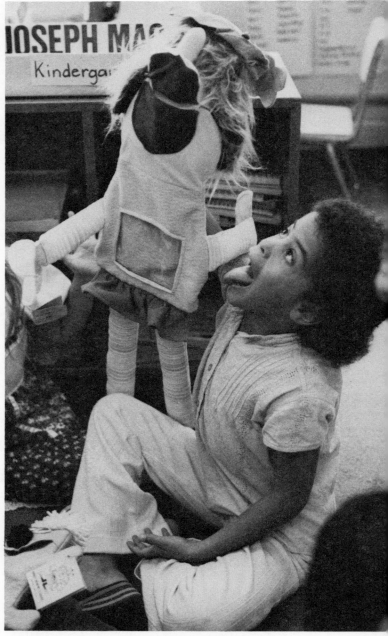

Children are explorers of many languages.

20

● **Builds social skills.** The nature of creative puppetry as a group activity requires that young children listen to each other, take turns, observe, respect and accept one another's ideas, feelings and creations. Since cooperation is essential for the activity to succeed, children are motivated to develop those skills necessary for positive group interaction.

● **Enables children to experience life situations.** Wouldn't it be nice if we could rehearse our life before we lived it, if we could meet new situations with a sense of preparedness because we had practiced them before they actually occurred? One advantage of creative puppetry is that it offers the child a chance to experience life events vicariously. While the child may never meet the "Troll" of *Three Billy Goats Gruff*,

he may certainly run into a neighborhood bully with demands equally devastating. The young child's practice in thinking quickly and expressing ideas will help him to face many daily experiences with more confidence and self assurance than if he had had no preparation whatsoever.

● **Helps children distinguish between fantasy and reality.** One of the most difficult tasks for young children is to determine what is real in their world and what is not. One way they accomplish this delineation is through dramatic or fantasy play. They act out what they have seen or heard by testing their own abilities and exploring the limits of their environments. Puppets are especially helpful in that

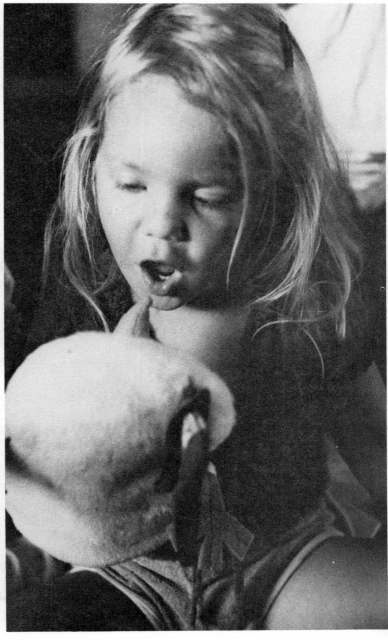

they encourage children to verbalize their inner confusions about reality. Puppets also perform in ways children *wish* they could but know they cannot. For example, puppets fly, engage in battle without injury and demonstrate super strengths and intelligence, while a child can only dream of such powers.

Even the simple act of bringing a puppet to life is an exercise in fantasy and reality. A child sees the puppet limp and lifeless on the table. Suddenly, through the child's own initiation, the puppet takes on a life and personality of its own. The very act of controlling what the puppet says and does is in itself a subtle message that things are not always what they seem to be.

The Teacher

Whether you are a curriculum specialist, art or drama specialist, student teacher, teacher's aide or a daily classroom teacher, there is a place for puppets in your work with children. The degree of personal involvement will depend in part upon the type of setting you choose and the specific activity planned. Indirect involvement is felt mostly in the Puppet Corner where Puppet Play is encouraged with the placement of puppets, puppet-making materials and related objects such as books and props. Simply through the arrangement of these objects you will subtly control and shape the quality of the children's activity. At Easter, for instance, you might put several bunny puppets in the Puppet Corner or even

Suddenly you are a "Puppet Person", a teller of tales, a maker of magic!

22

provide paper bags and pre-cut ears for the children to make their own. Then by displaying several books such as Margaret Wise Brown's *The Runaway Bunny,* Carolyn S. Bailey's *The Rabbit Who Wanted Red Wings,* and Beatrix Potter's *The Tale of Peter Rabbit,* you will inspire ideas for ways children can use the puppets.

More direct involvement occurs when the teacher-leader elects to interact with one or more children. You may use a puppet on an individual basis to encourage conversation with a child who seems reticent. Or after observing several children inter-acting with puppets, you may put on a puppet yourself and enter spontaneously into their improvisations. Another form of direct involvement is achieved in guiding a larger group through the Puppetization of a favorite song or story.

Regardless of the type of interaction chosen, there are numerous benefits that will come to you as a teacher.

● **Provides increased understanding of the child.** Puppets lead to a better understanding of young children in that feelings and thoughts can be transmitted through the medium of a puppet. The more you know about a child, the easier it is to facilitate her growth as a self-confident, fulfilled and creative individual. While playing with puppet characters, children often reveal information about their home relationships, personal concerns or fears and fantasy wishes. Even the less-verbal child may become surprisingly fluent when operating through the medium of a puppet.

● **Enables children to see you differently.** By participating in Puppet Play you may strengthen and even change your relationship with the children. Suddenly you become a "puppet person," a teller of tales, a maker of magic! The children see you as a teacher who brings pleasure and excitement to the day's activities, someone who genuinely shares the mutual enjoyment of dramatic play.

● **Enhances your own creativity.** Each of us is a creative being; the trick is to recognize our potential and learn to tap our hidden resources. Regardless of how long you have taught, by making puppets and using them with the children, you will discover in yourself hidden talents as an artist, performer and educator.

● **Provides alternative learning experiences.** Those who work with young children know

that equal importance must be given to the major areas of growth and development: the cognitive, social, emotional and physical aspects of the individual. Puppets can be easily integrated into these four areas and greatly enrich the content as well as the quality of the learning experience. For example, the identification of new words can be made more exciting when a "word-eater puppet" gobbles up the correct answers. A mechanical skill, such as scissor cutting is more fun when a child cuts a paper head for a puppet. Problem-solving techniques can be practiced ahead of time through Puppet Play, thus minimizing daily squabbles over objects and equipment. If a child is encouraged to inform a puppet, instead of an adult, about a particular concern, she may be more willing to reveal feelings and thoughts.

● **Provides an atmosphere of fun.** In a society where the educational system strongly rewards cognitive accomplishments, it is sometimes difficult to justify those activities that appear to develop only the affective domain of the child. Yet the affective or "feeling" side of the child is equally important and must be nurtured in early years by sensitive, caring teachers.

One never needs an excuse to engage children in puppetry activities. The value of the experience will be reflected by the children with their entire beings, the energy of their bodies, the excitement in their voices and the attentiveness of their minds. Puppets give pleasure and where there is pleasure, there are also opportunities for learning.

The Puppets

Puppets may be used effectively as visual tools to enhance curriculum, to stimulate verbal communication or just for fun. Usually puppets are viewed as facilitators in learning situations because of the tremendous identification children feel toward them. When making puppets, emphasis should never be placed on artistic merits but rather on the child's perception of his work. It is not what the puppet looks like that counts but rather how the child feels about the puppet. Remember, a child-made rabbit puppet does not have to look like a real rabbit—the child needs only to believe in it as a rabbit.

Any puppet that can be manipulated by a young child is suitable for creative puppetry: a simple marionette, a basic hand/mitt puppet or any variety of finger puppets. Puppets can be store-bought, teacher-made or child-made. However, young children do have a special fondness for soft cuddly puppets that convey the tactile warmth of stuffed animals.

puppets by Nancy Renfro Studios

24

The Physical Space

Creative puppetry generally involves two kinds of physical arrangements: one for *making* puppets and one for *using* puppets. Puppet construction is best done on a large table, similar to an art table. The amount of space needed for using puppets depends on the type of activity being planned. Small group activities of three to four children can take place in a small corner of the classroom, perhaps shared alternately with the reading or block corner. Large group activities such as story sessions, circle times and Puppetizations are best performed in spacious carpeted areas where children can sit comfortably and move about freely. If necessary, a nice shady tree would be quite acceptable. A space for making and using puppets actually can be anywhere as it is basically a place for people to come together and share in the fun of creating.

The Environment

Besides the tangible requirements of teacher, child, puppet and space, there is a fifth essential element: the environment. Creative puppetry cannot occur unless there is a psychological atmosphere free from failure and those traditional ideas of only "one right way" with everything else, by implication, considered wrong. Whatever a child produces, so long as it is candid and honest, should meet your expectations. Furthermore, the work of one child is never better than that of another—it is only different.

As the teacher, you must establish the environment. By enthusiastically accepting all sincerely produced creations and ideas you can eliminate the fear of error in the minds of the children. *A child who is free from failure is also free to experiment*, to find new ways of making puppets and to engage in Puppet Play. In essence, such freedom is at the core of creativity. An atmosphere of creativity in your environment may have a lifelong effect on a child's perception of learning and the entire process of education itself.

Books on Creative Puppetry

Jenkins, Peggy D., *The Magic of Puppetry: A Guide for Those Working With Young Children*—A useful book for anyone engaging children in creative puppetry. Written with sensitivity to the role puppets can play in children's lives, covering values and use of puppets in home, school, and elsewhere. Englewood Cliffs, New Jersey, Prentice-Hall, 1980.

25

A Puppet Clothesline

Photos by Ann Weiss Schwalb

PUPPET PLAYING
An Informal Puppet Corner

Creating a play environment through the selection of puppets can vivify the classroom, adding color, animation and a new focus where informal play can evolve. Such play is not usually teacher-directed but instead has a life and direction originating from the children themselves. Establishing a Puppet Corner in which the children can interact with puppets is one of the best and simplest methods to introduce children to the art of puppetry.

In setting up your Puppet Corner consider available space, possible stages and appropriate ways to display, use and store puppets.

Space

The first question to ask is: Where can I put a Puppet Corner? Remember the Puppet Corner is basically a place where children engage in spontaneous dramatic play by making and using puppets. Look for an inviting location away from main traffic patterns. If possible, find a carpeted area that can accommodate a small, low table and will enable four or five children to move about comfortably. Ordinary floor-space is adequate if paper is spread out for making puppets and an area is set aside for performing and playing with puppets. If you are among the fortunate few who have a large school or classroom, you may wish to partition off an area exclusively for the use of puppets. If your overall space is limited, then select a multi-purpose reading or dress-up corner or, as mentioned above, an open space that can be converted to accommodate puppet activities.

27

Simple Stages—appliance boxes

Circus Tent

Santa's Workshop

Shapeland
refrigerator carton

28

Simple Stages

A simple stage can add a playful touch to the Puppet Corner and provide a defined area where children may act out stories informally. If your budget does not permit the purchase of a store-bought or custom-built stage, you may easily construct a makeshift box-stage from a washing machine, television or refrigerator carton obtained from a local appliance store. Remove the entire back of the box and cut out a window area in front. Decorate the outside with paint, wallpaper or contact paper to create a school house, space ship or a forest. Any scene will enliven the play area and the box-stage serve to double-purpose as a crawl through toy.

Other types of quick stages you may wish to consider include a table turned onto its side with scenery taped to the front; a stick covered with fabric and stretched between the backs of two chairs or an instant chair stage. Some play centers already have small-scale play structures with windows that may easily function as puppet-theater openings.

Chair stage

Stick stage

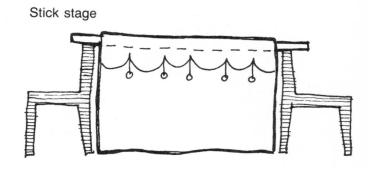

Table stage

Alternatives To Stages

Because Puppet Playing focuses on personal expression and small group interaction, alternatives to conventional stages are often more effective for stimulating dramatic play while de-emphasizing the notion of a formal performance as suggested by a stage.

- **Mirrors.** A large mirror fastened to a wall or panel will enable the children to see themselves operating their puppets. Not only do children love watching their reflections, but they derive positive self-concepts in becoming aware of their own personal roles as creators, as the generators of ideas, words and actions that they themselves are able to translate through the medium of puppetry.

- **Table Tops or Floor Spaces.** Table tops, especially round ones, provide excellent surfaces upon which to manipulate puppets. Seated around a table, interaction between children and puppets, as well as children and children, is casual and relaxed. This arrangement also offers flexibility to accommodate new children who may want to join the Puppet Playing. Cover the table or floor with a large piece of paper (mural paper, plain newsprint or anything similar) and let the children draw scenes of jungles, farms, cities, ponds, etc. Add three-dimensional trees, flowers, buildings or bridges made from paper plates, construction paper and discarded items to make inviting environments through which the puppets may wander.

Three Billy Goats Gruff with walking finger puppets

Puppets and toy props

30

A special wheelchair puppet stage by Nancy Renfro Studios.

Table top theaters also offer an excellent vehicle for handicapped children to participate in wheelchair style puppetry. Prop puppets up over a stand or plastic bottles weighted with sand for children to maneuver.

Formal Stages

If by chance a ready-made puppet stage is already at your disposal, it will undoubtedly find its proper niche in the Puppet Corner. Children particularly delight in stages with a curtain that opens and closes by means of a drapery cord. The advantage of a ready-made stage is its permanency and durability. Some toy shops sell stages. Or you may want to ask a local handyperson or carpenter to build a simple stage from plywood or masonite.

Puppets

Take an inventory to determine what puppets are already in your collection. Divide them into groups of animals, people, insects, etc. Once the puppets are organized, it is possible to set them out in small groups and alternate them on a regular basis so that the children have new characters with which to work.

You may wish to encourage Puppet Play based on literature. Familiar picture books provide a good source for launching ideas. By placing corresponding puppets nearby, you subtly invite the children to improvise and verbalize what they have already discovered in a book. Owl, tiger and bear puppets make a perfect combination for A. A. Milnes' *Winnie-the-Pooh*. By grouping puppets, you will be surprised as to how many corresponding book-and-puppet sets already exist at your school.

Holiday themes can be reinforced in the Puppet Corner. On Saint Patrick's Day, for instance, put out all the green puppets; on Valentine's Day, choose the red and pink ones; on Easter, display the rabbits and chicks. Seasonal themes can be suggested by winter characters such as Santa, snowmen and elves and spring by flowers, birds and butterflies. Perhaps your weekly curriculum activity is based upon the letters of the alphabet. If so, during "B" week set out bears, butterflies, bunnies and bugs; during "M" week set out monkeys, mice and moose puppets. Trust your own imagination and inventiveness to find clever ways to adapt puppets thematically.

When purchasing puppets, select those that are durable and if possible, washable. Avoid puppets made of felt since the fabric will wear out quickly with repeated use; cloth or crocheted puppets are usually long-lasting. Start with a collection of popular animals, community helpers and a set of people puppets that can serve as family members or be converted into fantasy characters. Check the Appendix of this book for puppet suppliers.

Simple Puppetmaking activities can be set up for the children to do by themselves in the Puppet Corner. Paper bags, a basket of felt-tip pens or crayons require minimal supervision and are practical for making instant puppets. A low table can double for both Puppetmaking and Puppet Playing!

The Farm

Colors

Letter "B"

Cooking

Matching Books with Puppets

The following represents a list of popular children's books suitable for matching with puppets for table-top theme displays or storytelling purposes:

Alligators/Crocodiles

Aliki. *Keep Your Mouth Closed, Dear.* New York: Dial, 1966.

DeGroat, Diane. *The Alligator's Toothache.* New York: Crown, 1977.

De Paola, Tomie. *Bill and Pete.* New York: Putnam, 1978.

Duvoisin, Roger. *The Crocodile in the Tree.* New York: Knopf, 1973.

Duvoisin, Roger. *Crocus.* New York: Knopf, 1977.

Marshall, James. *Willis.* Boston: Houghton Mifflin, 1974.

Peterson, Esther. *Frederick's Alligator.* New York: Scholastic, 1979.

Reinach, Jacquelyn. *Who Stole Alligator's Shoe.* New York: Holt, Rinehart, and Winston, 1977.

Shaw, Evelyn. *Alligator.* New York: Harper and Row, 1972.

Venable, Alan. *The Checker Players.* New York: Lippincott, 1973.

Waber, Bernard. *Lovable Lyle.* Boston: Houghton Mifflin, 1969.

Ants

Cameron, Polly. *I Can't Said the Ant.* New York: Coward, 1961.

Myrick, Mildred. *Ants Are Fun.* New York: Harper and Row, 1968.

Wolkstein, Diane. *The Visit.* New York: Knopf, 1977.

Anteaters

Waber, Bernard. *An Anteater Named Arthur.* Boston: Houghton Mifflin, 1967.

Armadillos

Hopf, Alice L. *Biography of an Armadillo.* New York: Putnam, 1976.

Badgers

Hoban, Russell. *Bread and Jam for Frances.* (series) New York: Harper and Row, 1964.

Bats

Kaufmann, John. *Bats in the Dark.* New York: T. Y. Crowell, 1972.

Bears

Alexander, Martha. *Blackboard Bear.* New York: Dial, 1969.

Bach, Alice. *Smartest Bear and His Brother Oliver.* New York: Harper and Row, 1975.

Berenstain, Stan and Janice Berenstain. *Bear's Picnic.* (series) New York: Beginner, 1966.

Bethell, Jean. *Look Who's Taking a Bath.* New York: Scholastic, 1979.

Bond, Michael. *Paddington's Garden.* (series) New York: Random, 1973.

Bonners, Susan. *Panda.* New York: Delacorte, 1978.

Duvoisin, Roger. *Snowy and Woody.* New York: Knopf, 1979.

Flack, Marjorie. *Ask Mr. Bear.* New York: Macmillan, 1958.

Freeman, Don. *Corduroy.* (series) New York: Viking, 1968.

Galdone, Paul. *The Three Bears.* Boston: Houghton Mifflin, 1972.

Gross, Ruth. *A Book About Pandas.* New York: Scholastic, 1972.

Gross, Ruth B. *A Book About Pandas.* New York: Dial, 1973.

Hoban, Lillian. *Arthur's Honey Bear.* New York: Harper and Row, 1974.

Hoff, Syd. *Grizzwold.* New York: Harper and Row, 1963.

Margolis, Richard. *Wish Again, Big Bear.* New York: Macmillan, 1972.

McClosky, Robert. *Blueberries for Sal.* New York: Viking, 1948.

Milne, A. A. *Winnie the Pooh.* New York: Dutton, 1971.

Minarik, Else H. *Little Bear.* (series) New York: Harper and Row, 1957.

Peet, Bill. *Big Bad Bruce.* Boston: Houghton Mifflin, 1977.

Reinach, Jacquelyn. *Scaredy Bear.* New York: Holt, Rinehart, and Winston, 1978.

Ward, Lynd. *The Biggest Bear.* Boston: Houghton Mifflin, 1952.

Weinberg, Lawrence. *The Forgetful Bears.* New York: Scholastic, 1981.

Wildsmith, Brian. *Lazy Bear.* New York: Watts, 1974.

Winter, Paula. *The Bear and the Fly.* New York: Scholastic, 1976.

Bees

Barton, Byron. *Buzz, Buzz, Buzz!* New York: MacMillan, 1973.

Carle, Eric. *The Honeybee and the Robber.* New York: Philomel, 1981.

Hawes, Judy. *Bees and Beelines.* New York: T. Y. Crowell, 1964.

Russell, Franklin. *The Honeybees.* New York: Knopf, 1967.

Wahl, Jan. *Follow Me Cried the Bee.* New York: Crown, 1976.

Birds

Eastman, Philip D. *Are You My Mother?* New York: Beginner, 1960.

Eastman, Philip D. *Best Nest.* New York: Beginner, 1968.

Fisher, Aiken. *Filling the Bill.* Los Angeles, CA: Bowmar-Noble, 1973.

Freeman, Don. *Fly High, Fly Low.* New York: Viking, 1957.

Gans, Roma. *Birds at Night.* T. Y. Crowell, 1968.

Hefter, Richard. *Kiss Me, I'm Vulture.* New York: Holt, Rinehart, and Winston, 1978.

Hefter, Richard. *Stork Spills the Beans.* New York: Holt, Rinehart, and Winston, 1977.

Hurd, Edith T. *Look for a Bird.* New York: Harper and Row, 1977.

Massie, Diane. *The Baby Beebee Bird.* New York: Harper and Row, 1979.

Nicklewiczowa, Maria. *A Sparrow's Magic.* New York: Scholastic, 1970.

Rabinowitz, Sandy. *The Red Horse and the Bluebird.* New York: Harper and Row, 1975.

Reinach, Jacquelyn. *Nuts to Nightingale.* New York: Holt, Rinehart, and Winston, 1978.

Reinach, Jacquelyn. *Quail Can't Decide.* New York: Holt, Rinehart, and Winston, 1977.

Rossetti, Christina. *What is Pink?* New York: Macmillan, 1971.

Stone, Harris A. *Last Free Bird.* Englewood Cliffs, NJ: Prentice-Hall, 1967.

Velthuijs, Max. *The Painter and the Bird*. Reading, MA: Addison Wesley, 1975.

Weiss, Leatie. *Heather's Feathers*. New York: Avon, 1978.

Butterflies

Carle, Eric. *The Very Hungry Caterpillar*. New York: Philomel, 1969.

Garelick, May. *Where Does the Butterfly Go When It Rains?* Reading, MA: Addison Wesley, 1961.

Kennedy, Mary. *Wings*. New York: Scholastic, 1980.

Camels/Dromedaries

Disney, Walt. *How the Camel Got His Hump*. New York: Western, 1976.

Freschet, Berniece. *Happy Dromedary*. New York: Scribner, 1977.

Kipling, Rudyard. "How the Camel Got His Hump" from *Just So Stories*. New York: Doubleday, 1946.

Reinach, Jacquelyn. *Fixed by Camel*. New York: Holt, Rinehart and Winston, 1977.

Swindells, R. *The Very Special Baby*. Englewood Cliffs, NJ: Prentice-Hall, 1978.

Tworkov, Jack. *The Camel Who Took a Walk*. New York: Dutton, 1974.

Waters, John F. *Camels: Ships of the Desert*. New York: T. Y. Crowell, 1974.

Cats

Blegvad, Lenore. *Mittens for Kittens, And Other Rhymes About Cats*. New York: Atheneum, 1974.

Brown, Margaret W. *When the Wind Blew*. New York: Harper and Row, 1977.

Calhoun, Mary. *Audubon Cat*. New York: Morrow, 1981.

Carter, Angela. *Comic and Curious Cats*. New York: Crown, 1979.

Charles, Donald. *Calico Cat Looks Around*. (series) Chicago: Childrens Press, 1975.

Gag, Wanda. *Millions of Cats*. New York: Coward, 1928.

Galdone, Paul. *Puss in Boots*. Boston: Houghton Mifflin, 1976.

Gantos, Jack. *Rotten Ralph*. Boston: Houghton Mifflin, 1976.

Mayer, Mercer. *The Great Cat Chase*. New York: Scholastic, 1975.

Seuss, Dr. *The Cat in the Hat*. New York: Beginner, 1957.

Weil, Lisl. *Walt and Pepper*. New York: Scholastic, 1974.

Chameleons

Carle, Eric. *The Mixed Up Cameleon*. New York: T. Y. Crowell, 1975.

Lionni, Leo. *A Color of His Own*. New York: Pantheon, 1976.

Massie, Diane. *Chameleon Was a Spy*. New York: Scholastic, 1979.

Chickens/Roosters

Ginsburg, Mirra. *Chick and the Duckling*. New York: Macmillan, 1972.

Hartelius, Margaret A. *Chicken's Child*. New York: Scholastic, 1977.

Hutchins, Pat. *Rosie's Walk*. New York: Macmillan, 1968.

Jeschke, Susan. *Sidney*. New York: Holt, Rinehart, and Winston, 1975.

Kent, Jack. *The Egg Book*. New York: Macmillan, 1975.

Mari, Iela and Enzo Mari. *The Chicken and the Egg*. New York: Pantheon, 1970.

Selsam, Millicent E. *Egg to Chick*. New York: Harper and Row, 1970.

Williams, Garth. *Chicken Book: A Traditional Rhyme*. New York: Delacorte, 1970.

Cows/Bulls

Cole, Joanna. *Calf is Born*. New York: Morrow, 1975.

Duvoisin, Roger. *Jasmine*. New York: Knopf, 1973.

Jewell, Nancy. *Calf, Goodnight*. New York: Harper and Row, 1973.

Kent, Jack. *Mrs. Mooley*. New York: Western, 1973.

Leaf, Munro. *The Story of Ferdinand*. New York: Viking, 1938.

Crawfish

Fontenot, Mary. *Clovis Crawfish and the Curious Crapand*. (series) Baton Rouge: Claitor, 1970.

Crickets

Caudill, Rebecca. *Pocketful of Crickets*. New York: Holt, Rinehart, and Winston, 1964.

Disney, Walt. *Pinocchio*. New York: Dutton, 1979.

Deer

Carrick, Donald. *The Deer in the Pasture*. New York: Greenwillow, 1976.

Miller, Albert G. *Walt Disney's Bambi Gets Lost*. New York: Random, 1973.

Dinosaurs

Bram, Elizabeth. *A Dinosaur Is Too Big*. New York: Greenwillow, 1977.

Daly, Kathleen. *Dinosaurs*. New York: Western, 1977.

Hoff, Syd. *Danny and the Dinosaur*. New York: Harper and Row, 1978.

Klein, Norma. *Dinosaur's Housewarming Party*. New York: Crown, 1974.

Kroll, Steven. *The Tyrannosaurus Game*. New York: Holiday, 1976.

Parish, Peggy. *Dinosaur Time*. New York: Harper and Row, 1974.

Rao, Anthony. *Dinosaurs*. New York: Platt, 1979.

Dogs

Annett, Cora. *The Dog Who Thought He Was A Boy*. Boston: Houghton Mifflin, 1965.

Birdwell, Norman. *Clifford at the Circus*. (series) New York: Scholastic, 1977.

Blegvad, Lenore. *Hark. Hark. The Dogs Go Bark: And Other Rhymes About Dogs*. New York: Atheneum, 1976.

Cole, Joanna. *My Puppy Is Born*. New York: William Morrow, 1973.

Flack, Majorie. *Angus and the Cat*. New York: Doubleday, 1971.

Gackenbach, Dick. *Claude the Dog*. Boston: Houghton Mifflin, 1974.

Hefter, Richard. *No Kicks for Dog*. New York: Holt, Rinehart, and Winston, 1978.

Keats, Ezra J. *Whistle for Willie*. New York: Viking, 1964.

Kroll, Steven. *Is Milton Missing?* New York: Holiday, 1975.

Miles, Miska. *Somebody's Dog*. Boston: Little, 1973.

Ness, Evaline. *Old Mother Hubbard and Her Dog*. New York: Holt, Rinehart, and Winston, 1972.

Perkins, Al. *The Diggingest Dog*. New York: Beginner, 1967.

Sharmat, Marjorie. *Taking Care of Melvin*. New York: Holiday, 1980.

Sugita, Yutaka. *My Friend Little John*. New York: McGraw, 1973.

Zion, Gene. *Harry the Dirty Dog*. (series) New York: Harper and Row, 1956.

Dolphins

Benchley, Nathaniel. *Several Tricks of Edgar Dolphin*. New York: Harper and Row, 1970.

Davidson, Margaret. *Dolphins*. New York: Scholastic, 1964.

Davidson, Margaret. *Nine True Dolphins Stories*. New York: Scholastic, 1974.

Morris, Robert A. *Dolphin*. New York: Harper and Row, 1975.

Donkeys

Calhoun, Mary. *Old Man Whickutt's Donkey*. New York: Parents, 1975.

Dumas, Philippe. *Story of Edward*. New York: Scholastic, 1977.

Duvoisin, Roger. *Donkey Donkey*. New York: Scholastic, 1968.

Reinach, Jacqueline. *Jackal Wants Everything*. New York: Holt, Rinehart, and Winston, 1978.

Steig, William. *Farmer Palmer's Wagon Ride*. New York: Farrar, Straus, Grioux, 1974.

Steig, William. *Sylvester and the Magic Pebble*. New York: Simon and Schuster, 1969.

Ducks

Alexander, Martha. *No Ducks in Our Bathtub*. New York: Dial, 1977.

Conover, Chris. *Six Little Ducks*. New York: T. Y. Crowell, 1976.

Delton, Judy. *Two Good Friends*. New York: Crown, 1974.

Delton, Judy. *Two is Company*. New York: Crown, 1976.

Flack, Majorie. *The Story About Ping*. New York: Viking, 1933.

Ginsburg, Mirra. *Chick and the Duckling*. New York: Macmillan, 1972.

McCloskey, Robert. *Make Way for Ducklings*. New York: Viking, 1941.

Shaw, Evelyn. *Nest of Wood Ducks*. New York: Harper and Row, 1976.

Weiner, Jane. *The Fuzzy Duckling*. New York: Western, 1949.

Werner, Jane. *Fuzzy Duckling*. New York: Western, 1949.

Wildsmith, Brian. *Little Wood Duck*. New York: Watts, 1973.

Elephants

Barton, Byron. *Elephant*. Boston: Houghton Mifflin, 1971.

Bednarik, Rosi and Susan Bond. *Elefish*. New York: Scroll, 1971.

Conklin, Gladys. *Elephants of Africa*. New York: Holiday, 1972.

Cutler, Ivor. *Elephant Girl*. New York: Morrow, 1976.

De Brunhoff, Jean. *Babar the King*. (series) New York: Random, 1937.

Disney, Walt. *Dumbo*. New York: Western, 1977.

Ets, Marie H. *Elephant in a Well*. New York: Viking, 1972.

Freschet, Berniece. *Elephant and Friends*. New York: Scribner, 1977.

Maestro, Betsy. *Where Is My Friend?* New York: Crown, 1976.

Mayer, Mercer. *Ah-Choo*. New York: Dial, 1976.

Petersham, Maud and Miska Petersham. *Circus Baby*. New York: Macmillan, 1950.

Reinach, Jacquelyn. *Elephant Eats the Profits*. New York: Holt, Rinehart, and Winston, 1977.

Seuss, Dr. *Horton Hatches An Egg*. New York: Random House, 1968.

Seuss, Dr. *Horton Hears a Who*. New York: Random, 1954.

Thomas, Patricia. *"Stand Back," said the Elephant, "I'm Going to Sneeze."* New York: Lothrop, 1971.

Fireflies

Hawes, Judy. *Fireflies in the Night*. New York: T. Y. Crowell, 1963.

Ryder, Joanne. *Fireflies*. New York: Harper and Row, 1977.

Fishes

Ipcar, Dahlov. *The Biggest Fish in the Sea*. New York: Viking, 1972.

Lionni, Leo. *Fish is Fish*. New York: Pantheon, 1970.

Lionni, Leo. *Swimmy*. New York: Pantheon, 1963.

Margolis, Richard. *Wish Again, Big Bear*. New York: Macmillan, 1972.

Reinach, Jacquelyn. *Fish and Flips*. New York: Holt, Rinehart, and Winston, 1977.

Fleas/Flies

Lionni, Leo. *A Flea Story: I Want to Stay Here I Want to Go There*. New York: Pantheon, 1977.

Conklin, Gladys. *I Watch Flies*. New York: Holiday, 1977.

Ross, Pat. *Hi Fly*. New York: Crown, 1974.

Winter, Paula. *The Bear and the Fly*. New York: Crown, 1976.

Foxes

Brown, Margaret W. *Fox Eyes*. New York: Pantheon, 1977.

De Regnier, Beatrice S. *Catch a Little Fox*. Boston: Houghton Mifflin, 1970.

Lindgren, Astrid. *The Tomten and the Fox*. New York: Coward, 1979.

Spier, Peter. *Fox Went Out on a Chilly Night*. New York: Doubleday, 1961.

Tompert, Ann. *Little Fox Goes to the End of the World*. New York: Scholastic, 1979.

Watson, Clyde. *Tom Fox and the Apple Pie*. New York: T. Y. Crowell, 1972.

Frogs/Toads

Chenery, Janet. *Toad Hunt*. New York: Harper and Row, 1967.

Dauer, Rosamond. *Bullfrog Builds a House*. New York:

Greenwillow, 1977.

Erickson, Russell. *Toad For Tuesday*. New York: Lothrop, 1974.

Erickson, Russell E. *Warton and Morton*. New York: Lothrop, 1976.

Hawes, Judy. *What I Like About Toads*. New York: T. Y. Crowell, 1969.

Hawes, Judy. *Why Frogs Are Wet*. New York: T. Y. Crowell, 1968.

Kraus, Robert. *Mert the Blurt*. New York: Simon and Schuster, 1980.

Langstaff, John and Feodor Rojankovsky. *Frog Went A Courtin'*. New York: Harcourt, Brace, Jovanovich, 1955.

Lobel, Arnold. *Frog and Toad Are Friends*. (series) New York: Harper and Row, 1970.

Mayer, Mercer. *A Boy, A Dog, and a Frog*. New York: Dial, 1967.

Naden, Corinne J. *Let's Find Out About Frogs*. New York: Watts, 1972.

Rockwell, Anne. *Big Boss*. New York: Macmillan, 1975.

Tarcov H., Edith. *The Frog Prince*. New York: Scholastic Book, 1974.

Zemach, Harve and Kaethe Zemach. *Princess and Froggie*. New York: Farrar, Straus, and Giroux, 1975.

Geese

Asch, Frank. *Macgoose's Grocery*. New York: Dial, 1978.

Duvoisin, Roger. *Petunia*. New York: Knopf, 1958.

Galdone, Joanna. *Gertrude, the Goose Who Forgot*. New York: Watts, 1975.

Reinach, Jacquelyn. *Goose Goofs Off*. New York: Holt, Rinehart, and Winston, 1977.

Sumera, Annabella. *What Lily Goose Found*. Wisconsin: Western, 1977.

Gerbils

Tobias, Tobi. *Petey*. New York: Putnam, 1978.

Weil, Lisl. *Fat Earnest*. New York: Scholastic, 1973.

Giraffes

Brenner, Barbara. *Mr. Tall and Mr. Small*. Reading, MA: Addison Wesley, 1966.

Cooke, Ann. *Giraffes at Home*. New York: T. Y. Crowell, 1972.

Duvoisin, Roger. *Periwinkle*. New York: Knopf, 1976.

Goats

Blood, Charles and Martin Link. *The Goat in the Rug*. New York: Scholastic, 1980.

Galdone, Paul. *The Three Billy Goats Gruff*. Boston: Houghton Mifflin, 1973.

Grasshoppers

DuBois, William Pene. *Bear Circus*. New York: Viking, 1971.

McNulty, Faith. *Woodchuck*. New York: Harper and Row, 1974.

Hedgehogs

Bodecker, Niels M. *Miss Jaster's Garden*. New York: Western, 1972.

Hippopotami

Duvoisin, Roger. *Veronica*. New York: Knopf, 1961.

Hefter, Richard. *Hippo Jogs for Health*. New York: Holt, Rinehart, and Winston, 1977.

Mahy, Margaret. *The Boy Who Was Followed Home*. New York: Watts, 1975.

Marshall, James. *George and Martha*. (series) Boston: Houghton Mifflin, 1972.

Mayer, Mercer. *Hiccup*. New York: Dial, 1978.

Mayer, Mercer. *Oops*. New York: Dial, 1977.

Shecter, Ben. *The Hiding Game*. New York: Scholastic, 1980.

Thaler, Mike. *A Hippopotamus Ate the Teacher*. New York: Avon, 1981.

Thaler, Mike. *What Can a Hippopotamus Be?* New York: Scholastic, 1975.

Horses

Anderson, Clarence W. *Blaze and the Forest Fire*. (series) New York: Macmillan, 1962.

Bonzon, Paul J. *Runaway Flying Horse*. New York: Scholastic, 1976.

Brett, Jan. *Fritz and the Beautiful Horses*. Boston: Houghton Mifflin, 1981.

Bridgmen, Elizabeth. *If I Were A Horse*. New York: Dodd, 1977.

Dennis, Wesley. *Flip*. New York: Viking, 1941.

Hoff, Syd. *Chester*. New York: Harper and Row, 1961.

Hoff, Syd. *Horse in Harry's Room*. New York: Harper and Row, 1970.

Hoff, Syd. *Thunderhoof*. New York: Harper and Row, 1971.

Rabinowitz, Sandy. *The Red Horse and the Bluebird*. New York: Harper and Row, 1975.

Richards, Jane. *Horse Grows Up*. New York: Walker and Company, 1972.

Selsam, Millicent E. *Questions and Answers About Horses*. New York: Scholastic, 1976.

Iguanas

Reinach, Jacquelyn. *Me Too Iguana*. New York: Holt, Rinehart, and Winston, 1977.

Kangaroos

Du Bois, William Pene. *Bear Circus*. New York: Penguin, 1973.

Hefter, Richard. *Who Can Trust You, Kangaroo*. New York: Holt, Rinehart, and Winston, 1978.

Hurd, Edith T. *Mother Kangaroo*. Boston: Little, 1976.

Mayer, Mercer. *What Do You Do With A Kangaroo?* New York: Scholastic, 1975.

Payne, Emmy. *Katy No-Pocket*. Boston: Houghton Mifflin, 1973.

Wiseman, Bernard. *Little New Kangaroo*. New York: Macmillan, 1972.

Ladybugs

Carle, Eric. *The Grouchy Ladybug*. New York: T. Y. Crowell, 1977.

McClung, Robert M. *Ladybug*. New York: Morrow, 19 .

Lions

Daughtery, James. *Andy and the Lion*. New York: Viking, 1938.

Freeman, Don. *Dandelion*. New York: Viking, 1964.

Mann, Peggy. *King Laurence, the Alarm Clock*. New York: Doubleday, 1976.

Fromm, Lilo. *Muffel and Plums*. New York: Macmillan, 1973.

Pape, Donna L. *Leo Lion Looks for Books*. New Cannon, CT: Garrard, 1972.

Peet, Bill. *Hubert's Hair-Raising Adventure*. New York: Houghton Mifflin, 1959.

Du Bois, William Pene. *Lion*. New York: Penguin, 1974.

36

Fatio, Louise. *Happy Lion Roars.* New York: McGraw Hill, 1957.

Galdone, Paul. *The Horse, the Fox and the Lion.* Boston: Houghton Mifflin, 1968.

Hefter, Richard. *Lion is Down in the Dumps.* New York: Holt, Rinehart, and Winston, 1977.

Lizards

Conklin, Gladys. *I Caught a Lizard.* New York: Holiday, 1967.

Anderson, Lonzo. *Izzard.* New York: Scribner, 1973.

Freschet, Berniece. *Lizard Lying in the Sun.* New York: Scribner, 1975.

Llamas

Eiseman, Alberta. *Candido.* New York: Macmillan, 1967.

Mice

Aliki. *At Mary Bloom's.* New York: Greenwillow, 1976.

Freeman, Don. *Norman the Doorman.* New York: Viking, 1959.

Goodall, John S. *Naughty Nancy.* New York: Atheneum, 1975.

Holl, Adelaide. *Moon Mouse.* New York: Random, 1969.

Ivimey W., John. *Three Blind Mice.* (complete version) New York: Frederick Warne, 1979.

Lionni, Leo. *Alexander and the Wind-Up Mouse.* New York: Pantheon, 1969.

Lionni, Leo. *Frederick.* New York: Pantheon, 1966.

Lionni, Leo. *Geraldine the Music Mouse.* New York: Pantheon, 1979.

Lionni, Leo. *The Greentail Mouse.* New York: Pantheon, 1973.

Lionni, Leo. *Theodore and the Talking Mushroom.* New York: Pantheon, 1971.

Lobel, Arnold. *Mouse Soup.* New York: Harper and Row, 1977.

Lobel, Arnold. *Mouse Tales.* New York: Harper and Row, 1972.

Miller, Edna. *Mousekin Finds a Friend.* (series) Englewood Cliffs, NJ: Prentice-Hall, 1967.

Steig, William. *Amos and Boris.* New York: Penguin, 1971.

Titus, Eve. *Anatole and the Cat.* New York: McGraw Hill, 1957.

Waber, Bernard. *Cheese.* Boston: Houghton Mifflin, 1967.

Moles

Conford, Ellen. *Eugene the Brave.* Boston: Little, 1978.

Quakenbush, Robert. *Detective Mole.* New York: Lothrop, 1976.

Monkeys/Gorillas

Bornstein, Ruth. *Little Gorilla.* Boston: Houghton Mifflin, 1976.

Carle, Eric. *All About Arthur: An Absolutely Absurd Ape.* New York: Watts, 1974.

Galdone, Paul. *Monkey and the Crocodile.* Boston: Houghton Mifflin, 1969.

Hurd, Edith T. *Mother Chimpanzee.* Boston, Little, 1978.

Maestro, Betsy. *Wise Monkey Tale.* New York: Crown, 1975.

Perkins, Al. *Hand, Hand, Fingers, Thumb.* New York: Random House, 1969.

Rey, H. A. *Curious George.* (series) Boston: Houghton Mifflin, 1958.

Rockwell, Anne. *No More Work.* New York: Greenwillow, 1976.

Thaler, Mike. *Moonkey.* New York: Harper and Row, 1981.

Wolkstein, Diane. *Cool Ride in the Sky.* New York: Knopf, 1973.

Moose

Hefter, Richard. *Moody Moose Buttons.* New York: Holt, Rinehart, and Winston, 1977.

Marshall, James. *The Guest.* Boston: Houghton Mifflin, 1975.

Pinkwater, Manus. *Blue Moose.* New York: Dodd, 1975.

Wiseman, Bernard. *Morris and Boris: Three Stories.* New York: Dodd, 1974.

Seuss, Dr. *Thidwick: The Big Hearted Moose.* New York: Random, 1948.

Moths

Mari, Iela. and Enzo Mari. *The Apple and the Moth.* New York: Pantheon, 1970.

Mosquitos

Aardema, Verna. *Why Mosquitos Buzz in People's Ears.* New York: Dial Press, 1975.

Octopi

Reinach, Jacquelyn. *Octopus Protests.* New York: Holt, Rinehart, and Winston, 1978.

Shaw, Evelyn. *Octopus.* New York: Harper and Row, 1971.

Opossums

Berson, Henry. *Henry Possum.* New York: Crown, 1973.

Brown, Margaret W. *Fox Eyes.* New York: Pantheon, 1977.

Conford, Ellen. *Impossible Possum.* Boston: Little, 1971.

Freschet, Berniece. *Possum Baby.* New York: G. P. Putnam's Sons, 1978.

Otters

Benchley, Nathaniel. *Oscar Otter*. New York: Harper and Row, 1966.

Owls

Benchley, Nathaniel. *Strange Disappearance of Arthur Cluck*. New York: Harper and Row, 1967.

Erickson, Russell. *Toad for Tuesday*. New York: Lothrop, 1974.

Garelick, May. *About Owls*. New York: Scholastic, 1975.

Hurd, Edith T. *Mother Owl*. Boston: Little, 1974.

Hutchins, Pat. *Good-Night Owl*. New York: Macmillan, 1972.

Lobel, Arnold. *Owl at Home*. New York: Harper and Row, 1975.

Peacocks

Alexander, Sue. *Peacocks Are Very Special*. New York: Doubleday, 1976.

Pelicans

Benchley, Nathaniel. *The Flying Lesson of Gerald Pelican*. New York: Harper and Row, 1970.

Freeman, Don. *Come Again, Pelican*. New York: Viking, 1961.

Penguins

Freeman, Don. *Penguins, of All People*. New York: Viking, 1971.

Penny, Richard. *The Penguins Are Coming*. New York: Harper and Row, 1969.

Mizumura, Kazue. *Emperor Penguins*. New York: T. Y. Crowell, 1969.

Pigs

Baker, Betty. *The Pig War*. New York: Harper and Row, 1969.

Bond, Felicia. *Poinsetta and Her Family*. New York: T. Y. Crowell, 1981.

Dyke, John. *Pig Wig*. New York: Methuen, 1978.

Goodall, John S. *Paddy's Evening Out*. (series) New York: Atheneum, 1973.

Hefter, Richard. *Pig thinks Pink*. New York: Holt, Rinehart, and Winston, 1978.

Hoban, Lillian. *Mr. Pig and Sonny Too*. (series) New York: Harper and Row, 1977.

Lobel, Arnold. *Small Pig*. New York: Harper and Row, 1969.

Lobel, Arnold. *A Treeful of Pigs*. New York: Scholastic, 1979.

Rayner, Mary. *Garth Pig and the Ice Cream Lady*. New York: Atheneum, 1977.

Steig, William. *The Amazing Bone*. New York: A. Hoen, 1976.

Porcupines

Freschet, Berniece. *Porcupine Baby*. New York: Putnam, 1978.

Hall, Malcolm. *Forecast*. New York: Coward, 1977.

Rabbits

Aardema, Verna. *Who's in Rabbit's House: A Masai Tale*. New York: Dial, 1977.

Bailey, Carolyn S. *The Little Rabbit Who Wanted Red Wines*. New York: Platt, 1978.

Brown, Margaret W. *The Golden Egg Book*. New York: Western, 1976.

Brown, Margaret W. *Goodnight Moon*. New York: Harper and Row, 1947.

Brown, Margaret W. *Home for a Bunny*. New York: Western, 1975.

Brown, Margaret W. *The Runaway Bunny*. New York: Harper and Row, 1972.

Cleveland, David. *April Rabbits*. New York: Scholastic, 1978.

Delton, Judy. *Rabbit Finds a Way*. New York: Crown, 1975.

Galdone, Paul. *The Hare and the Tortoise*. New York: Mc-

From *Golden Egg Book* by Margaret Wise Brown
Copyright © 1971, 1947 by Western Publishing Company, Inc.

Reprinted by permission.

38

Graw Hill, 1962.

Hoban, Tana. *Where Is It?* New York: Macmillan, 1974.

Lionni, Leo. *In the Rabbitgarden.* New York: Pantheon, 1975.

Potter, Beatrix. *The Tale of Peter Rabbit.* New York: Warne, 1902.

Reinach, Jacquelyn. *Rest Rabbit Rest.* New York: Holt, Rinehart, and Winston, 1977.

Wahl, Jan. *Doctor Rabbit's Foundling.* (series) New York: Pantheon, 1977.

Zolotow, Charlotte. *Mister Rabbit and the Lovely Present.* New York: Harper and Row, 1962.

Raccoons

Bourne, Miriam A. *Raccoons Are For Loving.* New York: Random, 1968.

Duvoisin, Roger. *Petunia, I Love You.* New York: Knopf, 1965.

McPhail, David. *Henry Bear's Park.* Boston: Little, 1976.

Miklowitz, Gloria. *Save That Raccoon.* New York: Harcourt, Brace, Jovanovich, 1978.

Wells, Rosemary. *Benjamin & Tulip.* New York: Dial Press, 1973.

Seals

Freeman, Don. *The Seal and the Slick.* New York: Viking, 1974.

Sharks

Copps, Dale. *Savage Survivors.* Chicago: Follett, 1976.

McGovern, Ann. *Sharks.* New York: Scholastic, 1976.

Sheep/Lambs

Beskow, Elsa. *Pelle's New Suit.* New York: Harper and Row, 1929.

De Paola, Tomie. *Charlie Needs a Cloak.* Englewood Cliffs, NJ: Prentice-Hall, 1974.

Skunks

Freschet, Berniece. *Skunk Baby.* New York: T. Y. Crowell, 1973.

Hess, Lilo. *Misunderstood Skunk.* New York: Scribner, 1969.

Snails

Byars, Betsy C. *The Lace Snail.* New York: Viking, 1975.

Lionni, Leo. *The Biggest House in the World.* New York: Pantheon, 1968.

Ungerer, Tomi. *Snail, Where Are You?* New York: Harper and Row, 1962.

Snakes

Bradbury, Peggy. *The Snake That Couldn't Slither.* New York: Putnam, 1976.

Kennedy, Mary. *Wings.* New York: Scholastic, 1980.

Leydenfrost, Robert. *Snake that Sneezed.* New York: Putnam, 1970.

Noble, Trinka. *The Day Jimmy's Boa Ate the Wash.* New York: Dial, 1980.

Ungerer, Tomi. *Crictor.* New York: Harper and Row, 1958.

Spiders

Brandenberg, Franz. *Fresh Cider and Pie.* New York: Macmillan, 1973.

Brinckloe, Julie. *Spider Web.* New York: Doubleday, 1974.

Chenery, Jane. *Wolfie.* New York: Harper and Row, 1969.

Conklin, Gladys. *Tarantula, the Giant Spider.* New York: Holiday, 1972.

Freschet, Berniece. *Web in the Grass.* New York: Scribner, 1972.

Goldin, Augusta. *Spider Silk.* New York: T. Y. Crowell, 1964.

Graham, Margaret B. *Be Nice to Spiders.* New York: Harper and Row, 1967.

Hawes, Judy. *My Daddy Longlegs.* New York: T. Y. Crowell, 1972.

McDermott, Gerald. *Anansi the Spider: A Tale from the Ashanti.* New York: Holt, Rinehart, and Winston, 1972.

Squirrels

Himler, Ann. *Waiting for Cherries.* New York: Harper and Row, 1976.

Hutchins, Pat. *The Silver Christmas Tree.* New York: Macmillan, 1974.

Sharmat, Marjorie W. *Sophie and Gussie.* New York: Macmillan, 1973.

Wildsmith, Brian. *Squirrels.* New York: Watts, 1975.

Tigers

Kraus, Robert. *Leo the Late Bloomer.* New York: E. P. Dutton, 1971.

Pore, Gerald. *The Tiger-Skin Rug.* New York: Prentice-Hall, 1979.

Tortoises/Turtles

Asch, Frank. *Turtle Tale.* New York: Dial, 1978.

Freeman, Don. *Chalk Box Story.* New York: Lippincott, 1976.

Freschet, Berniece. *Turtle Pond.* New York: Scribner, 1971.

Furrer, Jurg. *Tortoise Island.* Reading, MA: Addison Wesley, 1975.

Hefter, Richard. *Turtle Throws a Tantrum.* New York: Holt, Rinehart, and Winston, 1978.

Seuss, Dr. *Yertle the Turtle and Other Stories.* New York: Random, 1958.

Sharmont, Marjorie W. *Edgemont.* New York: Coward, 1976.

Williams, Barbara. *Albert's Toothache.* New York: Dutton, 1974.

Unicorns

Reinach, Jacquelyn. *Happy Birthday Unicorn.* New York: Holt, Rinehart, and Winston, 1978.

Walruses

Bonsall, Crosby N. *What Spot?* New York: Harper and Row, 1963.

Hefter, Richard. *Very Worried Walrus.* New York: Holt, Rinehart, and Winston, 1977.

Hoff, Syd *Walpole.* New York: Harper and Row, 1977.

Whales

Behrens, June. *Whalewatch.* Chicago: Childrens Press, 1978.

Broger, Achim. *Good Morning Whale.* New York: Macmillan, 1975.

Cosgrove, Stephen. *Maui-Maui.* Los Angeles, CA: Price, Stern, Sloan, 1979.

Goudney, Alice E. *Here Come the Whales.* New York: Scribner, 1956.

Hurd, Edith T. *The Mother Whales.* Boston: Little, 1973.

McGovern, Ann. *Little Humpback Whale.* New York: Scholastic, 1979.

McGovern, Ann. *Little Whale*. New York: Four Winds, 1979.

Mizumura, Kazue. *The Blue Whale*. New York: T. Y. Crowell, 1971.

Pluckrose, Henry. *Whales*. Fairmont, WV: Gloucester, 1979.

Ricciuti, Edward. *Catch a Whale by the Tail*. New York: Harper and Row, 1969.

Rockwell, Anne. *Tuhurahura and the Whale*. New York: Scholastic, 1971.

Selsam, Millicent and Joyce Hunt. *A First Look at Whales*. New York: Walker and Company, 1980.

Steig, William. *Amos and Boris*. New York: Penguin, 1971.

Wolves

Allard, Harry. *It's So Nice To Have a Wolf Around the House*. New York: Doubleday, 1977.

Benchley, Nathaniel. *Small Wolf*. New York: Harper and Row, 1972.

Galdone, Paul. *The Three Little Pigs*. Boston: Houghton Mifflin, 1970.

Sharmat, Marjorie. *Walter the Wolf*. New York: Holiday, 1975.

Worms

Craig, Paula M. *Mr. Wiggle's Book*. Minneapolis, MN: Denison, 1972.

Lionni, Leo. *Inch By Inch*. New York: Astor Honor, 1962.

Yaks

Hefter, Richard. *Yakety—Yak-Yak-Yak*. New York: Holt, Rinehart, and Winston, 1977.

Zebras

Arundel, Jocelyn. *Little Stripe*. New York: Hastings, 1967.

Hefter, Richard. *Zip Goes Zebra*. New York: Holt, Rinehart, and Winston, 1977.

Raskin, Ellen. *Moe Q. McGlutch, He Smoked Too Much*. New York: Scholastic, 1973.

40

Puppetuckers

Puppetuckers are places to "tuck" puppets for display or storage purposes in the Puppet Corner. A Puppetucker can be as simple as an empty soda carton or as elaborate as a giant fabric tree with "leafy" pockets for holding hand puppets. Whether plain or fancy, Puppetuckers offer a refreshing alternative to merely depositing your puppets in a basket or drawer.

Puppetuckers can visually brighten the Puppet Corner and give focus and direction to the children's Puppet Play. They can also serve as a tool for organizing your puppet collection. Whether you opt for a thematic fabric hanging or choose a multipurpose 'tucker such as a shoe bag makes no difference; in either case, the children will be enchanted to discover the puppets poking, peeking and hanging in the Puppet Corner, waiting to be brought to life.

The selection of the best Puppetuckers for a specific setting depends upon the availability of time, money and space as well as the types of puppets to be stored.

The Three Bears tucked in cut down milk cartons
Puppets by Nancy Renfro Studios

Hanger and Clothespins

Pajama Bag

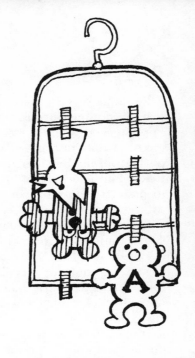

Multiple Skirt Hangers

Chest

Wine Rack

Beverage Pack

Storage Tuckers—hand puppets

Additional Ideas:
- pegboard
- grocery cart
- shoerack
- clothing drying rack
- kitchen utensil rack

42

Springtime Puppets

Supplies for Puppets -

Pup

Butterfly Puppet -   pg 14 "Good Apple"
 - egg cartons - 1 cup per child
 - chenille stem ? - pipe cleaners
 - thin wire for feelers

   Maybe we could have a discussion about monarch's
and then bring in some catepilars when they come
out - watch for them on milkweed. We could watch
them transform themselves into butterflies.

Turtle puppet - pg. 62
   ~~green pipe cleaners~~ paint
 - ~~egg cartons~~ stiff paper plates - construction paper

 - Easter Bunny - pg. 42

 - Duck   pg 61
   - paper plates   Lg + sm
   - yellow crepe paper

Snail - pg. 63
   sm paper plates
   socks
   felt (eyes)

Puppet Totes - pg 59
   Grocery Bags

Plastic Soda Bottles

Cut away top of plastic quart bottles and stack together; tape or glue together with contact cement.

8 Oz. Milk Cartons

Cut away peaks of cartons and stack with open ends facing frontwards; glue or tape together:

Stack a Story

Additional Ideas:

- stacking food bins
- flower pots

Strawberry Baskets—wired together

Hanging Basket

43

Lego Blocks

Plastic Divider Boxes

Egg Carton

Tinker Toy

Utensil Rack

Muffin Tin

Storage Tuckers—finger puppets

44

Good Morning!

Turn-a-round

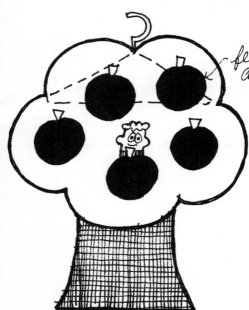

Good Night!

Alphabet
(See other side for rest of alphabet)

Apartment House

On fabric, trace around outer edge of hanger and add a seam allowance. Extend length of hanging for long displays. Cut out front and back pieces. Attach pockets and decorations. Sew right sides together leaving bottom open. Turn right side out and slip over hanger through a hole on center top of fabric hanging. Hem bottom.

Covered Hangers

Apple Tree
(finger puppets)

Easter Basket

Christmas Tree
(finger puppets)

45

The Sea

Outer Space

SPRING IS SPRUNG

Springtime

Pocket Pals

Train

Wall Hangings

These appealing hangings made from mural paper or fabric adds a vivid touch to any classroom. Here are some additional ideas:

- Village of Houses
- Mountains
- Zoo
- Circus
- North Pole
- Playland

Introducing The Puppet Corner

During the first few days a Puppet Corner is introduced, confusion may erupt. Children, overstimulated by their newly found friends, often become noisy and possessive. Therefore you may find it worthwhile to spend extra time in the vicinity of the Puppet Corner at its inception, helping the children to adjust. When disruptions occur, handle them just as you would any other dispute over toys or playing spaces. Rest assured that as the children become more accustomed to the puppets, they will become more relaxed in working with them as well.

Several suggestions may alleviate problems. Post a sign limiting the number of children who may use the Puppet Corner at a given time; four usually work well together. Or, have a sign-up sheet for the children to write their own names, thus ensuring them that they, too, will have a turn. As the novelty wears off, the children will begin to gravitate toward the puppets on a more equalized basis, just as they do the block or reading areas with which they are already familiar.

Within the first few weeks you will see the rewards of your efforts. The Corner will become a place where children's imaginations spark dramatic play improvisations with stories that have personal relevance. As time goes on, with little effort and almost no adult intervention, the children will be able to weave their puppet characters into adventures of great fantasy and fun.

Books on Puppet Playing

Renfro, Nancy, *A Puppet Corner in Every Library*—A valuable resource book in setting up a Puppet Corner, including: stages, storage suggestions, buddy puppets, puppet constructions and simple production techniques. Austin, Texas, Nancy Renfro Studios, Austin, Texas, 1978

48

I Want To Be A Puppeteer

1. _____

2. _____

3. _____

4. _____

5. _____

6. _____

7. _____

8. _____

Hi!

May be reproduced. Happy Puppetry!
Courtesy of **Nancy Renfro Studios**

With Puppetelling there is no stage, hence all the actions are revealed (Nerf Ball Puppet).

Photo by Robert W. Bethune

PUPPETELLING
Presenting Music and Literature with Puppets

To tell a story, teach a song, read a poem or share a book using puppets provides perhaps one of the most treasured aspect of puppetry. For the teacher, it offers an opportunity for creative interpretation and time to capture the magical world of make-believe while establishing a special bond with the children.

Puppetelling, as the name implies, is simply the telling of tales with puppets. It is not "putting on a show" or "performing" for an audience. Rather, it is an informal "presentation" and sharing of literature. There is a wealth of appropriate material in the language arts curriculum—fingerplays, poems, songs, stories and books that all take on new meaning when introduced or acted out by puppets.

When selecting and preparing material for Puppetelling consider the factors of enrichment, clarification and dialogue exchange.

● **Enrichment.** Puppets and stories are the two aspects of Puppetelling that children seem to enjoy most. This winning combination offers an enrichment to the language arts experience since puppets give color, texture and dimensionality to the characters as well as to actions and locations described. Imagine the children's pleasure when a favorite character like Dr. Seuss' *Cat in the Hat*, H. A. Rey's *Curious George* or Jean De Brunhoff's *Babar* suddenly appears in the classroom for the children to touch and watch.

● **Clarification.** What illustrations can do for picture books, puppets can accomplish for stories. They supply to young children visual information not yet acquired because of the children's limited years and experience. Stories about unfamiliar animals such as opossums, for example, become more meaningful when the child can visually associate the word "opossum" with a concrete image represented by a corresponding puppet. Therefore, Puppetelling can become a total sensory experience, combining visual and audio elements with action.

● **Dialogue.** Dialogue exchange is stimulated between puppets and children. A case in point is the reaction of my four-year-old son to Leo Lionni's *Swimmy*, his favorite bedtime story. Night after night he would listen quietly as I read each page. One night I surprised him with a black fish fingerpuppet that popped out from behind the book. His reaction was immediate. "Swimmy!" he squealed with delight, "How did you get here!?!" Swimmy and my son talked at great length about the ocean, the other fish and what it felt like to be afraid. The potential for discussion seemed endless. Because he had never talked to the illustrations before, it was definitely the puppet that made the difference!

Adapting music and literature to Puppetelling can be a comfortable and rewarding experience if you start simply and escalate in complexity as skills and confidence evolve.

Begin with a selection you personally like, perhaps a song or rhyme that is also familiar to the children. Think about the best ways to visualize the choice for the children. Fingerplays, for example, lend themselves well to Story Gloves because many are based on the number five. On the other hand,

The Three Billy Goats Gruff is better suited to a Lap Board for holding the Troll's bridge or table-top puppetry. It is not necessary to be too literal in scene interpretations. Children are just as happy to imagine a bridge as they are to see the actual prop.

Remember the intent in Puppetelling is not to hide the source of voice or puppet manipulation as in performing. With Puppetelling there is no stage, hence all the actions are revealed. This open quality, lacking a facade, helps children relate to the puppets at their own emotional levels. Those children who wish to suspend reality and see only the puppet, may unconsciously do so. Likewise, those children who wish to retain a sense of security by knowing the teacher is present and that an adult they trust is in control of the situation may do so as well. For young children, this elemental form of Puppetelling provides an excellent introduction to fantasy.

How To Puppetell

When choosing material for Puppetelling, select stories, poems and songs with a limited number of characters or, at least, characters that can be manipulated one or two at a time. Beginning Puppetellers often forget they have only two hands! A song like *Old MacDonald Had A Farm* is a good choice because each stanza features just one puppet character. Books such as Marie Hall Et's *Just Like Me* also adapt well because the animals in the story appear one after the other, rather than all at once. Look for clever ways to integrate various types of puppets. For example, Story Gloves and fingerpuppets enable the puppeteer to increase the number of characters that can be manipulated simultaneously. For instance, in *Old MacDonald Had A Farm*, as many as ten separate characters can be managed on the two hands of the Puppeteller.

Several elements of puppetry are at the disposal of the Puppeteller to embellish the story presentation:

● **Props.** Have fun with props! These very important focal points capture the children's interest. A puppet carrying a toy pop-gun in Mercer Mayer's *There's a Nightmare In My Closet*, for example, or a real carrot growing from the pocket of your story apron for Ruth Kraus' *The Carrot Seed* greatly enrich those particular episodes. In general, however, props should be kept to a minimum, limited to those items that are essential for illustrating the storyline. Otherwise, an overuse of props may lessen the impact or contribute to an unmanageable presentation.

● **Scenery.** In the form of background or "set pieces," scenery can be easily painted onto cardboard, story aprons or story panels. Simple sets such as a folded stand-up panel showing a volcano or barnyard scene can be stood up on a table top or Lap Board. Partial sets that only "suggest" the scenery such as a tree (to represent the forest) or house (to represent a village) may be clipped onto a box theater. Such background scenes bring a special charm to stories by adding mood and tone.

● **Sound effects.** Can be devised vocally, with records, instruments or improvised sounds (using pot lids, wood blocks and other objects). Children enjoy hearing new sounds, especially those that tantalize and cover a broad tonal range. Experiment with such sounds as a real whistle to signal a policeman, jingling bells to heighten suspense when Santa arrives or chiming finger cymbals to set the mood for a story in the Far East.

● **Special effects.** Add interest to a story by creating simple, but interesting effects. For instance, gently toss a handful of white confetti during a snow-scene, wave a cluster of Christmas tinsel (taped to the end of a stick) to represent rain or squeeze a plastic bottle of baby powder to simulate smoke.

Once all your material is selected and prepared, go through it to see if it works. Many beginning Puppetellers become uncomfortable at this point. Do not let stage fright inhibit your progress; take heart in the fact that bringing puppets to life is just a matter of holding them, moving them, making them talk, and believing in them, yourself, as real characters.

The Buddy Puppet

One of the most valuable tools for the teacher of young children to adopt and expand upon is a "buddy" puppet. This puppet becomes an invaluable friend, a reinforcer and accomplice for many classroom activities.

● Choose a lovable, appealing character with whom both you and the class can identify. From the teacher's standpoint, this puppet should be one with whom she can easily relate and for whom she can discover an appropriate voice and personality. From the children's viewpoint, it should be one that is naturally appealing and one with whom a bond can be formed. Furry, huggable animals are especially popular.

52

• Use at scheduled times for added effectiveness as a teaching tool. If the children know that this particular puppet will appear only at special times, whether five minutes daily or half an hour at the end of the week, they will look forward to this session with heightened anticipation.

• Avoid using the "buddy" puppet for free play by the children. This puppet should remain a special guest who visits at allotted times. If children are allowed to play at liberty with it, the "buddy" puppet will soon be taken for granted and lose much of its effectiveness.

• Establish a home for your puppet in the classroom. A dog should have a doghouse; a mouse might live in a drawer with a blanket and pillow (under which to hide his cheese); a spider in a giant web; a squirrel in a tree or a crab in a beach pail. (See Page 58 for additional ideas).

• Spend time refining the puppet's personality. Over the year, mold into it traits and idiosyncrasies so that in due time the puppet's personality will emerge as a real entity to the children. (The puppet may even have a birthday date the children can help to celebrate.)

Ways to Use the Buddy Puppet:

• Introduce a story

• Quieten the class, preferably in an indirect manner. For example, when the puppet requires "quiet" so it can sleep, the children will be eager to cooperate.

• Help the children articulate particular difficulties. For example, in the case of a toothache, the puppet can talk about its own toothache; in an argument, the puppet can sympathize with the children; with inferiority complexes, the puppet can share its feelings to bolster the child's sense of self-identity.

• Celebrate Holidays
  Bring out a pumpkin for Halloween
  Make Christmas decorations with the children
  Bake cakes on birthdays

• Teach Curriculum
  Count a stockpile of puppet's food (nuts for squirrel, bones for dog, etc.)
  Classify (shapes, colors, etc.)
  Measure things
  Briefly enact historical events such as the landing at Plymouth Rock or the discovery of America
  Lead singalongs, poetry readings and nursery rhymes
  Role-play community leaders (by adding hats or props)

Developing A Puppet's Personality

Many adults are shy to use puppets in front of children not realizing that young children are rarely overly critical. The ideas and impressions conveyed through the puppet are of far greater interest to them than the expertise of the puppeteer. Also, children believe in the puppet and what it says and does; therefore any mistakes are attributed to the puppet rather than to the puppeteer. Moreover, puppets are naturally positive creatures that, in turn, elicit positive responses from children. In such a strongly supportive atmosphere, the adult is only encouraged to become emboldened in the use of puppets, more relaxed and creative.

53

To become acquainted with your puppet, spend some quiet time, alone, in front of the mirror and experiment with the puppet's movement, voice and gestures. Savor the experience of molding a new personality, building in idiosyncrasies to give it distinction and bring it to life. This shaping of a puppet into a fully blossomed personality is a process that is actually more crucial and creative to puppetry than the making of the puppet itself. Even the simplest puppet can have an outstanding personality!

Selecting a Puppet

Choose a puppet that is personally appealing and one with whom you can identify. It is important to feel comfortable with your puppet before you bring it to life. At the start, not even a voice is required; instead, the puppet can respond merely with a peculiar laugh or a simple action like hugging thumbs, stroking noses or repeating an appropriate sound. For example, a cow may respond to all questions with a "moo" in various intonations to imply certain meanings.

Puppets with moving mouths are easiest to manipulate and can be adeptly synchronized with dialogue. Those without moving mouths may be considered as well, but require more skill in handling. The advantage of the puppet without a moving mouth is its ability to achieve certain action tasks with its flexible arms such as picking up an object, rubbing its tummy and opening and turning the pages of a book. In choosing between these two types of puppets, decide first what important function your puppet must serve in the story in terms of presenting either dialogue or action.

The Voice

Discover a voice contrasting to your own. Look at the puppet and see what characteristics its physical features suggest. A deep, commanding voice, for example, may be appropriate for a large mouth while sleepy eyes may connote a slow, tired voice; many teeth imply a chattering voice while stand-up ears, a snappy voice. Become fully involved with the character and experiment freely. There are many voices never discovered within us, undiscovered simply because our whole range of tones and cadences has never been fully explored. A puppet's personality does not develop immediately; rather it evolves over a span of days, weeks, sometimes months. By reading aloud a paragraph from time to time, or responding to questions, you will have the chance to practice the puppet's voice and mannerisms. These exercises will give you the opportunity to refine the puppet's personality until it becomes almost second nature. You may wish to invest such efforts in a single puppet that will become your own "special buddy," to be reserved for particular occasions such as introducing stories and celebrating holidays.

Puppets without moving mouths also require personality development and practice. The head and the hands should be manipulated in accordance with the words spoken as well as the tone of voice employed. A puppet with a deep voice, for instance, will require more exaggerated movements while

faster and smaller movements may be more suitable for a shrill-voiced puppet.

When using more than one voice with puppets, practice making the transition between your own voice and that of the puppet until the process becomes smooth and does not sound or feel awkward.

Here are some exercises to exemplify how to create a voice for a given puppet as well as how to develop your own voice range. Recite this nursery rhyme using the suggestions that follow:

> Hickory, dickory dock,
> The mouse ran up the clock.
> The clock struck one,
> The mouse ran down,
> Hickory, dickory dock.

1. Recite it in a low voice, slowly.

2. Repeat it in a high-pitched voice, quickly.

3. Now, alternate high and low voices for every other line with appropriate speed variations.

4. Change voice while reading a line. For instance, when the mouse runs up the clock, make your voice run up in frequency also.

5. Recite the verse exploring other descriptions for character voices sad, happy, sleepy, grumpy.

6. Find more advanced material with which to practice similar techniques.

Character voices are easier to acquire than might be imagined. In another exercise, recite the following rhyme in the "first person" as Old Mother Hubbard might say it. Try to create voices that are alternately cackly, sleepy, grumpy or forgetful.

> I'm Old Mother Hubbard.
> I went to the cupboard,
> To get my poor dog a bone.
> The cupboard was bare,
> And nothing was there,
> And so my poor dog had none.

Now try a squeaky voice in the first person of a mouse:

> I'm a little squeaky mouse,
> Sneaking through the house.
> Can't make a sound,
> Or knock things down.
> 'cause the cat might come around!

Your voice can also be changed by speaking softly or loudly as well as high and low. A good practice story is *The Three Billy Goats Gruff* in which the smallest goat has a high-pitched fast voice, the middle goat has a normal speaking voice and the biggest

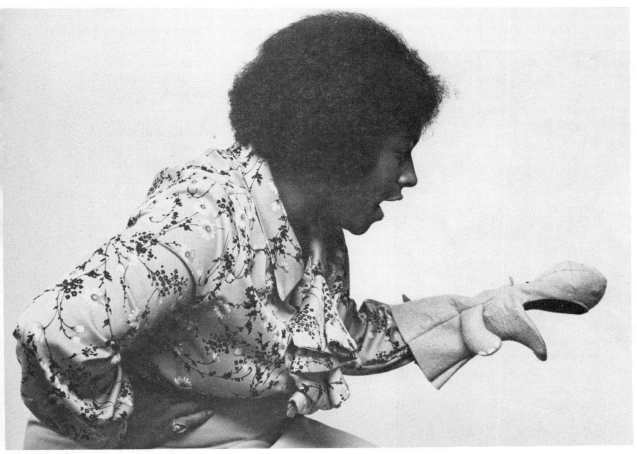

Hippo Puppet made by the Puppet Factory

55

goat has a deep, loud, slow-speaking voice. Give the Troll a fierce, cackly voice to convey the terror he strikes in those he meets.

Animal puppets, of course, can speak with sounds instead of words. A great range of feelings, both comic and poignant, can be conveyed through puppet growls, barks, chirps, buzzes, purrs, quacks and so forth. Practice animal sounds to become familiar with recognizable tones and cadences.

Ventriloquism is not necessary in order to project your voice through a puppet. As long as the puppet's head, mouth or body is moving during the dialogue, children will be unconcerned about the actual origin of the voice.

Puppet Movements

When using puppets:

● Be sure that all the children can see and hear.

● Keep action both continuous and lively enough to retain the children's interest.

● Vary the puppet's movements; for example, let the puppets do something besides jump around. Use linear movements as well as up and down motions.

● Create only purposeful puppet movements. Do not let your puppet suffer from "jigolitis." Instead, each movement or action should be well defined and meaningful.

● Allow the primary puppet, the one (or ones) on whom the attention is focused, to command the limelight. Rather than having *all* puppets move *all* the time, let the puppet(s) speaking or directing the action, be the only one(s) to move, thereby avoiding "upstaging" and confusion.

Manipulation of a puppet is primarily a matter of simplifying animal or human movements and adapting them to a smaller scale. Consider how to make the puppet:

run	crawl	march
jog	hide	peek
climb	walk	yawn
slither	bounce	wave
strut	swing	bow
hop	sneak	fly

Personality

In developing a puppet personality, it is sometimes easier to pattern a character after a real person than to try to create one that is entirely imaginary. For example, think of a distinct screen or television celebrity, a friend, former teacher, child or even a member of your own family to offer credence to the puppet character. Give the puppet a name and, in so doing, try to answer the following questions:

What does the puppet look like or represent? Is it . . .

attractive?	dirty?
homely?	clean?
exotic?	funny-looking?
messy?	adorable?
neat?	

How will your puppet behave? Will it be . . .

regal?	charming?	pompous?
dignified?	forgetful?	strong?
friendly?	cheerful?	weak?
shy?	serious?	scatterbrained?
sophisticated?	silly?	organized?

How does your puppet usually feel? Is it . . .

happy?	nervous?	grouchy?
afraid?	sad?	excitable?
surprised?	angry?	calm?

Another way to enhance a puppet's personality is to give it an idiosyncrasy that sets it apart. Perhaps it has an allergy and is always sneezing. Or, maybe it falls alseep sporadically, trips over things or is forever confused. Little personality quirks will make the puppet seem more human and thus more endearing.

Let your puppet speak, describing itself in various ways until the personality that seems right begins to emerge. "Hi! I'm _____. I look very _____, don't I? I usually behave in a very _____ manner. Most of the time, I feel _____. Today I'm feeling _____. When I move, I like to _____. Don't I have a _____ voice?"

Another approach is to introduce the puppet to the children and let them fill in their own ideas about the puppet's personality.

Puppetotes

Puppetotes are "mobile homes" for puppets. Bags, purses, boxes, basically anything that will conceal the puppets while enabling you to carry them from place to place can serve as an effective Puppetote. Art specialists find 'totes convenient for transporting puppets from one class or school to another. As a teacher, a Puppetote will aid you in keeping the puppets out-of-reach (and out-of-sight!) until you are ready to Puppetell. In selecting a 'tote, be sure it is big enough to hold the puppets yet small enough to be placed nearby during Puppetelling-time.

When using 'totes with the children, think of them as curiosity motivators. "What's inside?" is certain to be asked. If you have a canvas bag painted like a barn, you can inquire "Who do you suppose lives in my barn?" an excellent lead-in to the singing of *Old MacDonald Had A Farm* with puppets. A colorfully wrapped box wih a big bow on top suggests Santa, birthdays and other popular gift-giving occasions. The Puppetote may even double as a Story Box or as background for a puppet presentation. In general, Puppetotes are fun to make, easy to use and stimulating for the children.

Character Totes

Sometimes puppets like to have permanent homes of their very own. Whenever you bring "that" container out, the children will anticipate with great joy the arrival of a favorite character. Cookie Monster would dearly love to live in a cookie jar while Mr. Tooth Decay would feel right at home in a Whitman candy box. What better place for a fish puppet than in a pocket of a sea-scene mural, a small fish bowl or beach pail. Assorted baskets can be easily converted into birds' nests as well as a host of other habitats; flower pots make excellent homes for plants and blossoms. You may even have a class mascot who lives in a box that is painted to look like your school!

Many of the suggested containers can be used "as

is" while others may need to be spruced up with fabric trims, contact paper or a coat of paint. A good corresponding art project is to let the children decorate the puppet homes themselves. If containers are needed, circulate a "wish list" among parents and staff, also check garage sales and flea markets for small and large cookie tins, lunch boxes, wastebaskets, canisters, bread boxes, picnic baskets, purses, shoe boxes, jewelry boxes (for fingerpuppets), bird cages and pots and pans with lids.

Holiday Totes

Puppetotes are superb for holiday themes.

Valentine's Day. Any container that is pink or red is apt, especially empty heart-shaped candy boxes.

Easter. Easter baskets and break-open plastic eggs of all sizes will accommodate bunnies, chicks or spring characters. Save L'Egg stocking containers for silver or colored eggs.

Halloween. Witches, goblins and ghosts can live in a plastic jack-o-lantern, mysterious black boxes or even trick-or-treat bags.

Thanksgiving. A cornucopia or a pilgrim's hat turned upside down makes an appropriate 'tote.

Christmas. Try using a red and white Santa bag, a colorful stocking or a gift box with a bright ribbon for a festive touch.

57

		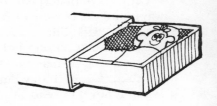
Fishbowl	Spaceship	Matchbox

Carry Bag	Felt Log	Beach Pail

Watering Can	Pocketbook	Picnic Basket

Bird Cage	Candy Box	Christmas Stocking

Puppet Totes

Large grocery bags make excellent totes for puppets and can be converted into almost any theme.

Outer Space

Tree

Ocean

Night/Day

Easter Basket

Mountainside

Christmas

To North Pole/North Pole

Bat's Cave

Haunted House

Halloween

City/Country

Turn-A-Round Totes

Finger Puppet Food

Good Food Tote

A Strange Thing Tote

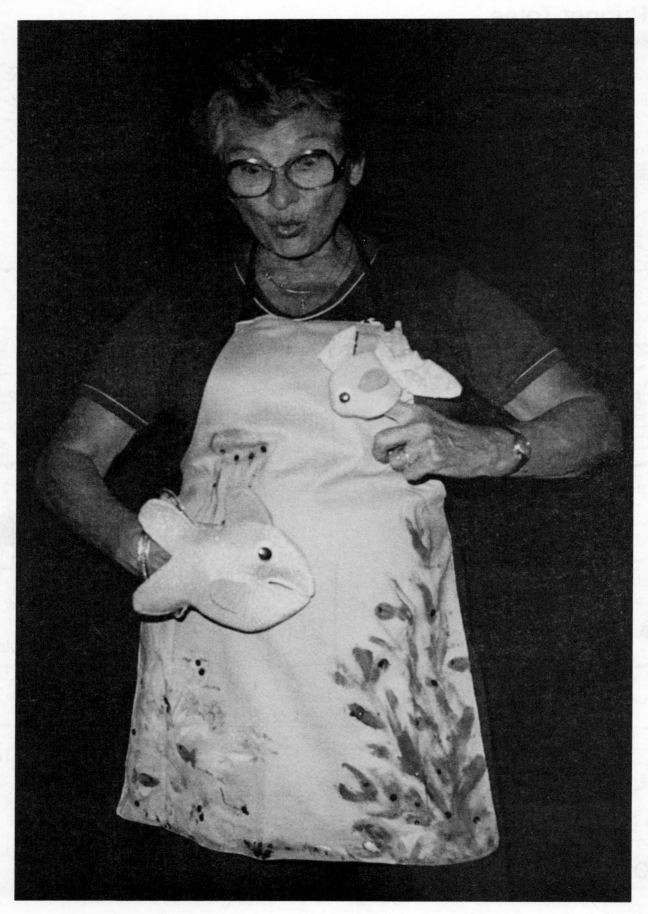

An underwater Apron Stage

Apron Stages

A colorful Story Apron is an ideal costume for you to wear as a Puppeteller. It signals that Puppetime is about to begin, it provides a background for your story, poem or song and it hides puppets and props until you are ready to use them.

Apron Stages are inexpensive to buy, easy to make and simple to customize. A brief survey of the kitchen section of most department stores will reveal a wide selection of styles and colors to use as the basic background. If you prefer making your own apron, look for apron designs in the craft section of pattern books.

When selecting a Puppet Apron, consider how you prefer to sit when performing and interacting with the children. If you like to sit cross-legged on the floor, then choose a short, circular or gathered apron to cover your knees. If you like to sit on a chair, select a fuller, circular apron that touches the floor. Or, if you prefer to be halfway up on your knees, opt for a butcher style apron. If creating the illusion of a background is not a concern, then a basic apron with pockets will be quite adequate, also less expensive.

To decorate an apron for puppet activities, review the fingerplays, poems, songs, stories and books that you most enjoy. Consider *where* the action will take place and, in so doing, determine a suitable setting for the action. You may find that your selections adapt well to one location. For example, a country scene that features a barnyard with a pond will furnish an ideal background for animal songs and stories like *Six Little Ducks, Old MacDonald, The Gingerbread Boy, The Ugly Duckling* and *The Little Red Hen,* to name just a few. On the other hand, your favorites might include diverse songs and stories such as *Rudolf, the Red-Nosed Reindeer* that connotes a winter scene or *The Lion and the Mouse* from *Aesop's Fables* that takes place in the jungle.

Most importantly, design your apron to be flexible! Buttons placed at the top of the apron will enable you to attach a new background panel for a change of scenery. Day can become night in Thurber's *Many Moons* or a rural scene can be converted to an urban setting in *The Country Mouse and the City Mouse.* Strips of velcro are also useful for attaching and removing puppets and scenery quickly from the background. For example, in the finger play *The Monkeys and the Crocodile,* the use of velcro allows the monkeys to be gobbled off the tree one-by-one. To simplify matters, think of the Puppet Apron as a flannel board. The country or city scene can grow up around the puppets in *The Country Mouse and the City Mouse* or a jungle can be created right before

the children's eyes when Max's room is transformed in Maurice Sendak's *Where the Wild Things Are.*

Rather than making a different apron or panel for each story or song, consider instead a set of general backgrounds that can be easily applied and removed from an all-purpose Puppet Apron. Most stories take place in these locations:

Desert	Country with river
Jungle	Meadow with pond
Zoo	Beach with ocean
City	Underground with cave/den
Farm	House (outside)
Tree	House (inside)
Garden	Outer Space

Themes are also appropriate as backgrounds.

Day	Colors
Night	Numbers
Summer/Spring	Shapes
Winter/Fall	Time
	Holidays

If time is short, omit the decorative panels altogether and let the children, instead, imagine the details of a background. In that case, select plain panels to suggest ideas or locations: blue for clear skies and daytime, white or silver for winter, green for springtime, grass or trees and brown for underground or darkness. By adding and removing suggestive details such as stars, sun, flowers, a small barn and such, one basic apron becomes amazingly versatile. Fabric with unusual but appropriate prints may also be adapted. For example, a fern design can represent the jungle, a blending of blues and turquoises, the ocean and metallic fabric for outer space. Holiday moods may be captured by green/red/white panels for Christmas, green panels for St. Patrick's Day and an orange/black combination for Halloween. Holiday prints are also appropriate.

There are many ways to decorate aprons and background panels. The following are some suggestions:

- **Permanent Ink Markers** come in all colors and are easy to use on fabrics. Simply draw the image desired. Always test fabrics first to see if colors blot.

- **Ball Point Paint Tubes** offer the benefit of paint without mess and inconvenience. Stocked in most craft stores or fabric departments, these tubes come in a multitude of colors and are operated like a ball point pen, but the effect is paint-like.

● **Fabric Crayons** are wonderful for giving a "child crafted" look to Puppet Aprons. The appearance is that of crayon drawings, with one important difference: they are wash resistant.

● **Textile and Acryllic Paints** are available in most art stores and produce vivid, dense colors on fabrics. The effect is similar to that of oil paints. When using, be sure to work away from carpets or use several layers of newspaper to protect floor area.

● **Fabric Applique and Stitchery** can produce a textured, rich looking apron. The crafts section of most fabric pattern books contain applique ideas with scenic backgrounds and a variety of figures. Just adapt the patterns or copy scenic designs from children books.

If you lack the time or still feel you cannot create a background, let the children do it for you. They will enjoy the process of making backdrops with crayons, paints, and pens on scraps of fabric or plain newsprint. Imagine the children's pride when they see you enact a story with scenery of their own design.

During Puppetelling sessions, participation on the part of the children is a natural and important part of the experience. Children will happily assist by turning book pages or holding a puppet prop. You can even make child-size Story Aprons, like your own, for the children to wear when assisting.

If the children have been unable to hold the puppets during the story, an opportunity should be set aside for them to do so afterwards. Intimate contact with a puppet, especially after seeing it in a dramatic situation, greatly heightens the child's overall impression. Each child should have a few minutes to satisfy his curiosity by talking to, holding and loving the puppets. By so doing, you will assure warm memories of the experience as well as a strengthened link between the story, the puppets, the children and yourself.

A Basic Story Apron

A general all-purpose story apron can be made by adding pockets to a storebrought apron or by creating your own custom-apron from selected fabric. A basic apron composed of a variety of calico cotton print pockets makes a cheerful background for most stories. If you desire an apron with a special theme, consider choosing holiday prints for Christmas; flower patterns for spring or ginghams and denim for barnyard themes.

Procedure: Hem along entire top edge of pocket strips. Turn under sides and bottom edges of pocket strips and sew to apron as shown. Sew vertical separation seams of each pocket strip down to apron. Gather apron top and pull gathers until 19 inches wide. Sew waistband to apron.

Inspired by Nancy A. Cole

Basic Story Aprons

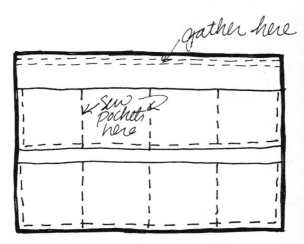

gather here

Sew pockets here

Sew pocket strips to apron panel before gathering and attaching waistband. Stitch pockets down as shown to make four pockets per strip.

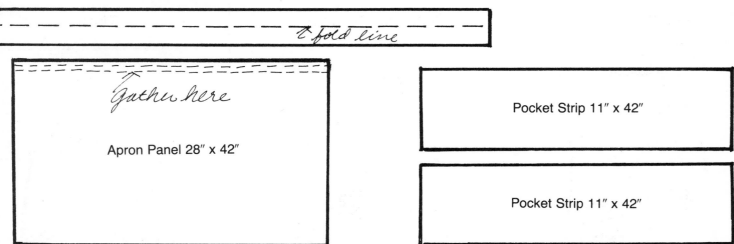

Waistband 4″ x 72″

fold line

Gather here

Apron Panel 28″ x 42″

Pocket Strip 11″ x 42″

Pocket Strip 11″ x 42″

Pocket Strip 12″ × 28″

Basic Pattern

63

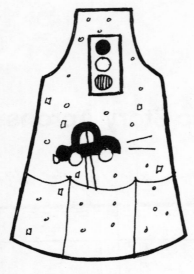

Traffic Safety

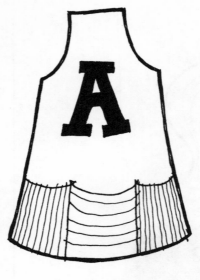

Letter "A"

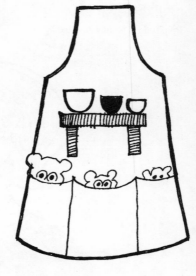

Goldilocks

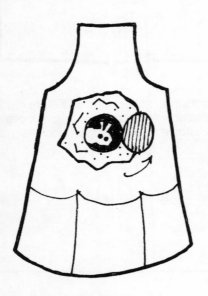

Rabbit's Hole

"Jack Be Nimble"

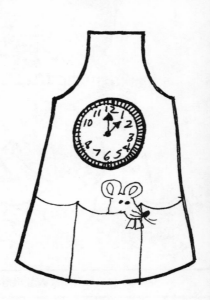

Time

Landscape

Snowscape

Oceanscape

Decorated Story Aprons

Aprons on top two rows on opposite page have velcro tabs attached to upper area of apron for changing scenic pieces (made from felt or decorated Pellon)

Aprons on bottom row are decorated or painted to match a particular theme.

Tree Apron

Use a brown textured fabric for butcher apron "trunk." Add a furry owl with wiggle eyes to front "knot hole." "Nest" can be made from a cardboard crown covered with fringed tissue paper or felt and tied to puppeteer's head with an elastic band. Large black felt or paper "roots" add a final, humorous touch when secured to your feet with ribbon ties.

Christmas Tree

Day/Night

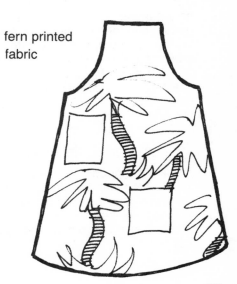

fern printed fabric

Jungle

65

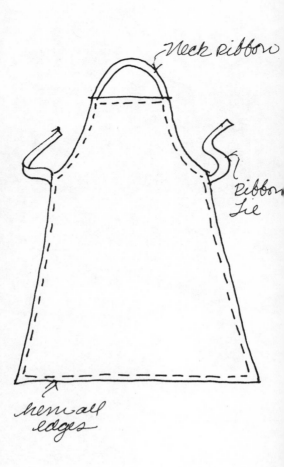

neck ribbon

Ribbon Tie

hem all edges

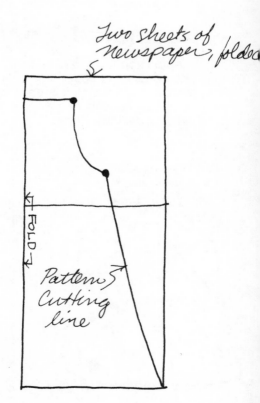

Two sheets of newspaper, folded

FOLD

Pattern Cutting line

Basic Butcher Apron

To make a basic butcher apron for ideas shown on these pages use denim, muslin or other heavyweight cotton fabric. Tape two large sheets of newspaper together and fold in half. Draw a shape as shown, following measurements indicated. Cut shape out and open up pattern. Cut a fabric apron and hem a $3/8''-1/2''$ hem around all edges.

Attach a 1" x 20" neck ribbon (grosgrain or other) to neck; also 1" x 24" ribbon ties to apron sides as shown.

Apron with Changing Scenery

Interchangeable, colored 11 by 11 inch Pellon scenery panels can be arranged in sequential order and buttoned in place onto the upper edge of a 12 by 12 inch pocket sewn to apron front. As each scene is finished, simply flip it up and back and tuck it into the pocket.

66

Idea by Clara Oshima

Interchangeable Scenery Panels

Pancho Stages

Cut a 4′ diamater fabric circle (or 4 quarter sections from varied fabrics, sewn together to create a complete circle). Cut out a 8–9″ neck hole in center. Try on Pancho and locate where to cut armslits, as shown. Color scenes with coloring medium. Rotate Pancho around for scenic changes.

Idea by Anna Fleming

67

velcro on scenery

| Pond | Sky | Rainbow | Stone Soup |

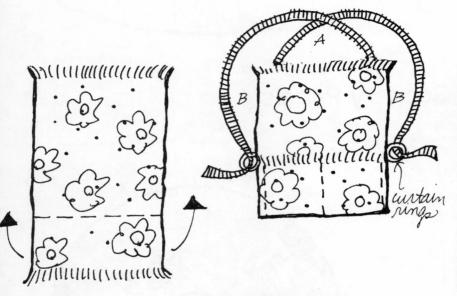

Idea by Maxine Nu'chiwa

Towel Aprons

A simple, versatile idea for Puppetelling is to create an apron from a small or medium sized bath towel. Select appropriate colors or patterned backgrounds to correspond with themes. For example, a flower print connotes a garden, bright stripes a carnival and azure blue a water theme. A solid colored towel serves well as a simple background on which to change felt or Pellon scenery; for this added versatility, add velcro pieces to towel apron.

Procedure: Fold bottom of towel upwards at the 1/3 point line. Sew down ends and center of pocket area as shown. Attach two 2½ foot lengths of 1 inch wide grosgrain ribbon to upper corners of apron. Sew small plastic curtain rings to both sides of apron and thread grosgrain ribbon through rings. Slip neck through area *A* and arms through areas *BB* and adjust grosgrain ribbon while tieing ends behind back of wearer.

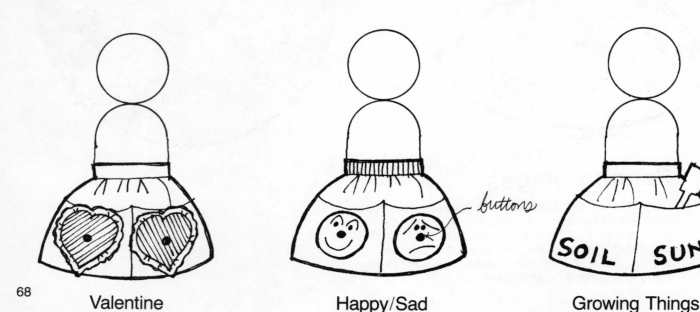

| Valentine | Happy/Sad | Growing Things |

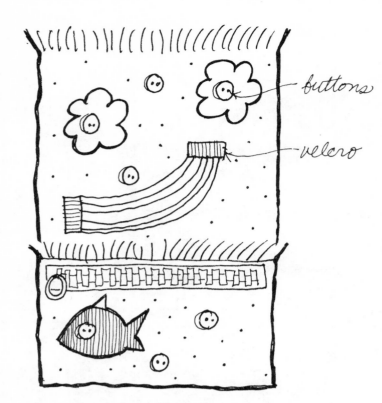

buttons

velcro

Small Motor Skills Apron

This towel apron is superb for teaching young children small motor skills and can include a variety of devices for them to manipulate, such as a zippered pouch, buttons for attaching felt scenic pieces (fish, flowers, butterflies, etc.), velcro tabs for securing additional scenery, buckles, ties and other fasteners.

See opposite page for attaching loops, arms and neck ribbons.

Short Aprons

A carpenter apron is a useful ready made apron for puppetry activities. Consider making your own short apron if a ready made one is not available by condensing an apron pattern. Buttons attached to pockets can be used for interchanging decoration.

Books on Puppetelling

Bauer, Caroline, *Handbook for Storytellers*—All facets of storytelling are covered: planning; promotion; story sources; multi-media storytelling (including puppets); and programs. A must for all storytellers. Chicago, Illinois, American Library Association, 1977

Engler, Larry, and Fijan, Carol, *Making Puppets Come Alive*—An essential handbook for the beginning puppeteer showing movement, manipulation, and voice synchronization of hand puppets. Includes excellent skits for building pantomime skills. New York, Taplinger Publishing Co., Inc., 1973

Ross, Ramon R., *Storyteller*—A superb book on developing skills in storytelling. Imaginatively and simply presented, this book includes ideas on utilizing songs, puppetry, flannelboard and game exercises to enrich storytelling. Columbus, OH, Charles E. Merrill, 1975

You will undoubtably find many ways to use these Story Gloves.

Story Gloves

Story Gloves complement fingerplays. Almost any glove will work well: garden, rubber, knitted, dress or home-sewn. By gluing velcro tabs to the fingertips you can interchange puppets, thus making the same glove adaptable to a variety of five- or ten-character poems. You may also wish to collect different types of gloves and employ a variety of colors. (A wonderful solution for what to do with the leftover glove that used to make a pair!) Black makes an ideal background for showing off colorful puppets. Brown connotes earth, holes, beehives, ant hills and tree trunks while green gloves are effective for poems about grass, flowers, tree-tops and spring. The fingers can also represent stems of flowers. Light blue can represent the sky or a body of water (ocean or pond) while dark blue can depict the night sky. White, of course, means snow. Consider also the application of appropriately colored gloves for holidays.

You will undoubtedly find many ways to use these Story Gloves. An effective technique with children is to tuck the fingers into a fist. As the poem is said, hold up one finger at a time to reveal flowers growing, bees swarming from a hive or ants marching out of their hill. A little clown velcroed to the thumb could even become Jack popping out of his box!

Since these tiny puppets are easily lost, it is imperative to find a safe way to store them such as a plastic box with dividers or small drawers.

Refer to the Teacher's Puppetmaking chapter for construction methods on fingerpuppets.

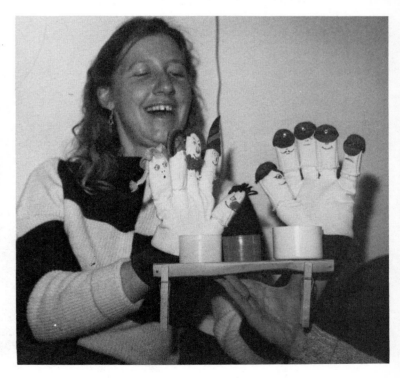

Books on Fingerplays

Beall, Pamela and Susan Nipp. *Wee Sing: Children's Songs and Fingerplays.* Los Angeles, CA: Price, Stern, Sloan, 1979.

Brown, Marc. *Finger Rhymes.* New York: Dutton, 1980.

Glazer, Tom. *Eye Winker Tom Tinker Chin Chopper.* New York: Doubleday, 1973.

Leighton, Audrey O. *Grandma Moon's Fingerplays.* Order from: A. Leighton 11837 S.W. Riverwood Road Portland OR 97219 (Total cost: $4.95)

71

Turtle in a Box

Humpty Dumpty

Mary, Mary, Quite Contrary

My Favorite Pet

Peacock Garden—Paper Tissue Box

Stories in Cups and Containers

Individualized theaters made from paper cups or food boxes are intriguing visuals to depict stories, poems, songs, and curriculum-related material. Children can make their own mobile theater to aid in verbalization or dramatization. Once completed theaters can be brought home as a memory of the puppet experience. Tape a small drawing or picture (magazine, coloring book or greeting card) to end of a drinking straw; slip other end of straw through hole punctured in bottom of container. Attach scenic suggestions to edge of container and decorate exterior to match story theme.

The Sea

Eeency Weency Spider

Shapeland

The Circus

For interchangeable scenery, create a series of pictures on several small paper plates. Staple the last scene to back edge of cup theater. Arrange other plates in sequence and secure together with a paper clip.

73

Book Theaters

A storybook itself may provide a natural theater with the front and back covers as well as interior illustrations furnishing background scenery for Puppetelling. Characters related to those in the book can introduce a story and conduct preliminary discussions. For example, a zookeeper may introduce an animal story while Mother Goose may present a nursery rhyme. Lead puppets can be used within the story itself such as a donkey in William Steig's *Sylvester and The Magic Pebble* or a mouse in Leo Lionni's *Frederick*. The Book Theater method is especially helpful for beginning Puppetellers since it serves to develop skills for handling more complex casts later on.

Place the book on a table with the outside covers facing the children. This positioning will allow the Puppeteller to read the inside text while gliding the puppets along the top edge of the book. Puppets can be made from paper cut-outs glued to drinking straws or popsicle sticks. Scenery and props, attached to spring clothespins, may be secured to the top of the book. If you are familiar enough with the story so that the text does not have to be read, then turn the pages of the book toward the children, thus allowing each page to create a different scene. Fingerpuppets are excellent for use with Book Theaters.

Theaters-to-Wear

Children love to take turns trying on this novel theater to tell their own versions of stories. It also provides an excellent theater for the teacher to Puppetell. A Theater-To-Wear can be attached around the neck and hung within easy reach in front of the standing Puppeteller. Fingerpuppets and small rod puppets are particularly well-suited for dramatizations. The advantage of this theater is that many characters can be maneuvered at one time with the use of rods. Rod puppets on very thin dowels or drinking straws can be made to adhere to double-backed carpeting tape that has been affixed to the front inside edge of a cut-down box. Several rod puppets that have already been introduced early in the story can remain in position while other puppets are brought into play.

To make a basic box, find a sturdy grocery carton. Cut away the entire back of the box then cut down the front side and ends to a height of six to eight inches. Attach a heavy cord or ribbon length to both sides of the box and adjust to a comfortable fit for hanging around your neck. The bottom of the box makes an ideal surface for laying a storybook or puppets presently not in use.

Lapboards

Lapboards make good "stages" for Puppetelling sessions when you need a surface on which to move puppets or place props. Simple to construct, Lapboards can be made by covering a piece of rigid cardboard with plain felt or contact paper. Scenery and props can be arranged on top of the Lapboard. For example, a circle of blue will represent the pond in Leo Lionni's *Fish Is Fish* while a small toy house and city buildings may provide the setting for Virginia Burton's *The Little House* and a railroad track sets the scene for Watty Piper's *The Little Engine That Could.*

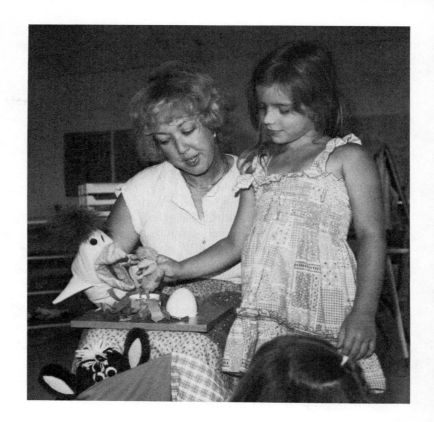

Lap Theaters

If a "puppet show" approach is desired, consider a Lap Theater with finger or small rod puppets as an alternate to a conventional stage. A sturdy cardboard box can be adapted into a successful Lap Theater by cutting out an opening in front and then removing the entire back section to accommodate the puppeteer's arms and hands. A curtain can be easily attached in the front opening to shield the puppeteer's movements. Additional puppets may be stored behind the stage on your lap. For practical purposes, when using the Lap Theater, it is best to select simple stories with a minimum number of characters, scenery and props.

75

Story Panels

A Story Panel can be propped up on a table top as a means for presenting stories or for informal use by the children in the Puppet Corner. These panels are especially practical for stories where several scenes need to be shown simultaneously. The background can be painted or colored with marker pens or pasted with pictures from magazines or children's drawings.

Panels with front openings or swinging panels are recommended for stories where characters go "into" something such as a cave, house or a hole. For stories where the puppets need to move from one locale to another, a horizontal series of panel arrangements would be better. For example, in *Goldilocks and The Three Bears* each panel may depict a separate room. In *The Night Before Christmas* one panel could show a house and the rest a snowscape with the North Pole and Santa's outpost at the opposite end.

To construct, make panels from poster board or other stiff cardboard. If panels are cut to equal size, they can be hinged together with tape and conveniently folded for storage. Cut two to three inch cardboard strips to match widths of panels and staple strips along the bottom edges of the panels. Cardboard or paper puppet figures can then be slipped along inside these strips and be moved about during the story. For permanency, you may wish to laminate the panels in plastic.

Granny's House

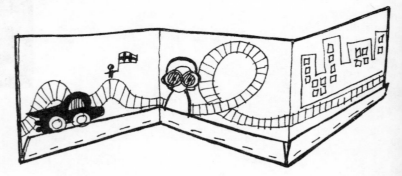

The Race

Story Panel by Diane Go

76

Variation on Story Panel for Peter, Paul and Mary's song *I'm Going to the Zoo!* can be operated from the back with fingers poking through to wiggle elephant's trunk, monkey's tail and other animation.

Story Boxes

Story Boxes combine puppet storage with puppet presentations. A composite of puppets, props and scenery with songs, books and poems contained in a single unit constitute a Story Box. Inside this kit are all the things necessary for the puppet presentation: puppets, props, text and scenery. Almost any type of box with a lid, that will rest comfortably on your lap, is suitable: for example, a shoebox, an under-the-bed storage box or file box. Miniature stories packaged in small jewelry boxes are also fun to explore.

Scenery may be constructed from lightweight cardboard featuring pasted-on magazine pictures or a scene of your own drawing. Include only key items that best illustrate the action of the story and keep things simple. By gluing spring clothespins onto the back of scenery parts, the scenery illustrations can then be clipped onto the top edges of the box. Beforehand, tie a party ribbon around the box to untie in the presence of the children. The Story Box then takes on the aura of a very special gift.

A sample Story Box for *The Three Pigs* might include:

Three Piggy puppets
A Bad Wolf puppet
Three cardboard houses of straw, wood and brick (each house-scene may be reversed to show an interior)

An *Old Mother Hubbard* may include:

Old Mother Hubbard and Dog puppets
Cardboard cupboard
Newspaper, flute, fruit and other props

Little Miss Muffet

Little Miss Muffet
Spider
Bottle cap bowl

finger puppets

Little Red Riding Hood

Turn-a-round scene panel:
- exterior house
- interior house

Little Red Riding Hood
Granny
Bad Wolf
Tiny basket

Miniature Story Boxes

77

Peek-a-Boo Boards

Peek-a-Boo Boards, an adaptation of the Story Panel, activate young children's reveling in peek-a-boo games and hide 'n seek. The children enjoy pointing to hiding puppets and are especially thrilled when the teacher cannot find the character. To create the boards, simply paste or draw a picture onto a piece of poster board. Cut holes in the appropriate places and let fingerpuppets peek through.

Poems like A. A. Milne's *Has Anybody Seen My Mouse?* or songs like *Where Has My Little Dog Gone?* are excellent for Peek-a-Boo Boards. If you have no specific story in mind, show the board to the children and let them make up a collective story. The children may want to construct their own little fingerpuppets to use while Puppetelling their new story.

Peek-a-Boo Boards also aid in learning about plants and habitats. For example, with a picture of a country scene, ask the children to guess what animals live in places depicted on the board (such as barns, holes, nests, etc.). When they guess the correct answer, poke the puppet through the hole.

For another exercise, draw a picture of a large tree and ask "What grows on a tree?" Puppets of apples, oranges and grapefruit, for instance, can peek out. A variety of trees such as papaya, coconut and mango can serve to teach children about their own geographic regions as well as those in other parts of the world. Also ask "What lives in a tree?" and let the children create the birds, worms, insects and so forth. To elaborate further on this idea, ask "What grows on a vine?" (grapes, beans, etc.) or with a garden theme "What grows underground?" (carrots, potatoes, beets and such).

Holiday themes also adapt well to Peek-a-Boo Boards. A Christmas tree, for example, can be decorated with puppet ornaments. A Haunted House at Halloween can be inhabited by ghosts, witches and skeletons. In addition, a Peek-a-Book Board can become a meadow or a house where Easter eggs are hidden.

For teaching spatial concepts such as top, bottom, under, over, near, far, left and right, ask the children to label the puppet's position in relation to something else on the board. The applications are seemingly endless; your own imagination will undoubtedly find many more ways to adapt Peek-a-Boo Boards and puppets to best serve the needs of the children in your school. Consider laminating Peek-a-Boo Boards in plastic, for permanency.

The Apple Tree

Sea Chanty

78

Bear hand puppet peeking through a large hole in book with flip-over scenic pages

Rabbit peeking through his hole

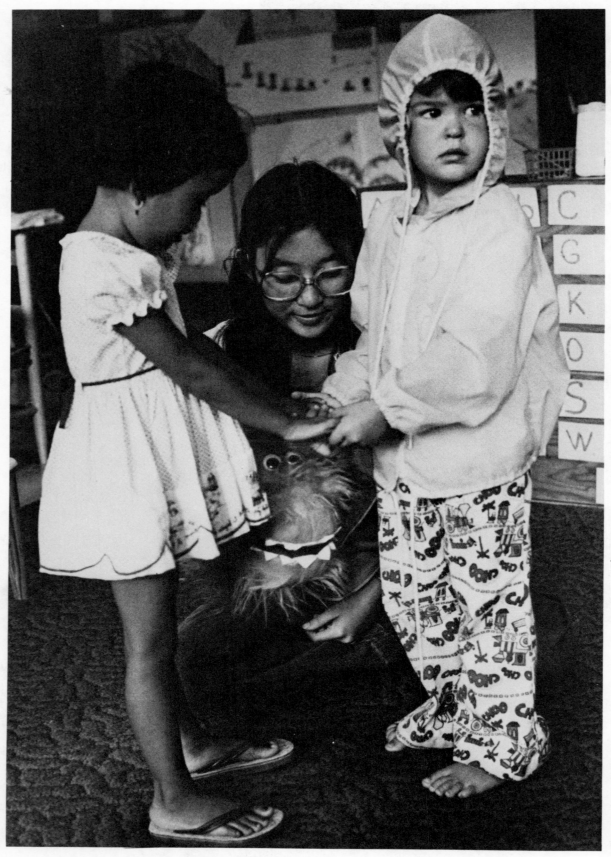

The Troll hides underneath the security of his "Bridge"

PUPPETIZING
Playacting with Puppets

Under the guidance of a teacher, Puppetization engages the children in informal dramatizations with improvised action and dialogue. Since there is no stage, the children are not confined to the limits of a small proscenium. Instead, they are free to roam throughout a large playing area and explore their own body movements in relation to those of the puppets. Because there is no script to follow or text to memorize, the children are at liberty to contribute spontaneously their own ideas by adding new action and dialogue as deemed appropriate. Furthermore, there is no audience, thus no pressure to "perform." As a result, the success of Puppetizing depends only upon the technical expertise and talents already possessed by the children; it does not exceed the collective abilities of the group. In essence, through the Puppetization process, the children are able to share ideas, characters, a poem or story with each other and, in so doing, they partake of an invigorating experience for learning and growing.

Development of a lesson plan for Puppetization requires two major steps: preparation and implementation. Preparation occurs *before* you meet with the children and implementation takes place while you are *with* the children.

Preparing the activity before you meet with the children is critical even to the success of seemingly "unplanned" activities in that it enables the leader to assess what is actually necessary as well as what is realistically available. Children, space, time, equipment, supplies and puppets are all important considerations. Your creative puppetry ventures will be greatly enhanced by investing a small amount of time in mapping out each of these aspects.

Children·

Children are the pivotal point for planning the puppet activity. The primary factor to consider is the age of the children since it indicates their psychosocial developmental level as well as verbal and physical abilities. In addition, the group's attention span and interest areas must be taken into account. For preschool children, simplicity and familiarity with a particular frame of reference are relevant factors to consider. There are several types of story themes that are especially suitable for Puppetizations with young children, including:

- **Reality-Based Situations** that deal with home or school life, animals, community workers, moving vehicles and other categories that children are familiar with in their daily lives.

- **Fantasy-Based Stories** based on imaginative leaps to which the children have had some exposure, such as storybook characters who fly or do other remarkable feats.

- **Stories With Repetition** help to facilitate a child's ability to assimilate new material. For example, a child listening to P.D. Eastman's *Are You My Mother?* grasps the story content with increasing delight as the basic action sequence is repeated several times. Many cumulative stories such as *Henny Penny* or stories with repeated refrains such as "Cats here, cats there, cats and kittens everywhere . . ." in Wanda Gag's *Millions of Cats* also are excellent vehicles for memory development.

- **Classic Stories** especially please young children who never tire of hearing them "one more time." The greatest pleasure comes from the children's anticipating ahead of time exactly what will happen next and how the story will end. Such all-time favorites as *Little Red Riding Hood*, *Jack and the Beanstalk* and *The Ugly Duckling* provide a constant in a world of daily changes, bringing a special comfort and sense of security to the child.

Children like to move about more and talk less in dramatic situations. By emphasizing movement rather than dialogue, the teacher can insure success for reaching a broader range of children. This is important especially in the case of children's first experiences with creative puppetry. In the beginning, let actions dominate and as children gain more experience in Puppetization, their verbal skills will naturally develop, as will their sense of self-confidence.

Always take into account the number of participants involved when selecting a story or scene to enact. The larger the group, the simpler the puppet project must be. Thus the preparation required for a puppetry activity for five children will be different than that for twenty.

In selecting material for both Puppetmaking and Puppetization activities for groups of ten or more, consider adapting stories with:

- **Unlimited Numbers of Same Characters.** For example, puppet construction is facilitated if all the children make bird puppets for *Sing A Song of Sixpence* or fish puppets for Leo Lionni's *Swimmy*. Children can still express their own individuality in the way they design and manipulate their puppets, even if they all make the same character.

- **Groupings of Characters with Similar Actions.** In *Old MacDonald Had A Farm* the children can be grouped together into various animal classifications. Then during the Puppetization, all the cows can "moo," hens "cluck" and ducks "quack" in unison, each group acting as a single unit. Such parallel structuring provides some interesting examples of group dynamics and unity of action.

Space

Puppetization is most effective when a clearly delineated play area has been chosen that will allow all the participants to see and hear easily, also to move about comfortably. The size of the area depends, of course, on the availability of floor space that, in turn, will determine the number of children who will be able to participate at a given time. For example, a small room with a playing space of five feet in diameter may be ideal for eight to ten children to take part in finger plays that require a minimum of physical movement. A large playing space, on the other hand, may be required for a full story dramatization using larger puppets. An overcrowded space should be avoided as it will tend to discourage creativity. Based on these spatial factors, the leader will need to decide in advance how many children can be accommodated for each given activity.

Several options include:

- **The Playing Circle.** Mark the outline of a circle on the floor with masking tape, chalk or even a long rope. This technique is suggested especially for younger children in helping them to maintain a circular seating

pattern. It also gives them a visible place to return after participating in a puppetization.

- **The Semi-Circle.** Using the method described above, mark a semi-circle. This plan is recommended for Puppetelling as some children, in their eagerness to touch the puppets, may come too close and block the views of others. With a semi-circular delineation, they may be politely asked to remain behind the "magic puppet line." This shape is also beneficial for activities in which the children create a mural or backdrop for their Puppetizations. These can be arranged in front of the semi-circle.

- **The Playing Carpet.** Roll out a large area rug or carpet remnant. The spectators may sit around the edge of this well-defined acting area while the puppeteers enact a scenario in the center.

- **Table Tops.** When a small number of children is involved, from two to six persons, a table top provides an ideal setting. Tables are suggested for finger-walking puppets, also for hand-puppets tht need to "hide" under something during the play action.

Time

The amount of time available needs to be coordinated with the amount of time required to complete all phases of an activity. Otherwise, too much time or too little will cause the experience to be frustrating rather than pleasurable. Sufficient periods must be allotted to motivate the children as well as for Puppetelling, Puppetmaking and Puppetizing, in any or all combinations. Since creative puppetry activities can be as brief as five minutes or as long as several weeks or even months, it is important to anticipate a time schedule in the preparation and planning stages. Factors of concern in determining time estimates include:

- The type of activity selected;
- How often you will meet with the children;
- Ways the activity will be integrated into the daily routine at school; and
- Whether the children will make their own puppets.

Specific activities may be chosen to suit the amount of time available. For example, a simple Puppetization of *Five Little Ducks* may take just a few minutes if pre-made duck puppets are to be used.

The class can sing the song while the puppeteers "wiggle-waggle" the duck puppets "down to the water and back." On the other hand, a fairy tale such as *Goldilocks and The Three Bears* may require twenty minutes or longer to Puppetize because of the complex storyline.

The amount of contact time you will have with the children may further determine the scope of your puppetry projects. For instance, a curriculum specialist touring the schools will be limited to shorter projects, usually less than an hour. In such a case, you may wish to skip Puppetmaking and focus instead on Puppetizations that make use of your collection of ready-made puppets. A classroom teacher, by comparison, will have ample time blocks for organizing a more comprehensive schedule of related puppetry activities.

Daily classroom routines may also affect the structuring of puppetry experiences. A complete activity may need to be compressed into the span of one day or spread out over a period of several days or weeks.

A one-day schedule may be arranged with:

- Puppetmaking in a large group during a designated working period or in smaller groups throughout the morning.
- Prior to lunch or before the children go home in the afternoon, set aside time for Puppetelling with the completed puppets.

A weekly schedule may be arranged as follows:

- Monday—Introduce the material to be Puppetized.
- Tuesday—Puppetell the material to the children.
- Wednesday and Thursday—Make the puppets.
- Friday—Puppetize the material with the children and their completed puppets.

Sound Equipment and Effects

Although a dynamic puppetry session can be achieved without the use of sound equipment, the addition of a record player, tape recorder or various musical instruments and sound effects are fun to use and add a stimulating audio dimension to the activity. Music can set a mood: for example, carousel music for a circus theme, electronic music for outer space scenes and country hoedowns for a farm story. Sound effects also can be cleverly interwoven into the story action such as beating a drum or tapping wood blocks together to simulate the Three Billy Goats' hoof-beats as they cross the Troll's bridge. A kazoo makes a wonderful Troll's voice while sandpaper blocks, maracas and handmade shakers suggest the sounds of mice scurrying up the clock in *Hickory Dickory Dock*.

It is great fun to have a sound effects bin! Fill it with items such as bells, blocks, styrofoam packing material, pot lids and kitchen utensils, basically anything that makes a distinctive sound or musical tone. Children enjoy experimenting with the rhythms and tones of these instruments in their attempt to create appropriate sound effects to synchronize with action segments.

Materials

To determine what materials and supplies will be needed for making or acquiring puppets, ask yourself:

"What do I need?
"What is available?"
"What can the children bring from home?"
"Will I have money enough to purchase materials?"

These questions need to be raised while preparing for an activity. Do not be discouraged if supplies and budgets are limited. Think positively! Many teachers have overcome similar difficulties and created effective programs by stockpiling throwaway items such as egg cartons and cereal boxes, wax paper containers and other similar types of commercial packaging materials that suggest interesting puppet characters.

Story Cup Theaters in action

The Puppets

Puppets are, of course, the essential element in any creative puppetry activity. You may need to decide in advance how to integrate puppets into your project to include both the making and the application. Several options are available to the teacher in terms of the types of puppets and the extent to which they will be utilized in the program. The amount of time available for a particular project may determine whether to buy commercially-produced characters or to rely on child-made puppets. Both approaches are valid as the children will benefit from the balance of the two experiences. Young children like to manipulate ready-made puppets, to touch soft textures and see how realistic the characters appear. On the other hand, they feel a tremendous sense of satisfaction in creating a puppet of their own and using it to bring a story to life.

Be sure to include a rich diversity of Puppetmaking activities in your Puppetization program. Children enjoy the opportunity to explore new construction methods and materials for various types of puppets. Refer to the Children's Puppetmaking chapter for an assortment of Puppetmaking ideas.

Implementation

A well-prepared Puppetization plan is like a blueprint for action; it is a way to predict what will happen when you meet with the children. In essence, it is an invaluable composite of information you have already assimilated about the children, the puppets, time, space, equipment and materials. Once formulated, this plan may be re-used year after year with variations and expansions upon the central ideas. While such a plan is important, you should also remain flexible at all times to assure that an input of fresh ideas from the children can be easily incorporated into the program. To present and develop your ideas, it is helpful to follow these step-by-step procedures for (1) Motivating the children, (2) Puppetelling the activity, (3) Making the puppets, (4) Puppetizing the activity, (5) Talking it over and (6) Replaying the Puppetization with improvements suggested by the class.

Motivating the Children

At the beginning of each creative puppetry session it is wise to build a transitional bridge between what the children have been doing and what is about to happen next. For example, if the children have just come in from the playground, they will need to

84

become mentally and physically ready for the new activity. The first few minutes required to make that transition constitute what is known as the motivation period, a time when you will need to spark imaginations and spur conversations and enable the children to get into the proper frame of mind for the activity

During this period you may wish to:

- **Set The Mood**. For example, to quieten the group and encourage the children to think in an imaginative direction, you may ask them to close their eyes and envision a large meadow with a blue sky overhead, a house with a grass roof and a stone fence around the garden. In the garden grow big, beautiful round cabbages. When the children open their eyes out pops a Peter Rabbit puppet, ready and eager to participate in the Beatrix Potter's well-known story.

- **Arouse Curiosity**. By raising a few thought-provoking questions before Puppetizing the story, you may sharpen the children's curiosity for more details. For example, before singing the song *I Know an Old Lady Who Swallowed a Fly*, you may stimulate inquisitiveness by asking some silly questions such as "What would happen if *you* swallowed a horse?" or "What could the Old Lady swallow that is even *bigger* than a horse?"

- **Explain Unfamiliar Words Or Concepts**. It is often helpful to discuss in advance some of the words or ideas in the song or story that may be new or potentially confusing to the children. Greater satisfaction will be gained from singing *The Itsy Bitsy Spider* with the children if they know, for example, what a water spout looks like. Clarifying abstract terms such as "nightmare" in Mercer Mayer's *There's A Nightmare In My Closet* may be advisable before Puppetizing that particular story.

Puppetelling the Activity

This period marks the introduction of the material that eventually is to be Puppetized by the children. Its purposes are to familiarize the children with the story content, to make the characters believable and to propel the children's creative thinking toward the visualization of their own interpretations later on. One of the simplest ways to introduce the activity is to let a puppet do it. A bunny puppet, for example, holding up Margaret Wise Brown's *Home For A Bunny* may signal the beginning of that story and subsequently can be interwoven into the plot. Or a bird puppet may chirpily conduct a sing-a-long session. Fingerpuppets are also effective for introducing material. Because of their miniature size, they are extremely popular with young children. An imag-

inative selection of additional techniques for Puppetelling can be found in the Puppetelling chapter.

Puppetelling Eric Carles' *The Very Hungry Caterpillar*
New York: Philomel, 1969

Making the Puppets

It is important to understand how to integrate the Puppetmaking experience into a coordinated Puppetization activity. Puppets are meant to be used and brought to life not merely to be regarded as inanimate objects of art. In actuality, more time should be devoted to the use of puppets than to Puppetmaking; however, a strong relationship should be established between both disciplines, the doing and the using. Once a puppet project has been presented to the children, they are usually eager to begin. Encourage the children to think of their puppets as characters. Choose your words and ask questions in such a way that will stimulate creative talents. For example, ask "*Who* are you making?" instead of "*What* are you making?" Or "Tell me about your puppet" instead of "What is it?" Questions such as "Can you describe your puppet's personality?" or "What kind of voice does your puppet have?" or

"How does your puppet move?" can be easily integrated into the Puppetmaking process and enable the children to begin to visualize their puppets as total characters.

In some cases, it may be more desirable to create the puppets *before* the story is presented so that the children may actually participate in the story with their completed puppets. This technique is especially effective in the case of a familiar story such as *Little Red Riding Hood* that the children will be eager to perform.

For Puppetmaking sessions to be as efficient as possible, you may consider constructing mostly those characters that appear repeatedly in songs and stories, especially farm animals, fish and other sealife and characters such as monsters and witches. Frequently used puppets can give mileage to your collection. Also children derive satisfaction in realizing that what they make can have reoccuring value; oftentimes children's productions are seen or used once and then discarded. As the puppets await future role assignments, you may wish to display the characters and thus add a touch of color to the classroom by hanging the creations on the wall or suspending them from a clothesline above the children's reach. Future Puppetizations with childmade characters may be enriched by allowing the children to take turns using each other's puppets and, in so doing, become familiar with another child's style or technique. At the end of the school year, the puppets should, of course, be given to the children to take home.

Apportioning the puppet characters among the class members may be handled in various ways.

- **Theme-Based Puppets** such as barnyard or zoo animals or ocean creatures. Within a thematic scope, invite the children to make a puppet depicting their favorite animal or fish to fit a particular story. For example, almost any form of sealife is suitable for Leo Leonni's *Swimmy*.

- **Group Characters**. For Puppetizing Aesop's Fable *The Sun and The Wind*, for instance, ask half the class to make Sun puppets and the other half, Wind puppets. When you read the story, the puppets of each group can enact as units in the Sun and Wind roles.

- **Many Different Characters**. In a story such as Ruth Kraus' *The Carrot Seed*, puppets representing the entire cast need to be constructed. In advance, list all the characters required and ask the children to indicate by a show of hands who wishes to make which puppet. Or, the selection process can be structured as a game by putting all the characters' names in a bag and letting each child pick a slip with the name of the character to be made. In a full-cast, if the lead puppet, such as Carrot, for some reason cannot be made, do not despair. There are several easy options: the teacher can quickly improvise the needed puppet; a child can play the role of the missing character by simply using her hand as a make-believe puppet or she can use an all-purpose "actor" puppet to fill in. For a spare puppet, keep available a plain garden glove or mitten (with simple eyes and nose features attached, if desired) to serve as a standby whenever the circumstances warrant.

- **Child Actor Without Puppet.** Such characters as "Carrot" or "Goldilocks" or the "Troll" can be successfully played by a child actor while other members of the cast utilize puppets. You may also choose commercial puppets to play the "stars" in combination with child-made puppets for supporting roles.

Once the puppets are finished and before the Puppetization begins, you will need to decide whether the children will manipulate their own puppets or if the puppets should be interchanged among members of the class. Some children become enotionally attached to certain characters they have created and as a result consider it imperative to bring those pup-

pets to life in the dramatization. On the other hand, a child who has made the lead puppet may be reticent or uncooperative to participate in which case it would be better to interchange puppets so that a more vocal or willing child can manipulate the lead puppet. The premise of interchangeability allows for a greater flexibility while the use of the child's own puppet usually works best in those instances when the children all create the same character and manipulate them as a group to pantomime actions.

Puppetizing the Activity

The responsibility of the teacher during the period when the scenes are being played out is to maintain a comfortable, absorbing pace. This pacing can be accomplished through direct or indirect participation in the Puppetization on the part of the leader. With young children, the leader may take a dominant role by telling the story as the children pantomime the action with puppets. Or, the leader may play the central character to assure a suitable pace and to salvage a scene should it suddenly become bogged down. Playing a lead role affords the additional advantage of being on-the-scene when a child has a lapse of memory. For example, in Beatrix Potter's *Tale of Peter Rabbit* prompting sentences such as "Look, there's a rabbit in the garden!" or "Quick, catch him and we'll have rabbit stew for dinner tonight!" can jog a child's memory and keep the action

flowing smoothly. Prompting, when needed, will vitalize a scene, keep the storyline going forward and—most importantly—rescue the child from feeling humiliated due to a forgotten line.

Another advantage for the leader's active participation is to deter those children who might be "carried away" by silliness or disruptive behavior. Instead of interrupting the Puppetization, try instead to distract the children by directing their attention to more sincere expressions of character portrayals. For example, in Puppetizing *The Three Billy Goats Gruff*, the first two Billy Goats, after crossing the bridge, may start to butt at one another. Such behavior is disruptive and diminishes the effect of one of the most important scenes of the story. You may skillfully resolve this conflict by entering the story as a fourth Billy Goat who already lives on the grassy side of the bridge and says "Look what's happening on the bridge! Let's watch and see." With remarks of this nature you may effectively redirect attention to the original storyline. Moreover, it is a rewarding experience for the teacher to participate simply for fun! Imagine the children's delight when an adult puts aside a pedagogic role to become a "Troll" or "Goldilocks." The children will love interacting with the teacher as part of the Puppetization.

There is danger in playing a character, however, that the children will tend to mimic the teacher in subsequent Puppetizations of that same story. To counter the tendency to imitate, encourage the children to add some word or action of their very own that will enhance the characterizations. As the children mature and acquire more Puppetization skills, the need for the teacher to participate directly in the actual playing will decrease. At a more advanced level, the teacher's responsibility will shift to that of "side-coaching." For example, in *The Three Billy Goats Gruff* the "goats" may be playing together at one end of the bridge and become uncertain as to when they should start "trip-trapping" over the bridge. Instead of actually entering the scene, you may comment from the side "I wonder which goat will walk across the bridge first?"

Talking it Over

The conversation that follows the Puppetization constitutes one of the most significant aspects of the entire puppetry process. The mood should be quiet, intimate and encouraging with the leader sensitive not only to *what* is said but also *how*. For it is in this setting that the child is presented with opportunities to make some giant leaps in building perception and evaluation skills as well as a sense of self-esteem.

With careful preparation, the leader may use this valuable discussion period to aid the children in developing cognitive skills such as vocabulary-building, memory recall, sequencing and competence in other areas related to the entire spectrum of creative puppetry.

To assure that the "backstage review" is a constructive, rewarding experience for everyone, the leader should adhere closely to the following rules.

- **Always Ask Open-Ended Questions.** "What," "Why" and "How" are words that evoke descriptive responses rather than just "Yes" or "No" answers. A question such as "How did you know that the Troll was angry when he discovered the Goats walking over his bridge?" requires that the children recall the actions of the scene and respond with some degree of detail.

- **Use The Puppets' Names.** To eliminate any negative feelings of personal criticism, avoid using the name of the child who played the part. Instead, use that of the character. In so doing, you will focus on the task, not the child.

- **Accentuate The Positives.** Praise those words and actions that worked well in the dramatization rather than criticizing those that did not. Comment on specific characters and episodes that were particularly well executed by the children. Encourge constructive suggestions that will lead to improvements.

- **Avoid Judgmental Terms.** Use words such as "interesting" or "believable" rather than comparative terms like "good" or "bad."

- **Refrain From Comparisons.** If a child played a role in a believable fashion relative to his own potential, then that is what is important, not how his rendition measured up to that of another child. Puppetry is *not* an appropriate arena for competition among the children. Indeed, what makes puppetry special is its capacity to open up new avenues for personal growth and creative self-expression. In puppetry, there are no criteria for measurement, no one way that is the "right" way.

- **Give The Children Deserved Praise.** Children need praise throughout Puppetization activites, especially those who are shy or withdrawn and reluctant to participate; likewise, those whose contributions may have been overlooked by the rest of the class. Sup-

88

portive comments for group as well as individual efforts are required.

Replaying the Puppetization

Once the dramatization has been discussed constructively and shared within the intimacy of the group, the children will be eager to play it again. Give them the opportunity while interest is still high. Try to set new objectives each time a scene is enacted. For example, the children might try various interpretations of attempts by the Three Billy Goats Gruff to cross the Troll's bridge. Variations maintain interest through subsequent repetitions of the same story. Encourage the children to trade puppets or dramatize the entire story without puppets for a creative dramatics experience. After the final replay, retire the puppets to the Puppet Corner for informal play. An attractive table top display accompanied by the matching book and props will entice the children to Puppetize the scenes on an improvisational basis again and again.

Coping with Disruptive Behavior

Even the most creative, innovative plans can be shattered in an instant when the children's behavior becomes uncooperative and disruptive. Your own personal experience, as a teacher, in knowing what to expect from the children, how to avoid possible negative situations and what to do about them when they arise, will bolster your own feelings of self-confidence and thereby help to limit potential difficulties.

Problems, if they occur, usually erupt during the playing period. Therefore, consider first what kind of behavior you can realistically expect from the children.

- **Sincerity**. The children's effort to bring the puppets to life should be honest and believable in terms of their own talents and abilities.

- **Respect For The Puppets**. Puppets represent characters, not weapons, and thus are not appropriate for punching or abusing other puppets or people.

- **Cooperation**. Creative puppetry is a group experience, the success of which depends on everyone's working together.

By anticipating well in advance the potential difficulties, you may side-step some of the troublesome areas. In the planning stage, ask yourself what situations could possibly go wrong, what could get out of

hand and then decide in your own mind ways to handle those problem-spots effectively. One technique is to limit excessive verbal explanations in Puppetizing activities and thereby minimize the amount of time the children will sit idly. Young children are virtual masses of energy and want to do, do, do! Also, try to include as many children as possible in each Puppetization.

Another effectual measure is to build control agents into your activity. Control agents are devices which, unbeknownst to the children, prevent them from becoming disruptive. For instance, the teacher's active participation in the Puppetization, as discussed earlier, is a superb method of controlling group behavior. Also, you may interject logical restrictions into the story context such as Monkeys that only whisper, Wild Things that always sleep after their wild rumpus and Billy Goats that lie down to rest after crossing bridges. Ingenuity and subtlety in the use of control agents will usually forestall most difficulties and ensure cooperative puppeteers.

If, however, matters do get out of hand and there is difficulty in controlling disruptive behavior, even after the technique of entering the Puppetization has been employed, then stop the action and proceed with these suggestions in sequential order.

(1) **Talk About How You Feel**. Say, for example, "It disturbs me to see you damaging the puppets that were so carefully made for you." Or "I cannot believe you are really puppeteers! Do you suppose you could convince me that you are the characters?" Start the Puppetization again and if the problems still persist, proceed to Step Two.

(2) **Re-Cast The Roles**. Ask the unruly puppeteers to leave the playing circle and let new puppeteers assume the respective roles. When the initially disruptive children feel they can be more honest with their roles, invite them to rejoin the Puppetization. If difficulties erupt on a large scale with the entire group, proceed to Step Three.

(3) **Cancel The Activity**. Matter-of-factly explain to the children that Puppetization requires everyone to work together harmoniously to make the story come to life. You may observe, for example, "Our group is not working well today but we will try again another time." Children love puppets and once they understand what is expected of them, they will usually seek to cooperate in every possible way.

89

The Puppetization Plan

Charting out the Puppetization plan is an extremely important procedure the leader needs to undertake for determining which puppets will be included in the activity as well as how, when and where the action will take place. This master blueprint for implementation should be based on several factors: the ages of the children involved, their experiences, to what extent they will participate and what type of activity will be utilized. No matter how elementary the activity may appear, it is worth investing time and effort to develop a plan. It will aid you in organizing your material, giving structure to the story elements and serving as a basic guide when you Puppetize with the children. Such a well thought out plan can be used continuously throughout your future programming with variations upon the central ideas.

Consider, for example, a full dramatization of The Little Red Hen. If the children-puppeteers are providing all the dialogue and action then it will be necessary first to divide the story into playing scenes. This scene division is needed to reduce the story into workable segments that the child can remember for dramatization purposes. The story may be divided as follows:

Scene 1: The Little Red Hen finding and planting the wheat.

Scene 2: The wheat growing and the Little Red Hen cutting it.

Scene 3: The Little Red Hen threshing the wheat.

Scene 4: The Little Red Hen taking the wheat to the mill.

Scene 5: The Little Red Hen baking the bread.

Scene 6: The Little Red Hen eating the bread.

Once the leader and the children agree on what actions will comprise each scene, it will be time to help the children plan how to act out Scene One.

First, review the basic storytelling to clarify the beginning, middle, and end. By raising questions you will aid the children to visualize those actions they will soon be dramatizing. For instance: "Where did the Little Red Hen find the grain of wheat?" or "Why do you suppose the other farm animals wouldn't help her?" or "How should we end this scene?"

Second, decide which character will be included in Scene One and to what extent each will speak and act. The children should be encouraged to contribute new ideas yet remain faithful to the basic storyline. For example, questions such as "What do you suppose the other animals would do and say while the Little Red Hen planted the grain?" will inspire appropriate dialogue and actions.

Third, determine where each scene will be played. All the events should take place at various points within the playing circle. To assist the children making site-decisions, you may ask, for example, "Where shall we put the barn?" or "Where shall we put the fence and wheat field?" The designated areas can be easily remembered if marked by chalk or the placement of a symbolic object, such as a box barn or a paper-circle of brown wheat.

Finally, decide who will play which parts. The teacher should ask for volunteers and remind the children that scenes will be repeated so that everyone will have the chance to play a "favorite character." Once the children have put on their puppets, refer to them as "puppeteers." This terminology not only promotes a sense of purpose but moveover implies the need for group cooperation.

Preparing a step-by-step Puppetization Plan delineates clearly the educational objectives of the lesson and the means requisite to accomplish those goals. Using the example of *The Three Billy Goats Gruff*, the following outline is offered as a sample plan. Remember, however, that this plan is only a guide. When you are with the children, the activity should bend and flow to accommodate the children's ideas and actions.

Puppetization Plan

Project	The Three Billy Goats Gruff
Age Level	4 and 5-year-olds
Number of Children	10
Type of Puppet	Three Billy Goat rod puppets (child-made) Troll puppet (adult-made or commercial)
Materials	Skewers, drinking straws or dowels for rod control Crayons/Markers Assorted construction paper scraps Glue Tape Stapler Fake fur, if available
Playing Space	8-foot diameter circle
Estimated Time	40 minutes: 20 minutes for construction 20 minutes for Puppetization
Objectives	Oral expression Reinforcement of concepts: small, medium, large
Motivation	Clarify terms by asking the children "What is a bridge?" "What does a goat look like?" "What does a Troll look like?" Differentiate fantasy/reality figures by asking "Can you think of other imaginary characters, like the Troll, that are frightening?" (For example, ghosts, witches, goblins, skeletons, etc.) Ask the children to close their eyes and imagine a large meadow joined by a bridge. On one side it is brown and ugly; on the other, it is covered with green grass and flowers.
Puppetelling	Read or tell the story with or without puppets.
Puppetmaking	Rod puppets for the goats, made by the children, can be cut from construction paper and taped to the end of the rod control (skewer, dowel or drinking straw).

Puppetizing

Gather the children, with puppets, around the playing circle for discussion and planning.

(A) Review the story to establish scene division.

Scene 1: The Three Billy Goats decide to cross the bridge.

Scene 2: The first Billy Goat crosses the bridge and meets the Troll.

Scene 3: The second Billy Goat crosses the bridge and meets the Troll.

Scene 4: The third Billy Goat crosses the bridge and butts the Troll.

Scene 5: The three Billy Goats celebrate their new life on the green side of the bridge by eating and eating and eating!

(B) Set the Scene. Decide where to situate the two meadows and the bridge.

(C) *Prepare To Act out Scene 1*.

1) Decide how the scene will begin and end.

2) Determine what the three Billy Goats will say and do.

3) Ask for three volunteer puppeteers to play the Three Billy Goats and three volunteers to make the bridge with their bodies.

During the remaining scenes the leader should play the Troll until the children know the story well enough to enact that role without adult participation.

Talking It Over

Apply the following rules:

Use opened ended questions. ("What clues tell us which was the smallest Billy Goat?")

Use character names. (What did the Big Billy Goat do that made him seem so large?")

Begin with positive statements. Ask for suggested improvements. ("What did you like about the fighting scene? How could we make it more believable next time?")

Never use evaluative terms such as "good" and "bad". ("What else could the Big Billy Goat do to make us believe he is stronger—*not better*—than the other Billy Goats?")

Re-Play

Re-cast the same scene or the next one to incorporate suggestions for improvements offered during the "Talking It Over" period.

Variations and Expansions

Use a number of circle shapes (more than three) in gradated sizes, from very tiny to super large, to represent a series of goats of ascending sizes, thus incorporating additional children into the Puppetization. Each time a goat crosses the bridge, another one could proceed that is just a "little bit larger" (or a little bit smaller) than the previous goat.

The Middle Billy Goat crosses the "Bridge"

The Troll hides under the Bridge, then appears!

Review

This review is intended as a checklist for planning and guiding creative puppetry sessions:

Before The Children Arrive

Preparation. Consider space, number of children, amount of time, equipment and puppets to be included. Match what is available with what is needed, as effectively as possible.

Material-Selection, Presentation and Use.

1) Think in terms of scenes, props, music and literature that might be included to augment effectiveness of production.

2) Present material by a variety of methods: playing, singing, telling or reading.

With the Children

Motivation. Consider how to introduce the material or idea to the children in order to heighten interest and enthusiasm.

Puppets. Decide whether to use commercial puppets or to construct them with the children as an integral part of the activity.

Planning. Decide answers to the who, what, when and where questions to determine how the puppets will be incorporated into the dramatization. For example, with a story dramatization:

1) Review the story to establish plot outlines and to make scene divisions.

2) Go through each scene from beginning to end to clarify action.

3) Decide what each character will say and do.

4) Decide where objects will be located and where events are to take place within the playing circle.

5) Decide who will play each character.

Playing. Act out scene-by-scene.

Assessing. Talk about the dramatization and suggest new ideas.

1) Use open ended questions.

2) Use character names, rather than children's names.

3) Emphasize the positive aspects of the production.

4) Never use "good" and "bad."

Books on Puppetizing

Champlin, Connie. *Puppetry and Creative Dramatics*—A highly imaginative resource book of clearly structured creative dramatic activities based on modern and classical children's literature. Contains sections devoted to pantomiming, characterization, sound and action stories. Austin, Texas, Nancy Renfro Studios, 1980

Champlin, John and Connie Books, *Puppets and the Mentally Retarded Student*—Shows an accumulative approach in developing literary comprehension with the mentally retarded student. Though written for the special child, its cleverly composed procedures are easily adaptable to preschool. Omaha, Nebraska, Special Literature Press, 1980

McCaslin, Nellie, *Creative Dramatics in the Classroom*—Although designed for use with elementary children, this book provides an excellent description of basic techniques used for engaging children in creative drama. New York, Longman, 1974

Pereira, Nancy, *Creative Dramatics in the Library*—Though written for the library setting, this book contains many basic ideas on an improvisational level that can adapt to preschool. Covers excellent structuring methods for group control and participation. Rowayton, Connecticut, New Plays, Inc., 1974

Renfro, Nancy, *Puppetry and the Art of Story Creation*—A valuable book for teachers just beginning to involve children in creative drama and puppetry who need pointers in creative story development. Chapters on the "special child" and making clever and simple puppets are included. Austin, Texas, Nancy Renfro Studios, 1979

Siks, Geraldine B., *Creative Dramatics, An Art for Children*—A standard text in creative drama providing the basic themes and techniques in this field. New York, Harper & Row, 1960 (Same author wrote *Children's Literature for Dramatization*. Harper & Row, 1964.)

Ward, Winnifred, *Playmaking With Children*—One of the oldest texts in creative drama, containing a fine chapter on creative experiences with young children. New York, Appleton-Centy-Crofts, 1957 (Same author wrote *Stories to Dramatize*. Anchorage Press, 1952.)

As learning tools, puppets expedite the absorption of knowledge by capturing and sustaining the interest of young children.

PUPPETEACHING
Puppets as Teaching Tools

The cognitive domain of the child is one that is ever-changing, ever-expanding and that profoundly affects the social, emotional and physical growth of the child. With a primary focus on intellectual development, Puppeteaching opens up new avenues to advance and enrich this domain. Through the medium of puppetry, the teacher may impart information to the children while, on the other hand, the children may employ puppets to absorb this same information. For example, the teacher may mobilize a fireperson puppet to lead a discussion about fire safety, thus reinforcing certain rules about "do's" and "don'ts." Subsequently, the children may role-play with puppets potentially hazardous scenarios and thereby recall what to do in case of a fire.

Puppeteaching provides first-hand sensorial experiences that are essential to concept development in early childhood. As learning tools, puppets expedite the absorption of knowledge by capturing and sustaining the interest of young children. Puppets therefore become commendable vehicles for assisting children to assimilate life's information and, as a result, to build concepts.

Alphabet and Words

The Old Lady

The Old Lady from the song *I Know An Old Lady Who Swallowed A Fly* makes an instructive and popular puppet for helping young children learn to match letter sounds with symbols. A delectable "menu" may be invented for her by changing the words of the traditional song to include all the letters as in the following example.

> I know an Old Lady
> Who swallowed an "A (all letters)
> Do you know why she swallowed an *A*?
> So she could read!

• Before singing the song, give the children cards on which simple words are written. If they can find the letter "A" in their word, they can feed their card to the Old Lady. Do the same with all the vowels, the consonants, hard letter sounds, soft letter sounds, silent letters and so forth.

• Older children can be asked to think up their own words with specific letters included for the Old Lady to swallow.

• When time is limited, ask the children instead simply to whisper the word into the Old Lady's mouth. After all, she can gulp down whispers, too!

• The Old Lady puppet can be adapted for classification activities. Use a panel board to display cutouts of objects such as fruits, vegetables, numbers, shapes, flowers and colors. Let the children take turns selecting an item from the board and feeding it to the Old Lady. One day she might prefer only red things and on another, merely objects associated with winter.

• Since there are only two variable words in the song, it is easy to originate new verses for teaching all kinds of subjects. Children never tire of hearing deviations of the Old Lady song, as in this example for nutrition:

> I know an Old Lady
> Who swallowed an apple,
> Do you know why she swallowed an apple?
> So she could grow!

MATERIALS

Two supermarket bags; stiff paper or poster board; construction paper; cotton; clean acetate (book report cover); fabric.

PROCEDURE

Cut a rectangle hole in stomach area.

Tape a piece of acetate to back of window hole.

Cut out a mouth hole as shown.

Cut a slit on either side of bag, close to window, large enough for hand to pull out cardboard figures.

Slip outer bag over inner bag (which has no cutouts or preparation). Fit together so bags match up perfectly.

Staple together bags around entire bottom edge.

Cut out a face shape (larger than flap of bag) from poster board. Glue to flap of outer bag. Paint on a face or make features from construction paper. Yarn or cotton serves well for hair.

Glue a piece of fabric on front of outer bag for a gay costume. Use trim to decorate.

Add poster board arms and legs. Perhaps a funny hat, too!

98

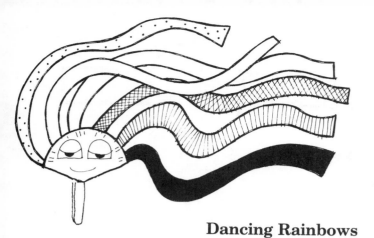

Dancing Rainbows

Colors

Simple color identification for very young children can be enhanced with a Rainbow puppet. By taping onto a third of a paper plate, six strips of colored construction paper, each representing a color of the rainbow, children can create their own rainbows. Attach the rainbow plate to cardboard tube or skewer. Once the puppet is constructed, encourage the children to experiment by circling their arms in the air to mimic a rainbow arch and running with their puppets to make them "fly" across the sky. Children like to dance with these puppets by moving them in time with music. Select gentle music to inspire graceful body movements. Particularly suited to this activity is Don Freeman's book, *A Rainbow of My Own*.

Precut colored paper rainbow strips

99

Community Helpers

When placed in the Puppet Corner, Community Helper characters inspire young children to Puppet Play various occupational roles such as that of the Bus Driver, Baker, Doctor, Nurse, Fireperson, Policeperson, Postperson, Teacher, Principal and Telephone Repairperson. Most puppets can be easily converted into role-characters by simply adding a hat or stethoscope, telephone or other prop. The Sesame Street song *Who Are the People in My Neighborhood?* may introduce the characters and stimulate dialogue about how these people help us in the communiy.

MATERIALS

Paper cup; paper features.

PROCEDURE

Make photocopy of hat patterns and let children color and glue a chosen hat onto an upside down paper cup.

Add paper features or decorate with coloring medium.

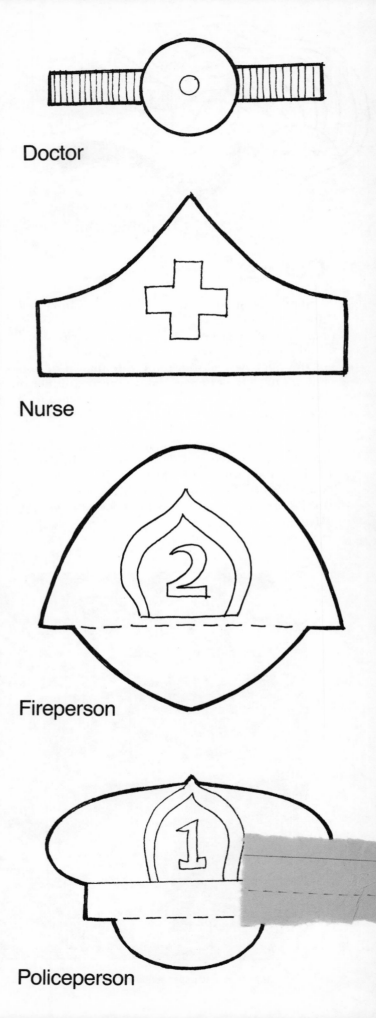

Doctor

Nurse

Fireperson

Baker

Policeperson

100

Cooking

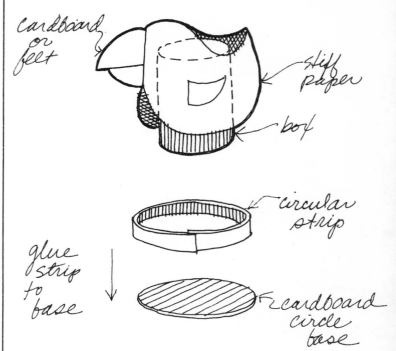

Young cooks can be enticed to partake in culinary adventures when puppets and literature lead the way. An enactment of the story *The Little Red Hen and the Grain of Wheat*, for example, is an apt introduction to bread-baking projects. *The Gingerbread Man* is ideal for Puppetizing on table tops with a real gingerbread cookie as the central character. Dr. Seuss' *Scrambled Eggs Super!* inspires marvelous egg creations, beginning with the elemental scrambled egg and progressing into the more advanced souffle or quiche.

Puppets also provide imaginative ways to make visual the sources for ingredients in recipes. For example, a cow puppet can explain how we get milk, butter and dairy products while a farmer puppet can talk about how produce is grown on a farm. Fruits and vegetable puppets can each tell the story of how they sprouted from a tiny seed. A chicken puppet will certainly delight the children by demonstrating its egg-laying prowesses!

Laying Hen

MATERIALS

Salt or oatmeal box; cardboard construction paper; felt features; red shag fur, paper or real feathers.

PROCEDURE

Hen: Remove lid from oatmeal box or cut end off a salt box; turn upside-down.

Cut out two side shapes for Hen's body, large enough to cover box area.

Add a cardboard or felt beak and other features. Hen's body can be decorated by covering with red shag fur, tissue paper fringe or real or paper feathers.

Nest: Curve a two-inch wide strip of cardboard into a 7-inch diameter circle and staple ends together.

Glue circular strip down onto a lightweight cardboard circle of corresponding size and let dry.

Glue straw or fringed paper onto outer surface of nest.

Place hen on nest with eggs hidden under the box.

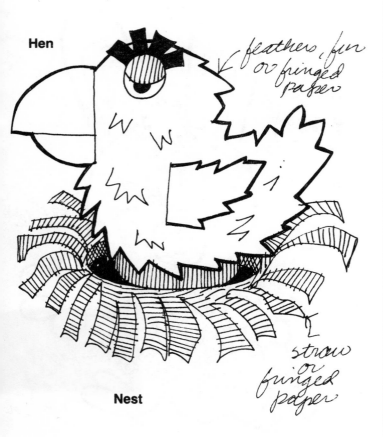

Hen

Nest

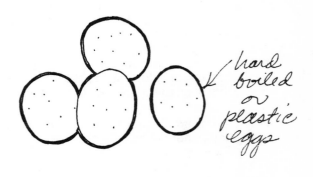

101

Counting

Counting Bunny

A Counting Bunny puppet is a versatile puppet to aid in various curriculum activities. Not only is it skillful at counting numbers, but through a repertoire of interchangeable "talking" paper-plate discs this puppet can be used to teach sounds, alphabet, colors, shapes, musical notes, math factors and so forth.

• Using two Counting Bunnies, paint numbers on one disc and a grouping of dots on the other. Let children match corresponding numbers to dot groupings.

• Revolve the back plate to display a number. Ask the chldren to find the corresponding number of objects from the Bunny's basket (eggs, beads, jellybeans, nuts) to match the number on display.

• Counting Bunny can sell some eggs, apples and carrots to the children. Different objects sell for different prices. Make a disc with different cents on it. Then let the children have real money in cents to equal a penny, nickel, dime, quarter, half dollar and dollar. The Counting Bunny might say "I'm selling this egg for 5¢" (appears on the disc). Whoever has the nickel and recognizes it, can drop the money in the Bunny's basket and take the merchandise. This exercise will also help the children to reinforce the relationship between numerical values and labels on coins.

MATERIALS
Two paper plates; paper fastener.

PROCEDURE
Cut a 2-inch diameter hole in lower section of one plate. Lay a second plate behind the first plate with the hole and line them up. Locate exact center of plates and punch out a small hole through both plates; insert paper fastener through plates. Revolve back plate and draw images on each clear space that shows through the hole of the front plate.

Glue a pom pom or paper nose over top of paper fastener. Add paper bunny ears and a body.

Fingerplays

Many fingerplays are actually counting games for children. A garden glove with velcro tips (see Teacher's Puppetmaking chapter) may be used for rhymes that start with "Five little. . . ."

Five little monkeys jumping on the bed,
One fell out and bumped his head,
Mommy called the doctor and the doctor said,
"That's what you get for jumping on the bed!"

Four little monkeys jumping on the bed. . . .
(and so forth).

"Ten Little Indians" is another popular fingerplay that is adaptable to puppets. Instead of Indians, substitute other characters such as children, bakers, monsters and ducklings.

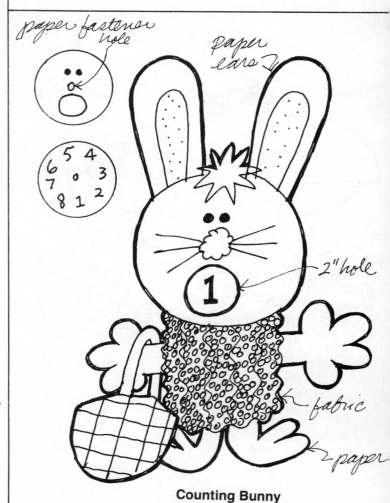

Counting Bunny

Health and Hygiene

Hygiene

Learning about health and hygiene can become far more intriguing when children are called on to instruct and interact with disheveled puppet characters in the finer details of "tidying up." The children can explain, for example, how to unsnarl messy hair, manage dirty nails or repair torn clothes. Young children will enjoy making a dirty, messy puppet of their own as a "model."

A turn-around Paper-Plate Puppet can be made by gluing a cardboard tube between two paper plates, to serve as a handle. Decorate plates with an untidy face on one side and a tidy face on the other.

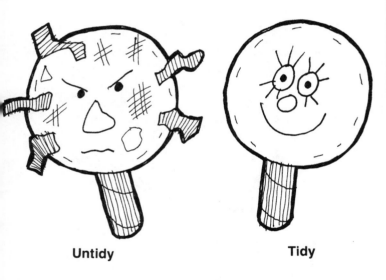

Untidy　　　　　　　　**Tidy**

Brushing Teeth

Brushing of teeth is an important part of the preschooler's daily routine. To inculcate the necessity of regular brushing, use a puppet to demonstrate correct (or incorrect, so that the children can correct) toothbrushing techniques. A "Mr. Tooth" puppet can distribute toothbrushes or squeeze the toothpaste. A puppet with very prominent teeth can serve as the model for children to use for practicing proper brushing. (A removable tooth can be devised on this puppet so that whenever the children mention a food with an abundance of sugar it can pop out!)

● The children's own toothbrushes can be made into puppets by sticking on self-adhesive stickers or gummed hole reinforcements for eyes and features.

● A dentist may be role-played by a puppet using a "play drill" and other instruments.

Big Teeth Puppet
MATERIALS

Large detergent, cereal or other type of box; white construction paper.

PROCEDURE

Slit open center of box on both ends and front only, leaving back of box intact.

Cut two finger holes in upper back of the box to maneuver upper portion of head back and forth.

Paint or use white construction paper to make big teeth. The tooth may become removable with the use of sticky-backed tape; paint tooth black on underneath side. Add a face with paint or paper.

Stand puppet on a table top so that the children can take turns brushing its teeth. They may also wish to feed it "healthy" foods from time to time.

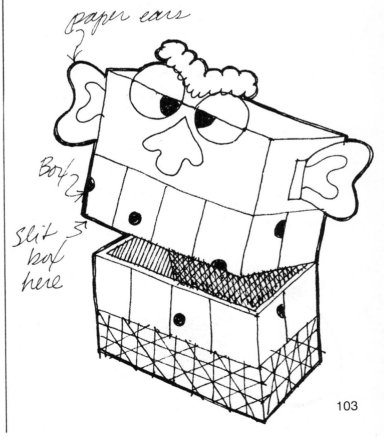

Measuring

The Longest Worm In The World

The "Longest Worm in the World" offers another clever way to help children conceptualize linear relationships while grasping the idea that many small parts comprise a whole. To construct the worm, invite each child to decorate a toilet tissue tube, paper cup or cardboard frozen juice can (with both ends removed). When finished, string all the parts together with sturdy cord to make a very long puppet. Let the children count the number of sections in the worm.

- To illustrate the concept "tall" as opposed to "long," hold the worm *up*, rather than lengthwise.

- Explore shapes, numbers and letters with the worm by forming it into a triangle, circle, "U", "S", "2" or other appropriate shape.

- Ask the children to count the number of children in the class and the number of sections in the worm. They will be delighted to discover that their totals are exactly the same. Keep this wonderful worm on display for several days and let the children re-count the worm's sections and the number of children when someone is absent. The class will be surprised to find that the worm's sections have remained constant, although their own numbers have decreased!

Following is a fun poem to recite with this activity:

The Longest Worm in the World
by Tamara Hunt

I'm the longest worm in the world,
I've got _____ sections in all.
You can count if you like,
But it might take all night,
'Cause *you* made me so long and so tall!

Size Gradation

Giraffes with necks that extend up and down are fitting animals for size/height comparisons. Ask each child to make a paper head and attach to tube neck. Insert other end of tube neck into a hole on top of a box. Decorate the bodies and neck with paint. Divide the class into groups of three. Let each child in the group "order" a puppet's neck to a specific length (in terms of so many inches or centimeters). Once the necks are in place, members can then line up their puppets in a circus parade according to relative heights. Older children may even write labels that identify which puppets are "tall," "taller" and "tallest." Another variation on this project is to use an expandable tube trunk for an elephant.

expandable tube-neck

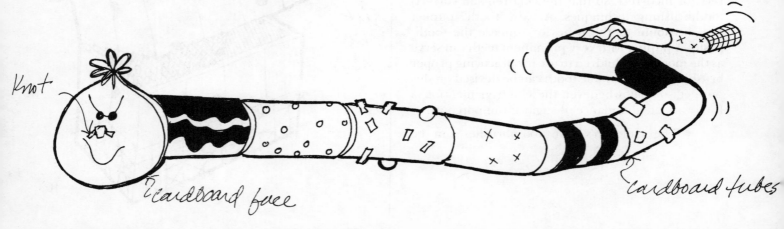

Knot

cardboard tube

cardboard tubes

Nature

Nature Cup Puppets

One of the most valuable gifts we can bequeath young children is a respect for Nature, coupled with an understanding and appreciation for the natural environment. By Puppetizing simple stories and poems, a child can begin to comprehend Nature's many fascinating and complex processes. Puppets-in-a-Cup illustrate well the notions of growth and transformation that occur in the great outdoor world.

To make a Puppet-in-a-Cup, give each child a paper or styrofoam cup, a plastic drinking straw and some scraps of construction paper. Ask them to create any kind of plant (flower, vegetable, fruit or tree) they desire. Tape the completed creations onto one end of the child's straw; place the other end of the straw in a hole, punctured in the bottom of the cup. Then ask the children to fill their cups with dirt, sand, grass or stone to represent the terrain. As the children manipulate their straw puppets up and down, sing this song:

This Is The Way We Plant A Seed
Adapted by Tamara Hunt
(sung to the tune of "Here We Go Round the Mulberry Bush")

This is the way we plant the seed,
Plant the seed, plant the seed.
This is the way we plant the seed,
So early in the morning.

This is the way our seeds will grow,
Seeds will grow, seeds will grow.
This is the way our seeds will grow,
So early in the morning.

Flower in Pot

Animal habitats may also be explored with these miniature "nature theaters." The exterior of a cup can be decorated to correspond with an animal or insect habitat such as a bee in a hive, an owl in a tree or a fish in an ocean.

Bird in Nest

Bee and Hive

Owl in Tree

105

Pets

Animal puppets can be useful in helping children learn how to approach and handle pets and strays. For example, a child can practice first by putting out his hand and letting the animal, represented by a puppet, smell it. Then he can practice petting the puppet "gently" and scratching "lightly" behind its ears or on its tummy. The child can even pretend to feed a horse by extending a carrot on a flat palm. The animal puppet should, of course, coo, purr or make other happy sounds to reinforce appropriate behavior on the child's part.

Safety

Safety rules are essential for children to know in order to protect themselves. Here are some innovative ways you can integrate puppets into your curriculum for teaching children when and how to apply specific "do's" and "don'ts":

● **Names and Numbers.** Children will enjoy giving to a puppet (far more than they will to an adult) their name, telephone number, address, parents' names and school. The process will quickly evolve into a game when a puppet, for example, misunderstands the information or keeps forgetting. If a child says her name is "Tammy" and the puppet repeats "Yammy!" the child will find great humor in the mispronunciation and seek to correct the puppet's mistake.

Puppets that depict Policepersons and Firepersons, who on occasion assist in classroom emergencies, will reinforce the idea that the children should regard persons in these occupations as sources of assistance in the event of a real crisis. In fact, it would be well for the children to recite their names and addresses to puppets wearing uniforms of the various helping professions. Similar puppet interactions repeated throughout the school year will serve to help the children remember those circumstances when they should apply certain rules.

● **Refusing Rides with Strangers.** People puppets may be used to depict strangers for role playing situations. For example, a stranger could tell the child he will give him a present if the child will leave the park with him or go for a ride in his car.

It is important that the child learn a rote response for such possible occurrences. As you Puppetize the scene, keep the puppet interaction *serious* and encourage the children to develop a sequence of verbal responses that will come automatically.

Another variation is for a child or another teacher to depict the stranger while you operate the child-puppet to better illustrate the serious nature of accepting overtures from strangers.

106

Traffic Light Rod Puppet

Make photocopy of pattern and color, leaving circles white. Laminate traffic light with cardboard and attach to a rod control. Make a red, yellow and green circle from colored paper to fit light's circles. Stick circles on and off with sticky-back tape and use as a visual for dramatizing traffic settings.

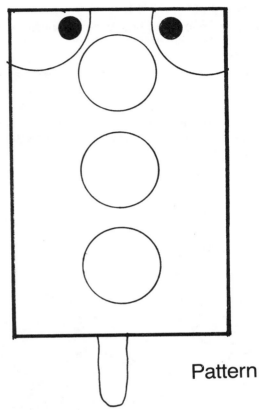

Pattern

● **Crossing the Street.** Convert a table top into a big intersection by laying strips of masking tape or paper at right angles to indicate corners. Using a traffic light puppet and assorted finger-walkers, let small groups of children Puppetplay how to watch a traffic-light before crossing the street. Each can take turns being the traffic-light puppet while the others walk their pedestrian puppets across the street in accordance with street-crossing rules. For street corners without traffic signals, let one child operate a small toy vehicle while the others, in the roles of finger-walking pedestrians, look both ways before stepping off the curb.

Table Top Traffic Play

Seasons

A calendar puppet is superb for checking off dates on the calendar. A life-sized puppet may be dressed regularly in the children's outgrown clothing. A concept as amorphous as seasons is best understood if personalized by things a child sees, wears and does, making these intangible concepts tangible. Ask the class to "advise" the puppet as to what is appropriate attire. The puppet design on this page can be easily dressed in a seasonal wardrobe.

Suggested accessories might be:

Rainy: Raincoat, rainhat, umbrella, galoshes
Snowy: Jacket, scarf, earmuffs, mittens
Windy: Sweater, scarf
Sunny: Bathing suit, sundress, T-shirt, sunglasses

Since weather often affects what we choose to do during a particular day, let the puppet reflect those choices through the use of props. For example, give the puppet a book to read on a rainy day; a cookie cutter to make cookies on a cold winter day; or a beach pail and shovel to play in the sand on a summer day.

Smaller types of puppets, as found in this book, can be used in conjunction with a seasonal wordrobe or props. Simply add paper or fabric costumes and cardboard or miniature props to create a year-round Calendar puppet. Consider using also paper dolls with accompanying clothing attached to a rod control.

MATERIALS

Cardboard; four hosiery legs; newspaper; paper features; cording.

PROCEDURE

Lay an average sized child in the class down on a sheet of carboard and trace around head and body area, omitting arms and legs.

Cut out torso and head shape and paint a flesh-tone. Decorate with proper features and "dress me" letters.

Stuff four hosiery legs with crumpled newspaper and cut legs down to length of average child. Attach to body as arms and legs.

Add cardboard hands and feet to ends of stuffed hosiery. Attach a length of cord to head for hanging puppet on wall.

Winter

"Dress Me" Puppet

Spring

Summer

108

The Puppet Tree

An enchanting addition to any Puppet Corner is a Puppet Tree made from felt or mural paper. This decorative wall hanging is an ideal gathering place for puppetime activities and provides a colorful backdrop for your Puppetelling ventures. Puppet friends of all kinds can live in its nest and knotholes. In autumn, you can ask the children to gather colorful leaves (or make their own) to attach to the tree; for winter, pin on puffs of cotton; in spring, attach children's drawings of flowers and fruits; and for summer, decorate with paper insects and butterflies.

- The Puppet Tree offers a woodsy backdrop for the sharing of nature stories such as A.A. Milne's *Winnie The Pooh*, Bernice Freschet's *Opossum Baby* and Margaret W. Brown's *Home For Bunny*.

- Buddy puppets in the form of woodland creatures can dwell in the tree. A squirrel family (including mama, papa and baby), a bird in the nest and a raccoon in a hole are all tempting suggestions. These puppets could even appear on a regular basis during story-time to meld a bond of friendship with the children. (See Puppetelling section for additional ideas.)

- The Puppet Tree may also serve as a visual tool to illustrate the life cycle of a living plant. Add paper or fabric strips to the base of the tree for a root system to achieve a realistic effect for explaining how water and minerals are absorbed and circulated throughout the tree.

- Many trees also produce fruits and nuts. Have the children cut out large paper nuts or fruit-shapes and tack onto the tree. Bring in a basket of real nuts or fruits, corresponding to the food shapes, for the children to taste. Perhaps explore some exotic tropical fruits such as mangos and papayas.

- Cactus for desert creatures may serve as an interesting alternative to a tree. A peek hole for an elf owl, brightly colored cactus flowers and bird life tacked onto the large stems will offer an entirely different sort of environment for discussions about reptiles and animals that live in a hot, dry climate.

Summer   Fall

Winter   Spring

109

Self-Concepts

Me Puppets

Children love seeing their own images in a mirror, a photograph or even a puppet-likeness of themselves. The idea of "Me" puppets can be initiated by asking the children to describe themselves and their peers (hair, height, color, shape, etc.). By commenting on how and why each child looks different from one another, they will come to value what makes each person special.

Here is a poem for children to recite in conjunction with their completed "Me" puppets.

People
by Tamara Hunt

Bodies have all shapes and sizes,
Thin or roundish, short or tall.
Arms and legs seem lean or chubby,
Some have big feet, some have small.

Eyes are found in different colors,
Hazel, brown, or green, or blue.
Hair is yellow, black or reddish.
Which of these colors is on you?

White and black and even brownish,
Skin has lots of different shades.
People grow in many ways . . . WOW!
Isn't it fun the way we're made!

Now you've had a chance to see,
Why people look so differently.
Alike in ways we must agree,
Yet still as different as can be!

To make "Me" puppets, ask the children to lie down on a long strip of mural paper, then draw an outline of their body shapes. Let each child cut out his own body outline and decorate it by detailing body features as well as the clothes he is wearing or would like to wear. Pleat the legs and arms to create the illusion of movement. Attach a paper plate to the head for the children to add facial features. Then make a hand grip on the back of the head by attaching a half of a paper plate. These puppets can be made to dance to music, jump, climb and play, in short, do anything a real child might do. When the body cut-outs are decorated as Superheroes, complete with capes and logos, an imaginative discussion can ensue beginning with the phrase "If I were a Superhero, I would . . ." Then the children can enjoy flying about the room with a new-found freedom.

Super "Me" Puppet

110

A clothesline of classmate "me" puppets

Sensorial

Puppetmaking activities, in general, stimulate an awareness of all the faculties of perception, especially the sense of touch. By providing a variety of contrasting types of construction materials and encouraging the children to articulate how the textures look and feel, you will help them to develop parallel powers of descriptive vocabulary and sensorial awareness. When gathering Puppetmaking supplies, consider tactile qualities such as:

Soft: Cotton balls
Rough: Sandpaper, burlap, metallic fabrics, carpet scraps
Hard: Buttons, macaroni
Smooth: Velvet, feathers, paper, plastics
Bumpy: Nutshells, bark
Furry: Synthetic fabrics and fake furs
Cold: Foil, metal, pennies

Mr. Sniff Snort's Stomach

MATERIALS

Grocery box; sock, construction paper for feet; party hat.

PROCEDURE

Cut a hole in front of box, large enough for a hand to fit through.

Glue or staple a sock (with toe cut out) to hole.

Add some funny feet and a party hat along with other features.

Fill Mr. Sniff Snort's stomach with assorted textured items as mentioned above for the children to feel and guess.

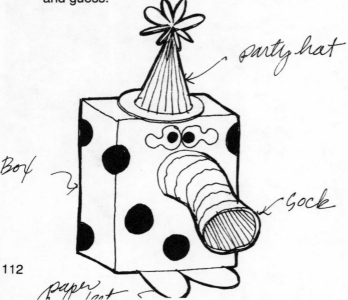

Shapes

Jack-in-the-Box

Labeling and differentiating between two-dimensional and three-dimensional objects can be achieved when the children make Jack-in-the-Box puppets. To begin, let each child choose a three-dimensional object. Stock up on a collection of assorted three-dimensional objects and place similar objects in separate bins. Let each child choose one object:

● **Cubes** should include a mixture of both rectangular and square shapes such as blocks, milk cartons (with top flattened down), styrofoam packaging forms, assorted food boxes (pudding, cereal, spaghetti, cake, etc.).

● **Cylinders**—Salt or oatmeal boxes, cardboard tubes (toilet tissue roll, foil, fabric and other tubes).

● **Pyramid**—Prism, cut down boxes

On a piece of lightweight cardboard, each child should trace around one side of her chosen object to make a flat representation of that object. Let her decorate this two dimensional shape with facial features. Attach the shape onto a rod control (drinking straw or skewer) and slip the rod through a hole in the bottom of a box container that houses the Jack puppet. Then ask the children to change Jack's position in relation to the box: in, out, under, over, behind, in front of, far away, near, right, left and so forth.

Jack-in-the-Box

Jack-in-the-box, all shut up tight,
Not a breath of air or a ray of light,
How tired he must be, all folded up.
Let's open the lid,
And up he'll jump!

112

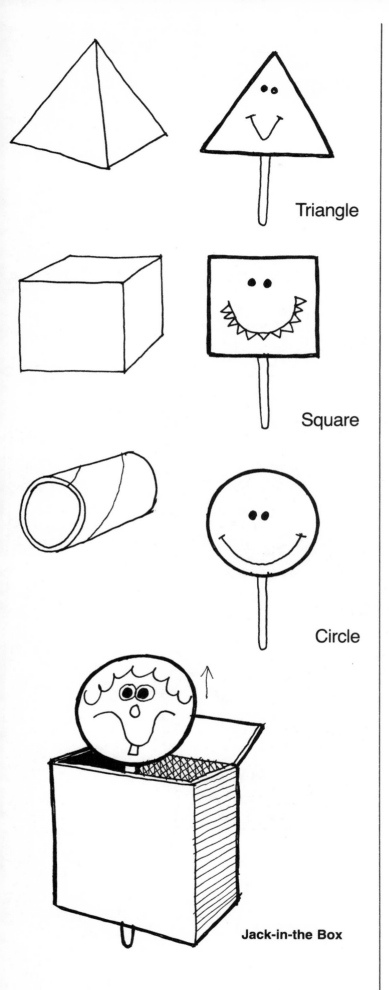

Triangle

Square

Circle

Jack-in-the Box

Time

It's Time To

Puppets are capable of helping children grasp the abstract concept of "time" as it relates to their daily activities. A "Time To" clock-puppet, for example, can move its hands to announce the time of day or night when certain routine chores are to be performed. The clock puppet can then proclaim "It's time to brush your teeth" or eat breakfast or take a bath. It can even ask the chidren to demonstrate, through pantomime, how they accomplish those tasks. With very young children a breakdown of morning, afternoon and nighttime activities is sufficient such as "In the morning it is time to . . ." With older children, number recognition can be coordinated with the scheduling of daily events as "At ten o'clock it is time to eat a snack" or "At seven o'clock it is time to go to bed."

The clock puppet may also show relationships between number recognition and unit-counting with the addition of a cuckoo-bird companion. It can invite children to join the bird as it vocalizes "cuckoo" sounds to correspond with the clock's time.

Those children who have already learned to tell time may practice their skills in teams with puppets. One puppet manipulated by one child may "set" the time, while a second puppet operated by another child identifies the correct time. Together they can discuss what they usually do at specific times of the day. This informal activity adapts well to the Puppet Corner.

113

Conversations with Bert
Puppet by Child Guidance Toys (see Bibliography)

SESAME STREET ACTIVITIES

Using Sesame Street Puppets to Teach Curriculum

Investing in several Sesame Street Muppet characters and an album of children's songs is a low-cost yet high-impact way to start working with puppets. Because of the strong recognition factors between Muppet puppets and their television counterparts, the children will be eager to cooperate with almost any suggestion these puppets make.

An imitation of the Muppeteers' voices is not required when manipulating the characters. Instead, you may create your own "special" voices and, in that way, tailor the scenarios to real-life situations. Actually, the children will become so engrossed in their own interactions with the puppets that they will never even notice that the voices of your puppets differ from those on records and television. You might consider purchasing the record album *Havin' Fun with Ernie and Bert* (CTW/CC #25506) to use in conjunction with a variety of puppet activities.

Kermit

Kermit the Frog is a willingly versatile puppet. Merely add different costume pieces and his role changes at a moment's notice. For instance, dressed in a lei and a hula skirt, he can become Kermit's Hawaiian cousin. Or, at storytime Kermit may introduce books about frogs, of course, reporting on all sorts of interesting tidbits about frog-habits and habitats. He might even spend the whole day just as himself, on your hand, chatting informally with the children about whatever topics they choose, just as Kermit does on television.

Besides being fun and easy to manipulate, a Kermit puppet is designed to sit comfortably on your lap or arm.

Oscar the Grouch

Oscar the Grouch is a favorite character among children because he pokes fun at customs and opinions that society holds dear. As a classroom puppet, Oscar may employ his customary role to help the children acquire a better understanding of social behavior and expectations. For example, in leading discussions, he can either mirror the children's feelings or play the devil's advocate. He might ask "How do you feel when you have to clean up your room?" or "What do you like to collect that other people call junk?" For the sake of debating, Oscar might argue "What does sharing mean? What's good about sharing?" or "What's so special about a kiss?"

Big Bird

Very young children identify closely with Big Bird's innocence and insecurities. His non-threatening personality encourages them to feel at ease in expressing their feelings and fears thereby enabling Big Bird to function well in Puppetalking situations. Older children, on the other hand, are more apt to teach Big Bird things they already know. For instance, when Big Bird visits the school, the older children may wish to explain to him what they do during the day or how they accomplish a particular task. Sometimes they may want to tell Big Bird about a forthcoming excursion or one from which they have just returned. Discussions of this nature are effective for determining at what level the children have comprehended certain experiences, also for ascertaining whether they have understood specific instructions.

With the song "Just Three Colors" from *Havin' Fun with Ernie and Bert*, Big Bird can stimulate an interest in colors. To begin, talk with the children about primary and secondary colors. Let them experiment with paints or food dyes. Then ask them to make a Color Puppet using their favorite color (see Puppeteaching section for ideas). As the song is played or sung, invite the children to hold up their Color Puppets when the appropriate colors are mentioned.

Ernie and Bert

Children perceive Ernie and Bert as good friends and derive pleasure from these two characters' sensitive yet comic interactions. When either one appears in the classroom, it is as if an old friend has come to spend the day. To observe the ways the children interact informally with Ernie and Bert, place the puppets in the Puppet Corner and watch for ideas on meaningful ways to integrate the characters into your general classroom program.

"Name the Animal" and "Tiger Hunt," two more songs from *Havin' Fun with Ernie and Bert*, suggest structured activities for Ernie and Bert puppets. For "Name the Animal," request that each child make a puppet depicting an animal with a distinctive sound. When the puppets are finished, invite the children to sit in a circle with their puppets hidden behind their backs. One by one, or in groups of "same animals," call on the children to make suitable animal sounds with their puppets as Ernie, with his eyes covered, guesses the name of each "noisy" animal.

"Tiger Hunt" is a splendid action-filled story involving lots of pantomime. In order to better visualize the storyline, the children should listen to the record with their eyes closed; then make tiger puppets. To Puppetize the adventure of this story, ask half the children to hide in one corner of the room with their tiger puppets while you act out the part of the Ernie puppet and lead the remaining children on a suspenseful journey. The tiger puppets, of course, should suddenly pop out at the end and scare the others. Repeat the story changing parts.

Cookie Monster

For discussing table manners and nutrition, Cookie Monster can hardly be surpassed. With his insatiable appetite, he may instruct the children on how to bake bread and, of course, he is especially adept at supervising student "cookie cutters" at holiday-time. Cookie Monster may also introduce the rhyme *Who*

Stole the Cookies from the Cookie Jar? while the children are seated in a circle so that all are in view of one another. The verses below may be repeated until each person's name has been called.

Cookie Monster: Who stole the cookie from the cookie jar?

Teacher: _____ (child's name) stole the cookie from the cookie jar.

Child: Who me?
Teacher: Yes, you.
Child: Not me.
Teacher: Then who?
Child: _____ (another child's name) stole the cookie from the cookie jar.

In the "Magic Cookie," also from *Having Fun with Ernie and Bert*, Cookie Monster becomes engulfed in an adventure of choosing between a magic cookie or everlasting joy and happiness. When you play this section of the record, ask the children to close their eyes and imagine the story in their minds. Afterwards, the class may make puppets from paper envelopes that depict these characters: Strange Little Man, Fire-Breathing Dragon, Wicked Wizard, Ogre, Witch, Gnome, Goblin, Six-Legged Bumblethunder Beast and Fairy. Try to get at least one puppet for each character. Then Puppetize the story with an adult playing the role of Cookie Monster.

Grover

Affectionate, endearing Grover bumbles his way through one situation after another on Sesame Street trying to conquer life's many skills. Through his successes and failures he no doubt elicits laughter and empathy from the children who have come to know him so well. Capitalize on Grover for teaching the alphabet, discussing the meaning of vocabulary words, and exploring the fantasy/reality elements of superheroes as portrayed by "Supergrover." Use the story "Grover Takes A Walk" from *Havin' Fun With Ernie and Bert* as motivation for learning body parts.

Fozzie Bear

Although not a Sesame Street character, Fozzie Bear is a good puppet to use with five year olds who are just learning the intricacies of language. Using jokes and riddles, quirks in language are readily explored with Fozzie's reputation as a stand-up comic

116

making him the ideal character to tell or guess the answers to children's jokes and riddles. The class could even make up jokes in an attempt to trick Fozzie.

The Count

The Count is a natural for helping children learn to count and classify objects in the classroom. For example, the Count may say: "How many objects in this room are red?" or "Count the number of triangles you see." or "Tell me how many people in the circle are wearing blue?" and "Whose names start with the 'B' sound?" also "How many children are absent today?"

Sesame Street puppets and sound tracks

Big Bird, Oscar the Grouch, Cookie Monster, Grover, Ernie and Bert are sold as hand puppets and finger puppets by Child Guidance Toys and can be purchased at most better toy stores. Inquire at your local store for more information.

A large selection of Sesame Street sound tracks are available in cassette, tapes or record form. Inquire at your local record store for ordering information, or write to the headquarters for Sesame Street Records at One Lincoln Plaza, New York NY 10023.

The Count Puppet by Child Guidance Toys

Books on the Alphabet

Anno, Mitsumasa. *Anno's Alphabet*. New York: T. Y. Crowell, 1975.

Azarian, Mary. *A Farmer's Alphabet*. Boston: Godine, 1981.

Baskin, Leonard. *Hosie's Alphabet*. New York: Viking, 1972.

Broomfield, Robert. *Baby Animal ABC*. New York: Penguin, 1968.

Brown, Marcia. *All Butterflies: An ABC*. New York: Atheneum, 1974.

Chess, Victoria. *Alfred's Alphabet*. New York: Greenwillow, 1979.

Crowther, Robert. *The Most Amazing Hide and Seek Alphabet Book*. New York: Viking, 1978.

Feeney, Stephanie. *A Is For Aloha*. Honolulu, HI: University Press of Hawaii, 1980.

Lobel, Anita and Arnold Lobel. *On Market Street*. New York: Greenwillow, 1981.

Mayer, Mercer. *Little Monster's Alphabet Book*. New York: Western, 1978.

Miller, Edna. *Mousekin's ABC's*. Englewood Cliffs, NJ: Prentice-Hall, 1972.

Milne, A. A. *Pooh's Alphabet Book*. New York: Dutton, 1975.

Seuss, Dr. *Dr. Seuss's ABC*. New York: Beginner, 1963.

Books on Colors

Brooks, Ron. *Annie's Rainbow*. New York: Philomel, 1976.

Charlip, Remy and Burton Supree. *Harlequin and the Gift of Many Colors*. New York: Scholastic, 1973.

Freeman, Don. *A Rainbow of My Own*. New York: Penguin, 1966.

Hirsh, Marilyn. *How the World Got Its Color*. New York: Crown, 1972.

Hoban, Tana. *Is It Red? Is It Yellow? Is It Blue?* New York: Greenwillow, 1978.

Lionni, Leo, *Frederick*. New York: Pantheon, 1966.

Reiss, John J. *Colors*. Scarsdale, NY: Bradbury Press, 1969.

Ross, Tony. *Hugo and the Man Who Stole Colors*. Chicago: Follet, 1977

Tison, Annette and Talus Taylor. *The Adventures of Three Colors*. Columbus, OH: Merrill, 1979.

Books on Community Helpers

Cameron, Elizabeth. *The Big Book of Real Fire Engines*. New York: Crosset and Dunlap, 1970.

Beame, Rona. *Calling Car Twenty-Four Frank: A Day with the Police*. New York: Messner, 1972.

Greene, Carla. *Doctors and Nurses: What Do They Do*. New York: Harper and Row, 1963.

Greene, Carla. *Truck Drivers: What Do They Do?* New York: Harper and Row, 1967.

Neigoff, Anne. *New House, New Town*. Chicago: A. Whitman, 1973.

Robinson, Barry and Martin J. Dain. *On The Beat: Policemen at Work*. New York: Harcourt, Brace, Jovanovich, 1968.

Books on Cooking

Cauley, Lorinda B. *Bake-Off*. New York: Putnam, 1978.

DePaola, Tomie. *Pancakes for Breakfast*. New York: Harcourt, Brace, Jovanovich, 1978.

De Paola, Tomie. *Strega Nona*. Englewood Cliffs, NJ: Prentice-Hall, 1975.

Galdone, Paul. *Gingerbread Boy*. Boston: Houghton Mifflin, 1975.

Galdone, Paul. *The Little Red Hen*. New York: Scholastic Book Services, 1975.

Sendak, Maurice. *In the Night Kitchen*. New York: Harper and Row, 1970.

Stadler, John. *Animal Cafe*. Scarsdale, NY: Bradbury Press, 1980.

Books on Counting

Brown, Marc. *One Two Three: An Animal Counting Book*. Boston: Little, 1976.

Carle, Eric. *One, Two, Three to the Zoo*. New York: Philomel, 1968.

Cartwright, Mary. *Mary Cartwright's One, Two Three*. Chicago: Rand McNally, 1981.

Charles, Donald. *Count on Calico Cat*. Chicago: Childrens, 1974.

Crowther, Robert. *The Most Amazing Hide and Seek Counting Book*. New York: Viking, 1981.

Feelings, Muriel. *Moja Means One*. New York: Dial, 1971.

Ginsburg, Mirra. *Kitten from One to Ten*. New York: Crown, 1980.

Hoban, Tana. *Count and See*. New York: Macmillan, 1972.

Nedobeck, Don. *Nedobeck's Numbers Book*. Milwaukee, WI: Ideals, 1981.

Peek, Merle. *Roll Over*. New York: Houghton Mifflin, 1981.

Wild, Robin. *The Bears' Counting Book*. New York: Lippincott, 1978.

Books on Dentists and Teeth

Bate, Lucy. *Little Rabbitt's Loose Tooth*. New York: Crown, 1975.

De Groat, Diane. *Alligator's Toothache*. New York: Crown, 1977.

McCloskey, Robert. *One Morning in Maine*. New York: Viking, 1952.

Rockwell, Harlow. *My Dentist*. New York: Greenwillow, 1975.

Showers, Paul. *How Many Teeth?* New York: T.Y. Crowell, 1976.

Williams, Barbara. *Albert's Toothache*. New York: Dutton, 1974.

Wolf, Bernard. *Michael and the Dentist*. New York: Four Winds, 1980.

Books on Hygiene

Manushkin, Fran. *Bubblebath*. New York: Harper and Row, 1974.

Silverstein, Sel. "The Dirtiest Man in the World" from *Where The Sidewalk Ends*. New York: Harper and Row, 1974.

Books on Measuring

Charosh, Mannis. *Straight Lines, Parallel Lines, Perpendicular Lines*. New York: Crowell, 1970.

Froman, Robert. *Bigger and Smaller*. New York: Crowell, 1971.

Lionni, Leo. *Inch By Inch*. New York: Astor-Honor, 1962.

Books on Pets

Chase, Catherine. *Pete, the Wet Pet*. New York: Dutton, 1981.

De Regniers, Beatrice. *May I Bring a Friend?* New York: Atheneum, 1964.

Gag, Wanda. *Millions of Cats*. New York: Coward, 1928.

Keats, Ezra Jack. *Hi, Cat*. New York: Collier, 1970.

Keats, Ezra Jack. *Pet Show*. New York: Collier, 1972.

Keats, Ezra Jack. *Whistle for Willie*. New York: Viking,

1964.
Kellogg, Steven. *Can I Keep Him?* New York: Dial, 1971.
Mayer, Mercer and Marianna. *A Boy, a Dog, a Frog, and a Friend.* New York: Dial, 1971.
Mayer, Mercer. *Frog Where are You?* New York: Dial, 1969.
Stevens, Carla. *Your First Pet and How to take care of it.* New York: Macmillan, 1974.

Books on Plants

Branley, Franklyn. *Roots Are Food Finders.* New York: T. Y. Crowell, 1975.
Cameron, Ann. *The Seed.* New York: Pantheon, 1975.
Carrick, Donald. *The Tree.* New York: Macmillan, 1971.
Jordan, Helene J. *How a Seed Grows.* New York: T. Y. Crowell, 1960.
Ringi, Kjell. *The Sun and the Cloud.* New York: Harper and Row, 1971.
Selsam, Millicent. *Apple and Other Fruits.* New York: Morrow, 1973.

Books on Safety

Dugan, William. *The Sign Book.* New York: Western, 1976.
Kessler, Leonard. *A Tale of Two Bicycles: Safety on Your Bike.* New York: Lothrop, 1971.
Leaf, Munro. *Safety Can Be Fun.* New York: Lippincott, 1961.
MacDonald, Golden. *Red Light Green Light.* New York: Doubleday, 1944.
McLeod, Emilie W. *The Bears Bicycle.* Boston: Little, 1975.
Poulet, Virginia. *Blue Bug's Safety Book.* Chicago: Childrens, 1973.
Shapp, Martha and Charles Shapp. *Let's Find Out About Safety.* New York: Watts, 1975.
Young, Miriam. *Beware the Polar Bear. Safety on the Ice.* New York: Lothrop, 1970.

Books on Seasons

Binzen, Bill. *Year After Year.* New York: Coward, 1976.
Branley, Franklyn M. *Sunshine Makes the Seasons.* New York: T. Y. Crowell, 1974.
Hazeltine, Alice and Smith, Elva. *The Year Around.* New York: Abington Press, 1956.
Ichikawa, Satomi. *A Child's Book of Seasons.* New York: Scholastic, 1976.
Lionni, Leo. *Mouse Days: A Book of Seasons.* New York: Pantheon, 1980.
De Paola, Tomie. *Four Stories. Four Seasons.* Englewood Cliffs, NJ: Prentice-Hall, 1977.
Zolotow, Charlotte. *Over and Over.* New York: Harper and Row, 1957.

Winter

Branley, Franklyn M. *Snow is Falling.* New York: T. Y. Crowell, 1963.
Briggs, Raymond. *Snowman.* New York: Random, 1978.
Bunting, Eve. *Winter's Coming.* New York: Harcourt, Brace, Jovanovich, 1977.
Busch, Phyllis S. *A Walk in the Snow.* New York: Lippincott, 1971.
Keats, Ezra J. *The Snowy Day.* New York: Viking, 1962.

Spring

Anglund, Joan W. *Spring Is A New Beginning.* New York: Harcourt, Brace, Jovanovich, 1963.
Carrick, Carol. *Swamp Spring.* New York: Macmillan,

1969.
Francoise. *Springtime for Jeanne-Marie.* New York: Scribner, 1955.
Tresselt, Alvin R. *Hi, Mister Robin.* New York: Lothrop, 1950.

Summer

Bourne, Miriam A. *Emilio's Summer Day.* New York: Harper and Row, 1966.
Low, Alice. *Summer.* New York: Beginner, 1963.
Schick, Eleanor. *One Summer Night.* New York: Greenwillow, 1977.
Tresselt, Alvin R. *Sun Up.* New York: Lothrop, 1949.

Fall

Kessler, Ethel and Leonard Kessler. *All For Fall.* New York: Scholastic, 1974.
Tresselt, Alvin R. *Autumn Harvest.* New York: Lothrop, 1951.

Books on Self Concepts

See page 132 for book list

Books on Sensorial Experiences

Aliki. *My Five Senses.* New York: T. Y. Crowell, 1962.
Showers, Paul. *Find Out by Touching.* New York: T. Y. Crowell, 1961.
Showers, Paul. *Follow Your Nose.* New York: T. Y. Crowell, 1963.

Books on Shapes

————. *Cat and Dog Raise the Roof.* New York: Watts, 1980.
Allington, Richard. *Shapes and Sizes.* Milwaukee, WI.: Raintree, 1979.
Emberley, Ed. *Ed Emberley's Big Orange Drawing Book.* Boston: Little Brown, 1980.
Emberley, Ed. *Ed Emberley's Big Purple Drawing Book.* Boston: Little Brown, 1981.
Emberley, Ed. *Ed Emberley's Drawing Book: Make A World.* Boston: Little Brown, 1972.
Emberley, Ed. *Ed Emberley's Drawing Book of Faces.* Boston: Little Brown, 1975.
Hoban, Tana. *Shapes and Things.* New York: Macmillan, 1970.
Kohn, Bernice. *Everything Has a Shape, Everything Has a Size.* Englewood Cliffs, NJ.: Prentice-Hall, 1966.
Lionni, Leo. *Pezzettino.* New York: Pantheon, 1975.
Pienkowski, Jan. *Shapes.* New York: Harvey, 1975.
Schlein, Miriam. *Shapes.* Reading, MA.: Addison Wesley, 1952.
Seuss, Dr. *The Shape of Me and Other Stuff.* New York: Random, 1973.
Youldon, Gillian. *Shapes.* New York: Watts, 1979.

Books on Time

Breiter, Herta. *Time and Clocks.* Milwaukee, WI.: Raintree, 1978.
Hutchins, Pat. *Clocks and More Clocks.* New York: Macmillan, 1970.
Shapiro, Arnold. *Mr. Cuckoo's Clock Shop.* Los Angeles, CA.: Price, Stern and Sloan, 1978.
Shapiro, Larry. *Pop-Up Time.* Los Angeles, CA.: Price, Stern, and Sloan, 1980.
Wade, Harlan. (ed.) *Time.* Milwaukee, WI.: Raintree Pub., 1979.
Youldon. *Time.* New York: Watts, 1980.

Young children sometimes find it difficult to confide with adults directly, yet will express themselves freely to or through a puppet.

Rabbit Puppet by "Steif" of Reeves International (See Bibliography)

PUPPETALKING
Social and Emotional Growth through Puppets

Young children are emotional beings who ride a roller coaster of feelings every day as they interact with their peers, their family and their environment. Anything that disrupts their expected routine can cause the child to feel disoriented and at odds with his world. Whether that disruption is a minor incident such as not getting a certain toy or an event of tremendous impact such as a death in the family, the effect on the child cannot be minimized. Unknowingly, adults sometimes assume that children who cannot verbalize their thoughts are incapable of experiencing any range in emotions; however, quite the contrary is true. Young children are not only very sensitive to the emotional timbre of their world, but are ruled in large part by it.

It logically follows that one of the most useful skills that can be developed in young children is the ability to *identify, understand* and *verbalize* inner thoughts and feelings. Puppets can add an exciting dimension in attaining this goal.

Young children sometimes find it difficult to confide with adults directly, yet will express themselves freely to or through a puppet. The process that an individual uses with puppets for interacting with a child or group of children is called Puppetalking. It is used to explore social and emotional growth in situations where the teacher-leader wants information about how the children are thinking or feeling. In such situations, the puppet becomes either a spokesperson for the child or a non-threatening confidant.

Puppetalking is effective because the puppet becomes a transparent facade behind which the child can hide. He feels no responsibility for the action and words he projects since, in his own mind, they are the words and actions of someone else. Likewise,

when a puppet is placed on the hand of an adult, the child ignores the adult's existence and focuses on the puppet, thus eliminating any communication barriers which might have existed.

In addition, Puppetalking offers an avenue for developing verbal skills in young children. If a child can label his feelings and articulate what caused them, he is generally closer to understanding them. Keep in mind however that because a child uses descriptive labels like "angry" or "afraid," there is no guarantee that he totally understands the concepts behind them. Observe the action to get a better grasp of the child's true feelings. For example, a child may say to a puppet that it is wrong to hit his friend, yet turn around five minutes later and punch him for not sharing a toy! Children need practice in using words to tell others what they want. Puppetalk can provide opportunities to "try on life's situations."

Puppetalking requires only a few puppets and a quiet place in which to exchange conversation. A quiet spot, away from general traffic patterns is best.

If you are new to puppets, then you may be unsure as to how and when to use them. Always keep in mind that your goal is to facilitate the child's ability to express thoughts and feelings. In so doing, several guidelines can be applied:

(1) Select puppets to encourage gentle responses from the children, preferably puppets that are soft, huggable, indestructible varieties in fabrics, that are interesting both in color and texture. Invite the children to touch and stroke the puppets as they make friends.

(2) Develop your puppet as a skilled, sensitive questioner who encourages a child to respond by identifying and expressing feelings, as well as ac-

tions: "I feel _____"; or "I don't like it when _____"; or "It makes me angry when _____." Let your puppet help the child perceive the relationship between his feelings and the resultant action. For example, when sad, a child might cry; when afraid, he might hit and so forth. The more children can understand about their own behavior, the more successful will be their interactions with others.

(3) Let your puppet be a sensitive listener. If the puppet treats the child's concerns with the utmost respect, then the child, in turn, will respond to the puppet as a trusted confidant. Be open and receptive, reflecting what the child says. Avoid value judgments that imply disapproval of the child's actions or thoughts. If discipline is required, *you* do it, not the puppet.

When applied to social or emotional growth, Puppetalking may be as simple as greeting the child every morning with a secret and a hug or as complex as helping the child verbalize his feelings over a parental divorce. Whatever the situation, you must find the technique that is most harmonious with your teaching style. Through experimentation and experience, the right combination of puppets and technique will evolve for teacher and children.

- Work on a one-to-one basis with each child rather than in small groups. In so doing, you may use a puppet who talks directly to the child.

- Give the puppets to the children so they can talk to each other instead of to you.

- Develop a four-way conversation between teacher, child and their individual puppets, treating each one as a separate entity. Keep in mind that the more you engage children in Puppetalking, the more creative you will be in applying the technique, so keep a puppet in your pocket ready to pull out at any time!

Puppetalking is basically an individualized experience thus making it difficult to develop activities for general use. However, there are many feelings and situations common to young children, and the following suggestions are presented as possible starting points. While most are conceived as Puppetalking, some can be expanded into more elaborate Puppetization experiences.

Before proceeding, however, one important point needs to be mentioned and, in fact, cannot be stressed enough: unless you are a trained therapist or working under the guidance of medical personnel, do not use Puppetalking for therapeutic purposes. It is one thing to engage children in Puppetalking to dis-

Let your puppet be a sensitive listener.

cern the extent of a problem but it is quite another to use Puppetalking as a form of treatment. Young children disturbed by turmoil at home, death, divorce or other serious events may need help beyond what you are trained to provide. Your responsibility is to inform the parent and, if necessary, to suggest professional help. A little knowledge can do a lot of damage if used improperly. Remember, it is better not to help at all than to seek to assist in an inappropriate manner.

Books on Puppetalking

Aleskovsky, Annie, *Learning Through Puppets*—Fairy tales and short stories are used to illustrate such concepts as "new baby," "moving in" and "self-concepts." Darien, Connecticut, Allen Raymond, Inc., 1975

122

Self-Concept

The single most important quality adults can nurture in young children is that of a positive self-image. Children need to feel good about how they are growing—intellectually, physically, socially and emotionally—in order to build self-confidence. Puppetalking is one means for reinforcing those features that help children perceive of themselves as special persons.

- Ask the children to make puppets that depict themselves. Let the puppet tell you what it likes best and least about itself, also what it can do that no other puppet can and what makes it special in the world.

- Using superhero puppets, let the children puppetize feats of bravery and strength that the children themselves would like to perform.

- Ask the children to make puppets that portray themselves as babies. Let them tell the baby puppets what it will be like when they grow up to be three, five, eight years old (whatever the age of the child).

Stand-up Tube puppets

Glue fabric around a cardboard tube; attach a photograph of child's face and add feet to bottom of tube.

Feelings

Emotions are the underlying core of children's developmental growth. The sooner children learn to identify, label and communicate their feelings, the easier it is for them to make social and emotional adjustments in their daily lives. The general exploration of their basic emotions (joy, sorrow, fear, anger) can be enhanced through puppetry.

- Read the following poem to the children. Ask them to make a puppet which shows on the *outside*, what they are feeling on the *inside*.

I Have Two Selves
By Tamara Hunt

I have two Selves or so I'm told,
My Outside and my In.
And if I take a thoughtful look
I'll see myself within.

Although I know my Outside Self,
I see it every day,
My Inside Self seems hidden,
So neatly tucked away.

It seems so strange I cannot touch
Or taste or hear or see . . .
I only *feel* all those things
That are inside of me.

Both my Selves are Special
That's what I'm about.
Feeling on the inside
Showing on the out!

Glad/Sad Cup Puppets: Use two cups. Cut window hole in one cup and place over second cup. Draw a happy face to fit window area; revolve outer cup and draw a sad face.

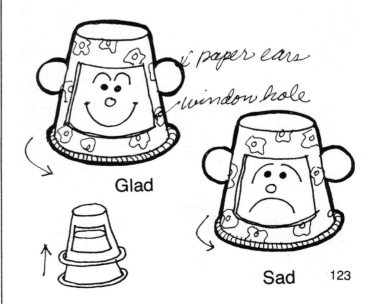

paper ears

window hole

Glad

Sad

123

Fighting

Preschool teachers and parents share the common goal of teaching children to use words instead of fists to communicate feelings and needs. Although fighting between the children may erupt out of anger, fear or basic hostility, these explosive feelings are often frustrating to the adult who must help children understand them.

- With puppets, stage an argument between the adults present over whose turn it is to play in the block corner. Make it as real as possible but stop before the puppets actually hit each other. Children generally find it funny when puppets hit and you want to maintain the seriousness of the scene. As a crowd gathers, let the puppets ask the children how to resolve the situation; repeat this technique throughout the year using a variety of conflict situations that occur regularly among the children.

- If two children start fighting and seem unable to resolve the issue themselves, invite them to sit down and mediate a discussion. When everyone is calm, give them each a puppet asking them to reverse roles. In so doing, they will each hopefully gain some insight into the other's point of view.

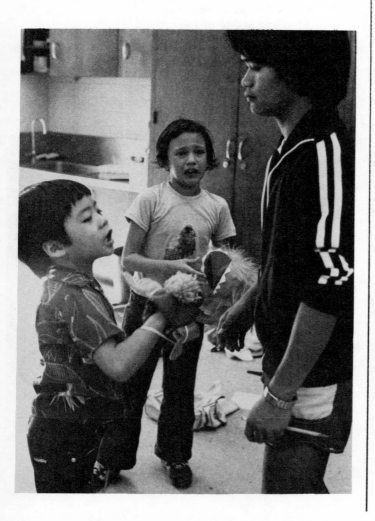

A New Baby

The arrival of a new baby sister or brother can be a disorienting, difficult to grasp experience for a child, especially a younger one who is unable to verbalize her feelings. One day she is the center of her parents' love and affection. The next she must share it with a wiggling, crying, attention-grabbing infant. The singlemost goal is to reassure the older child that although the family constellation has changed, her parents' love remains constant.

Young children desperately need to work through feelings of displacement for which Puppet Play offers a safe vehicle. The school environment gives a neutral setting to enact scenes where anger and hostility can be expressed without fear of parental disapproval. (At home the children are too apt to be confronted with parental reprimands for negative behavior toward a new sibling.)

Role-playing in which a child can say exactly what she feels about the new baby can provide an important emotional release. Sentiments like "I hate that baby!" or "Why do you always hold the baby?" or "Shut up, baby! You're hurting my ears!" express genuine feelings that are more acceptable when spoken through a puppet.

You will do a great service to the child by helping her identify and verbalize hostility. When the child no longer feels threatened, her jealousy will likely dissipate. Here are some suggested activities.

- You operate the mother or father puppet while the child operates a child puppet, preferably of his or her own sex. With a baby doll, pretend you are bringing an infant home from the hospital. Encourage the child to look at how *tiny* the baby is. Compare relative sizes of fingers, hands and toes. Talk about how the child was once that small. Ask questions such as "What do you suppose it's like being a baby?" "How can a baby tell someone it is hungry?" Try to develop in the child an understanding of why babies behave in certain ways.

- Using two child puppets, pretend you are the child with the new sibling. Complain to your friend that the baby always cries, that your mother never has time for you any more and that you do not like the baby. Try to verbalize the negative feelings that the real child is possibly experiencing. Encourage dialogue such as "Have you ever had a baby in your house? What did you do when _____?"

- After sharing some books about a new baby with the children, display them in the Puppet Corner together with the puppets representing family members and babies.

Adoption

The concept of adoption affects all children: directly if the child, a sibling or friend is adopted and indirectly if the child has just been introduced to the word for the first time.

In interacting with adopted children, it is important to talk with the parents to find out how they are handling the topic at home. A newly adopted child may be experiencing normal adjustment problems that can be eased through Puppetalking. These children may find it beneficial to role-play using puppets to represent themselves and their newly acquired families. Puppets can also be helpful in explaining "international families." Asian children, for example, who are adopted into Caucasian families may not understand why they do not look like their mother or father. By using puppets of various skin tones and facial features, life situations can be recreated with puppets and, in so doing, fears and doubts can be talked through and better understood.

Children who are not adopted usually become curious in two ways.

- First, they want to know about themselves. "Am I adopted?" "How do I know for sure?" "If I'm bad, will my own parents give me away to a new family?"

- Second, they want to know about the adopted child's home life. "What does it mean to be adopted?" "What does it feel like?" "Are your parents nice?" "Are your parents just like mine?" "Do they still love you even though you are adopted?"

Puppets can be used in a variety of ways to help children answer these questions and better understand the concept of adoption. Perhaps your class could "adopt" a puppet for the day. In the Puppet Corner you might speak for the adopted puppet and invite the children one-by-one to talk to, care for and generally see that the puppet is happy and feeling secure as a part of the school family. Later reverse roles and let the children become the "adopted puppet," thus affording them the opportunity to ask the questions that concern them.

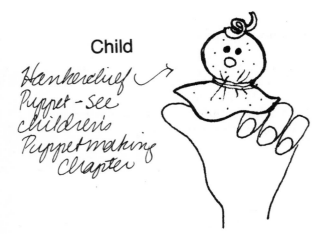

Child

Handkerchief Puppet - see children's Puppetmaking Chapter

Peer and Sibling Relationships

One of the major tasks confronting a young child is to grow from an egocentric being into someone capable of positive social interaction. For many children this task presents seemingly monumental hurdles to overcome. Learning to share and to wait turns, for example, require enormous amounts of restraint and patience on the part of a young child. When engaged in negative behavior, a child may not even know he is doing something inappropriate. Therefore, it is especially important to help a child recognize his role in social interactions. Puppetalking and Puppet Play provide excellent opportunities to heighten this awareness. Puppets can exemplify acceptable behavior as well as enable the child to try out various resolutions until a successful one is found. Whenever possible, improvisational situations should be similar to those that have occurred in actuality. Here are some beginning ideas for a puppet to demonstrate positive as well as negative forms of social interaction.

Have a puppet:

- Draw a picture for another puppet.

- Share a sandwich with a puppet that forgot its lunch.

- Invite another puppet to come to a secret place.

- Tattle on a puppet for taking away a toy.

- Push another puppet out of line.

- Prevent another puppet from having a turn riding the tricycle. (Use a toy tricycle as a prop.)

A New School

Every year a certain percentage of children will leave the nursery school to go to kindergarten or move up from one elementary school grade to the next. Most children approach such moves with mixed feelings. There is excitement in suddenly becoming a "big kid" and entering a more advanced school. Yet there is also the tremendous apprehension of leaving a comfortable, familiar environment.

Puppetalking can help to allay a child's anxiety and serve as a "rehearsal" for the real life situation. It is important to emphasize the positive aspects of the forthcoming experience: a friendly teacher, new friends and an attractive place with interesting things to do and learn. Yet it is important also to recognize those problems the child will likely encounter in not knowing anyone and being faced with a different set of regulations.

To prepare a child to change schools, create a Puppetalking scenario in which fears can be discussed in the safe forum of the Puppet Corner.

- Enact the role of two children entering a new school. Talk about things that are worrisome or frightening and encourage the child to do likewise through the puppet. Whenever possible, focus the dialogue on matters of concern to the child.

- Pretend you are an "old-timer" and tell the child what kinds of things you did when you were in kindergarten, first grade, second grade, sixth grade and up. In a confidential tone, admit you were frightened when you began a new school but emphasize how nice it was to have greater responsibilities with more freedom and opportunities.

- Pretend you are a younger child at a new school. Be somewhat awed by an older child who is moving up to the next grade. Ask what will happen when she gets there. This kind of Puppetalking will help to assess how much the child knows about her forthcoming experience.

Moving

Moving to a new neighborhood or city, even to a foreign country, should be treated in much the same way as entering a new school. To go from a known to an unknown location frequently has an unsettling effect upon the child as well as his family. As the moving date approaches and tension mounts, the strain on the child and his daily routine will surface.

If a child will be moving to a different country or environment then the move should be integrated into the curriculum as an enriching experience. Thus, the whole class may have the opportunity to contemplate what it would be like to live in France or go from a large city to a farm.

Here are some suggested activities.

- In the Puppet Corner set up a "neighborhood" tabletop display with toy houses and puppets. Work in small groups and let the adult, through the puppet, be the "new kid" trying to make friends. Later change roles with the children.

- On a one-to-one basis, interact with a child who is soon to change residences. If possible, consult beforehand with the parents for details as to when, where and how the move will occur. Pretend *you* are the one who will move and ask the child's puppet:

  "Do I have to move?"
  "Why do I have to go?"
  "Will my toys be packed?"
  "Can our dog go with us?"
  "What will our new house be like?"
  "Will there be other children to play with?"
  "Will I go to a new school?"
  "How will we travel to the new location?"
  "Are you coming, too?"

Then reverse roles.

- If a child is moving to a different environment as from one country to another, from a small town to a big city or from a warm to a cold climate, try some of the following exercises with whole class:

  Puppetize a story from the new country.
  Make a city mural and puppetize daily events that take place in the city.
  Show photographs of the snow and Puppetize snow-time activities.

Getting Lost or Separated

Separation from a parent can be a frightening experience for a young child. Being left at school or getting lost in a large department store may make a child feel that she will never see her parents again. A child may not understand why mother has to leave on a business trip or go somewhere without her. The child may even believe she caused the parent to go away. Puppetalking is a good way to help the child understand the circumstances surrounding a parental separation.

● Using two adult puppets, one operated by the child and the other operated by an adult, pretend that you are both going on a trip. Simulate the real life situation as closely as possible. Have the puppets talk about the child and the separation experience:

"Do you think my daughter Lisa knows where I'm going?"
"Do you know who will be taking her to school every morning?"
"I wonder if she'll be worried when she comes home from school and discovers I'm gone?"
"Do you suppose she knows I'm coming back?"
"What do you think she's doing while I'm gone?"
"Who will take care of her?"

Help the child verbalize what her daily routine will be like while the parent is away. Be sure to include adequate conversation about the parent's return and the anticipated reunion.

● Operate a child puppet while the child represents the adult who is going away. Ask the child questions that might be bothering her. Let her answer as she prefers and then use her responses to launch further discussion.

● Puppetize getting lost in a store. Help the child to think of ways to find the parent or store manager.

● With puppets, act out a child's being left for the first time at an unfamiliar school. Encourage the "old timers" to reassure the child.

Sleeping Away From Home

Spending the night away from home, whether by choice or necessity, can be unsettling for young children. When the excitement of playing at a friend's home gives way to the actuality of sleeping in a different bed apart from parents and familiar surroundings, panic may set in.

Although Puppetalking cannot altogether assuage the child's concern, it can prepare him for what to expect. Be careful to suggest only those situations likely to occur.

● Create a bed out of a box by cutting off the top half of the box; cover the remainder with a doll's blanket, a handkerchief or a scarf. Using two puppets, let the child be the host while you play the role of the guest spending the night. Ask questions that will reflect concerns the child is probably experiencing.

"Do you sleep with the light on or off?"
"Does somebody read you a bedtime story?"
"What happens if I wet the bed?"
"Will my mom pick me up in the morning?"

● Using mother and child puppets, you play the mother while the child enacts someone getting ready to spend the night at grandma's house. Help prepare for the event by asking the child puppet whether he will pack items such as a toothbrush, pajamas, toys or favorite stories. Help the puppet think of solutions to potential problems. "What will you do if you wake up in the middle of the night and you're afraid?" "What will you do if you hear strange noises?" Talk about happy things as well. "What games will you play with grandpa and grandma?" "What favorite foods would you like grandma to cook for your breakfast?"

Security Blankets

Young children frequently become attached to a special stuffed animal or toy during the first two years of life. This important "security blanket" is often dragged along wherever the child goes. When a child enters preschool, many parents and teachers feel it is time to wean the child from the object of dependency. Since children may not understand why they cannot take a teddy bear to school, Puppetalking can provide some of the answers.

- Let the child select a puppet to play the part of the "security blanket" or teddy bear. Operate the puppet and encourage the child to explain to the "security blanket" why it must stay at home today.

- Working in a small group of three children, Puppetize a scene in which two puppets take away the third puppet's stuffed animal. Operate the fourth puppet to resolve the situation. Change roles.

- Using two puppets, pretend that one is spending the night at the other's house and has forgotten to bring his special blanket. Think of ways to go to sleep without it.

- The subject of "security" toys can also be integrated into activities about separation.

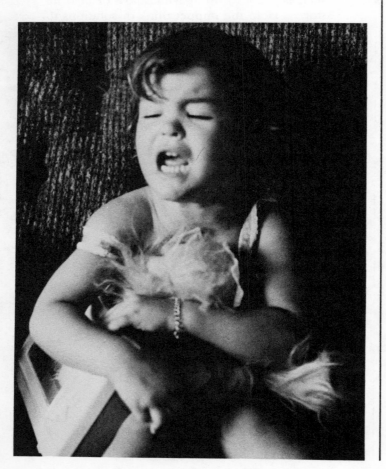

Haircuts

To a young child, getting a haircut can be a frightening experience. Although comfortable to an adult, this sometimes unfamiliar setting may seem overpowering to a child. The chair itself may be reminiscent of a dentist's chair or the scissors may look like weapons. These concerns that the child experiences may be associated with fears that more than just the hair (ears, nose and fingers!) might get cut off.

Children need to be reassured that scissors cut only the hair and that it will grow back in time. One of the best ways to prepare children for a hair-cutting experience is to simulate the scene in advance.

- Use a cardboard tube puppet with a yarn wig. Attach strands of yarn through the tube and extrude the yarn through the top of the puppet's head. Styrofoam or nerf ball puppets also work well; yarn strands can be easily taped onto the head. Let the child be the barber and the adult the puppet coming in for its first haircut.

- The puppet asks the barber: "Why do I have to get my hair cut?" "What are *those* (scissors) for?" "How do I know you won't accidentally cut off my nose?" "What are you going to do with my hair after it's cut?" While reassuring the puppet, the child can explain the procedures and, in so doing, allay some of his own fears.

The more questions you ask the child, the more you will know about how much the child understands about the process. Be sure to use blunt scissors and let the "barber" actually cut off the puppet's wig.

yarn hair

clothespin nose
cardboard tube
fabric

Fears of Nightmares, Darkness, Monsters

The inability of young children to distinguish between fantasy and reality sometimes gives rise to childhood fears. The most common are fears of monsters, strange shadows, nightmares and, of course, the dark. These are important concerns to young children and should not be minimized by adults. Puppetalking is an effective vehicle for helping young children verbalize fears.

- Describe the puppet as very fearful; let the puppet ask the children for reassurance by sharing its frightening experiences. "When I go to bed at night my mother says I have to turn out the light. I don't like it when my room is dark, do you? I see strange creatures in the shadows. What do you see?"

- Ask the children to transform their own versions of nightmares or monsters into paper string puppets (see instructions on page 177). Place them in the Puppet Corner for improvised Puppet Play.

Fears of Natural Disasters

Television has brought the reality of natural disasters into our living rooms for observation at close range. Sometimes these graphic descriptions create fear in the mind of the young viewers who begin to wonder if they might be caught in a similar disaster. Since children become confused and afraid of things over which they have no control, it is a good idea to use Puppetalking as a way of dispelling unnecessary fears. Remember, however, there is no reason to preoccupy children's minds if they have expressed no curiosity or concern.

Children may gain some reassurance from learning what to do in situations of natural disaster.

- Working in small puppet groups, enact what would happen if a specific natural disaster should occur. Help the children decide among themselves what would be the best procedure to ensure the safety of all.

- Let the child operate a puppet representing a fireperson, policeperson or rescue worker who saves a victim puppet from fire, drowning, etc. Encourage the children to verbalize safety rules by having them give instructions as part of the rescue attempt.

Basic hand puppet and police hat instructions on page 200   129

Medical and Dental Checkups

Some children are apprehensive about visiting the doctor or the dentist. Such fears may develop simply from not knowing what to expect or from former experiences in which they were fallaciously told "This won't hurt," causing their trust to be broken. Children want to know what is going to happen to them *before* it actually occurs and puppets offer an excellent vehicle for accomplishing this objective. A puppet can become the patient or the doctor, dentist or other health care personnel.

● Using a doctor puppet, perform a physical examination on the child to check the eyes, ears, nose, throat, height, weight, blood pressure and heart-rate; test the reflexes and feel the stomach and neck. Remember to take a pretend blood sample and to administer a vaccination. Then reverse roles and let the child be the puppeteer and examine you, the patient.

● Using a dentist puppet, set up a dental checkup for the child. Clean the teeth, treat with fluoride and talk about the equipment. Show how to brush and floss properly. Also give a shot of novocaine to fill a cavity. You may use this opportunity to discuss proper eating habits, nutrition and dental hygiene. Reverse roles. (See Page 103 for "Mr. Teeth" puppet.)

The Hospital

Hospital experiences may occasionally affect children at your school. A child who is going into the hospital for any reason—whether as a routine procedure or for a serious operation—will have questions about what is going to happen, as will the child's friends who may wonder if it will be their turn next.

Similar to the haircut situation, let the child's fears be discussed by way of the puppet. Talk about what happens when someone goes to the hospital (describe admission tests, special beds with rails and the roles of nurses and doctors); also mention where Mommy and Daddy will be while the child is being hospitalized. It is important to discover what the child is concerned about and then answer his questions.

Puppet by Poppets (see bibliography)

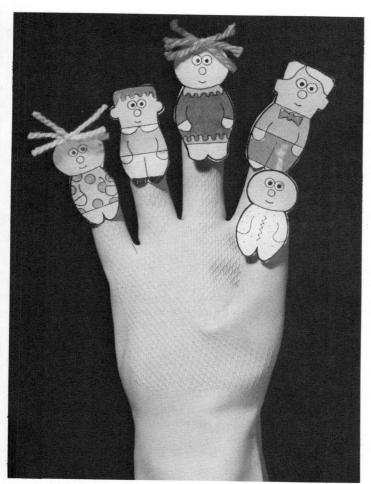

A rubber glove with stick-on paper finger puppets (See page 190) is an excellent vehicle for communicating about family oriented subjects presented in this chapter. Make photocopies of family characters on this page for glove Puppetalking.

A mitten can easily be converted into a sibling and parent for divorce or separation discussions. Add wiggle eyes and soft pom pom noses to thumb and finger sections of glove for faces.

Divorce

A large percentage of young children today live in single-parent homes. At every stage of a divorce, children need assistance understanding the complex situation that they did not wish upon themselves and over which they have no control. Puppetalking can be used to help the child understand that she did not cause the divorce and most importantly to reassure the child that both parents still love her even though one is no longer living at home. You may be able to engage the child in Puppet Play situations using child and parent puppets. Consult the parents first for their advice and approval. Possible Puppet Play situations might include:

- A father puppet taking his daughter puppet out on a Saturday afternoon.

- A mother and a father puppet arguing.

- A child puppet conferring with one parent about the other.

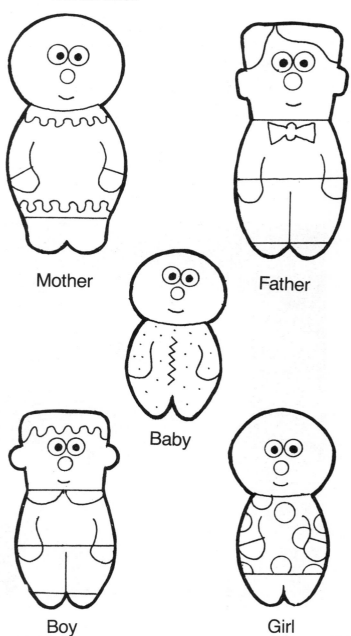

Mother

Father

Baby

Boy

Girl

Death

Death, whether it be of a pet, relative or peer, will affect children in varying degrees of intensity. Puppets are best used in these situations to facilitate the child's ability to express feelings and ask questions. Since death deals with personal and religious values, you should consult the parents before engaging children in Puppetalk on this subject. Conflicting viewpoints about death may totally confuse the child and, in fact, make matters worse. It is important to remember that children do not perceive death in the manner of adults, and unless it is the death of a mother, father or sibling, they may find the reactions of relatives more frightening and traumatic than the fact of the actual death itself.

Several things seem important in helping a child deal with death.

● Afford opportunites for the child to express verbally how she perceives the entire experience. What remains foremost in the child's mind? Is it the funeral, the ambulance, police or the reactions of adults? By Puppetalking about a situation in which a puppet dies, the child may be able to project her feelings about her own experience with death in her reaction to and treatment of the puppet.

● Be sure the child does not feel responsible for the death. If a child has been fighting with a brother and secretly wishing him dead, it is easy to understand why the child feels respon-

sible when a death wish becomes fulfilled. Puppetalking about things like "Why do people die?" and "Can you make somebody die?" may help determine whether the child is experiencing any of these feelings.

● Help him understand why everyone else is so upset. If the grandfather died, why is his mother crying so much? Perhaps the child could be a child-puppet and you, as a mother-puppet, could respond to the questions raised. Also try reversing the roles in order to let other feelings surface.

● Find out whether the child fears his own death or that of a loved one as a result of the event. Young children may wonder "Will I die?" "Will Mommy die?" "When will it happen?" "Will it hurt?"

As a teacher, you are probably the next closest adult to the child. A grieving family may not have the time or ability to elicit this information from the child. Remember that you are not a therapist. Your responsibility is to inform the parents or family counselor of your findings.

The death of a pet is a relatively commonplace occurrence to an adult, but to a child a pet's death can be quite traumatic. It should be treated with sensitivity, allowing the child to explore his emotions and ask whatever questions may arise.

Puppetalk Notebooks

Parents appreciate being included in their children's experiences during the school day. It might be useful to keep a Puppetalk notebook with a sheet for each child. Think of it as a diary in which you jot down information contributed by the children during Puppetalk-times. During morning drop-off or afternoon pick-up, parents can read the entries and write in ideas they would like for you to explore with their child.

Books on Self Concepts

Beim, Jerrold. *Smallest Boy in the Class*. New York: Morrow, 1949.

Blume, Judy. *Freckle Juice*. New York: Scholastic, 1971.

Charlip, Remy and Lillian Moore. *Hooray for Me*. New York: Scholastic, 1980. repro of 1975 ed.

Hazen, Barbara S. *Me I See*. Nashville, TN: Abingdon, 1978.

Klein, Norma. *Girls Can Be Anything*. New York: Dutton, 1975.

Krasilovsky, Phyllis. *The Very Little Boy*. New York: Doubleday, 1962.

Krasilovsky, Phyllis. *The Very Little Girl*. New York: Doubleday, 1953.

Levy, Elizabeth. *Nice Little Girls*. New York: Delacorte, 1974.

Thomas, Marlo et al. *Free to Be . . . You and Me*. New York: McGraw Hill, 1974.

Zolotow, Charlotte. *Someone New*. New York: Harper and Row, 1978.

Books on Feelings

Coombs, Patricia. *Lisa and the Grompet*. New York: Lothrop, 1970.

Castle, Sue. *Face Talk, Hand Talk, Body Talk*. New York: Doubleday, 1977.

Dunn, Judy. *Feelings*. Minneapolis, MN: Creative Education, 1970.

Hill, Elizabeth S. *Evan's Corner*. New York: Holt, Rinehart and Winston, 1967.

Kroll, Steven. *That Makes Me Mad*. New York: Pantheon, 1976.

Mr. Happy. (series) Los Angeles, CA: Price, Stern, Sloan, 1980.

Sendak, Maurice. *Where the Wild Things Are*. New York: Harper and Row, 1963.

Simon, Norma. *How Do I Feel?* Chicago: A. Whitman, 1970.

Simon, Norma. *I Was So Mad*. Chicago: A. Whitman, 1974.

Viorst, Judith. *Alexander and the Terrible, Horrible, No Good, Very Bad Day*. New York: Atheneum, 1976.

Wittels, Harriet and Joan Greisman. *Things I Hate*. New York: Human Sciences Press, 1973.

Books on Fighting

Bonsall, Crosby N. *It's Mine*. New York: Harper and Row, 1964.

Bonsall, Crosby N. *Mine's the Best*. New York: Harper and Row, 1973.

Lopshire, Robert. *I Am Better Than You*. New York: Harper and Row, 1968.

Zolotow, Charlotte. *The Hating Book*. New York: Harper and Row, 1969.

Books on the New Baby

Alexander, Martha. *Nobody Asked Me If I Wanted a Baby Sister*. New York: Dial, 1971.

Alexander, Martha. *When the New Baby Comes, I'm Moving Out*. New York: Dial, 1979.

Byars, Betsy C. *Go and Hush the Baby*. New York: Viking, 1971.

Greenfield, Eloise. *She Come Bringing Me That Little Baby Girl*. New York: Lippincott, 1974.

Hazen, Barbara S. *Why Couldn't I Be An Only Kid Like You*. New York: Atheneum, 1975.

Hoban, Russell. *A Baby Sister for Frances*. New York: Harper and Row, 1964.

Iwasaki, Chihiro. *A New Baby Is Coming to My House*. New York: McGraw Hill, 1972.

Keats, Ezra J. *Peter's Chair*. New York: Harper and Row, 1967.

Relf, Patricia. *That New Baby*. New York: Golden, 1980.

Schick, Eleanor. *Peggy's New Brother*. New York: Macmillan, 1970.

Stein, Sarah. *That New Baby*. New York: Walker and Company, 1974.

Walsh, Ellen. *Brunus and the New Bear*. New York: Doubleday, 1979.

Zolotow, Charlotte. *If It Weren't for You*. New York: Harper and Row, 1966.

Books on Adoption

Bunin, Sherry and Catherine Bunin. *Is That Your Sister?* New York: Pantheon, 1976.

Caines, Jeannette. *Abby*. New York: Harper and Row, 1973.

Lapsley, Susan. *I Am Adopted*. Scarsdale, NY: Bradbury Press, 1975.

Simon, Norma. *Why Am I Different?* Chicago: A. Whitman, 1976.

Wasson, Valerie. *The Chosen Baby*. New York: Lippincott, 1977.

Young, Mariam. *Miss Suzy's Birthday*. New York: Scholastic, 1974.

Books on Peer Relationships—Siblings

Alexander, Martha. *I'll Be the Horse If You'll Play With Me*. New York: Dial, 1975.

Berger, Terry. *Big Sister, Little Brother*. Milwaukee, WI: Raintree, 1975.

Bonsall, Crosby N. *The Days I Had to Play With My Sister*. New York: Harper and Row, 1972.

Bonsall, Crosby N. *Piggle*. New York: Harper and Row, 1973.

Bulla, Clyde R. *Keep Running, Allen*. New York: T. Y. Crowell, 1978.

Bonsall, Crosby N. *Who's a Pest*. New York: Harper and Row, 1962.

Hallinan, P. K. *We're Very Good Friends, My Brother and I.* Chicago: Childrens Press, 1973.

Hutchins, Pat. *Titch.* New York: Macmillan, 1971.

Viorst, Judith. *I'll Fix Anthony.* New York: Harper and Row, 1969.

Wells, Rosemary. *Noisy Nora.* New York: Dial, 1973.

Zolotow, Charlotte. *Big Sister and Little Sister.* New York: Harper and Row, 1966.

Books on Peer Relationships—Positive

Isadora, Rachel. *Max.* New York: Macmillan, 1976.

Manushkin, Fran. *Bubblebath.* New York: Harper and Row, 1974.

Sharmat, Marjorie W. *Goodnight, Andrew, Goodnight, Craig.* New York: Harper and Row, 1969.

Zolotow, Charlotte. *Hold My Hand.* New York: Harper and Row, 1972.

Books on Peer Relationships—Problems

Bonsall, Crosby N. *It's Mine.* New York: Harper and Row, 1964.

Bonsall, Crosby N. *Mine's the Best.* New York: Harper and Row, 1973.

Christopher, Matt. *Johnny No Hit.* Boston: Little, 1977.

Mallett, Anne. *Here Comes Tagalong.* New York: Scholastic, 1971.

Viorst, Judith. *Rosie and Michael.* New York: Atheneum, 1974.

Zolotow, Charlotte. *New Friend.* New York: Abelard, 1968.

Books on New Schools

Alexander, Martha. *Sabrina.* New York: Dial, 1971.

Amoss, Berthe. *The Very Worst Thing.* New York: Scholastic, 1972.

Anderson, Eloise. *Carlos Goes to School.* New York: Warne, 1973.

Breinburg, Petronella. *Shawn Goes to School.* New York: T. Y. Crowell, 1974.

Burningham, John. *The School.* New York: T. Y. Crowell, 1975.

Caudill, Rebecca. *Did You Carry the Flag Today, Charley?* New York: Holt, Rinehart and Winston, 1971.

Cohen, Miriam. *Will I Have a Friend?* New York: Macmillan, 1967.

Kantrowitz, Mildred. *Willy Bear.* New York: Scholastic, 1980.

Levy, Elizabeth. *Nice Little Girls.* New York: Delacorte, 1974.

Welber, Robert. *Goodbye, Hello.* New York: Pantheon, 1974.

Wells, Rosemary. *Timothy Goes to School.* New York: Dial, 1981.

Wolde, Gunilla. *Betsy's First Day at Nursery School.* New York: Random, 1976.

Books on Moving

Hickman, Martha W. *I'm Moving.* Nashville, TN: Abingdon, 1975.

Kantrowitz, Mildred. *Good-Bye Kitchen.* New York: Scholastic, 1969.

Tobias, Tobi. *Moving Day.* New York: Knopf, 1976.

Zolotow, Charlotte. *Janey.* New York: Harper and Row, 1973.

Books on Getting Lost and Seperation

Barnett, Moneta. *First Pink Light.* New York: Scholastic, 1979.

Brenner, Barbara. *Cunningham's Rooster.* New York: Scholastic, 1975.

Brown, Margaret W. *The Runaway Bunny.* New York: Harper and Row, 1972.

Carrick, Carol. *Lost in the Storm.* Boston: Houghton Mifflin, 1974.

Clymer, Eleanor. *Leave Horatio Alone.* New York: Atheneum, 1974.

Kraus, Robert. *Whose Mouse Are You?* New York: Macmillan, 1972.

Kroll, Steven. *Is Milton Missing?* New York: Holiday, 1975.

Lisker, Sonia O. *Lost.* New York: Harcourt, Brace and Jovanovich, 1975.

Myers, Bernice. *My Mother is Lost.* New York: Scholastic, 1971.

Raskin, Ellen. *Moose, Goose, and Little Nobody.* New York: Scholastic, 1980.

Rockwell, Anne. *The Story Snail.* New York: Macmillan, 1974.

Schick, Eleanor. *Katie Goes to Camp.* New York: Macmillan, 1968.

Sonneborn, Ruth A. *Friday Night is Papa Night.* New York: Viking, 1970.

Steig, William. *Sylvestor and the Magic Pebble.* New York: Simon and Schuster, 1969.

Tompert, Ann. *Little Fox Goes to the End of the World.* New York: Crown, 1976.

Books on Sleeping Away

Chorao, Kay. *Lester's Overnight.* New York: Dutton, 1977.

Waber, Bernard. *Ira Sleeps Over.* Boston: Houghton Mifflin, 1972.

Books on Security Blankets

Burningham, John. *Blanket.* New York: T. Y. Crowell, 1976.

Chorao, Kay. *Molly's Moe.* Boston: Houghton Mifflin, 1976.

Hoban, Lillian. *No, No, Sammy Crow.* New York: Greenwillow, 1981.

Hughes, Shirley. *David and Dog.* Englewood Cliffs, NJ: Prentice-Hall, 1978.

Mayers, Patrick. *Lost Bear, Found Bear.* Chicago: A. Whitman, 1973.

Pearson, Susan. *Izzie.* New York: Dial, 1975.

Schulman, Janet. *The Big Hello.* New York: Greenwillow, 1976.

Books on Haircuts

Freeman, Don. *Dandelion.* New York: Puffin, 1964.

Peet, Bill. *Hubert's Hair-Raising Adventures,* New York: Houghton Mifflin, 1959.

Books on Fears—Monsters

Bang, Molly G. *Wiley and the Hairy Man.* New York: Macmillan, 1976.

Crowe, Robert L. *Clyde Monster.* New York: Dutton, 1976.

Gackenbach, Dick. *Harry and the Terrible Whatzit.* Boston: Houghton Mifflin, 1977.

Hanlon, Emily. *What If a Lion Eats Me and I Fall into a Hippopotamus' Mud Hole*. New York: Delacorte, 1975.

Mayer, Mercer. *Liza Lou and the Yellow Belly Swamp*. New York: Scholastic, 1980.

Mayer, Mercer. *There's a Nightmare in My Closet*. New York: Dial, 1976.

Meddaugh, Susan. *Beast*. Boston: Houghton Mifflin, 1981.

Sendak, Maurice. *Where the Wild Things Are*. New York: Harper and Row, 1963.

Viorst, Judith. *My Mama Says There Aren't Any Zombies, Ghosts, Vampires, Creatures, Demons, Monsters, Fiends, Goblins, or Things*. New York: Atheneum, 1973.

Books on Natural Disasters

Anderson, Lonzo. *The Day the Hurricane Happened*. New York: Scribner, 1974.

Buckley, Helen E. *Michael Is Brave*. New York: Lothrop, 1971.

Dragonwagon, Crescent. *Will It Be Okay?* New York: Harper and Row, 1977.

Zolotow, Charlotte. *Storm Book*. New York: Harper and Row, 1952.

Books on Dentists and Teeth

Bate, Lucy. *Little Rabbitt's Loose Tooth*. New York: Crown, 1975.

De Groat, Diane. *Alligator's Toothache*. New York: Crown, 1977.

McCloskey, Robert. *One Morning in Maine*. New York: Viking, 1952.

Rockwell, Harlow. *My Dentist*. New York: Greenwillow, 1975.

Showers, Paul. *How Many Teeth?* New York: T. Y. Crowell, 1976.

Williams, Barbara. *Albert's Toothache*. New York: Dutton, 1974.

Wolf, Bernard. *Michael and the Dentist*. New York: Four Winds, 1980.

Books on Doctors

Black, Irmas. *Doctor Proctor and Mrs. Merriweather*. Chicago: A. Whitman, 1971.

Burnstein, John. *Slim Goodbody: The Inside Story*. New York: McGraw Hill, 1977.

Chalmers, Mary. *Come to the Doctor, Harry*. New York: Harper and Row, 1981.

Cobb, Vicki. *How the Doctor Knows You're Fine*. New York: Lippincott, 1973.

Rockwell, Harlow. *My Doctor*. New York: Macmillan, 1973.

Books on Hospitals

Blance, Ellen et al. *Monster Goes to the Hospital*. Los Angeles, CA: Bowmar-Noble, 1976.

Bruna, Dick. *Miffy in the Hospital*. New York: Methuen, 1976.

Rey, H. A. and Margaret Rey. *Curious George Goes to the Hospital*. Boston: Houghton Mifflin, 1966.

Stein, Sarah B. *A Hospital Story*. New York: Walker and Company, 1974.

Books on Divorce

Adams, Florence. *Mushy Eggs*. New York: Putnam, 1973.

Clifton, Lucille. *Everett Anderson's Year*. New York: Holt, Rinehart and Winston, 1974.

Eichler, Margrit. *Martin's Father*. Chapel Hill, NC: Lollipop Power, 1977.

Goff, Beth. *Where Is Daddy?: The Story of a Divorce*. Boston: Beacon Press, 1969.

Kindred, Wendy. *Lucky Wilma*. New York: Dial, 1973.

Lexau, Joan M. *Emily and the Klunky Baby Next-Door Dog*. New York: Dial, 1972.

Lexau, Joan M. *Me Day*. New York: Dial, 1971.

Lisker, Sonia O. and Leigh Dean. *Two Special Cards*. New York: Harcourt, Brace, Jovanovich, 1976.

Rogers, Helen S. *Morris and His Brave Lion*. New York: McGraw Hill, 1975.

Schick, Eleanor. *Neighborhood Knight*. New York: Greenwillow, 1976.

Simon, Norma. *All Kinds of Families*. Chicago: A. Whitman, 1975.

Stanek, Muriel. *I Won't Go Without a Father*. Chicago: A. Whitman, 1972.

Surowiecki, Sandra L. *Joshua's Day*. Chapel Hill, NC: Lollipop Power, 1977.

Van Leeuwen, Jean. *Too Hot for Ice Cream*. New York: Dial, 1974.

Zindel, Paul. *I Love My Mother*. New York: Harper and Row, 1975.

Zolotow, Charlotte. *Father Like That*. New York: Harper and Row, 1971.

Books on Death—Animals

Aliki. *Go Tell Aunt Rhody*. New York: Macmillan, 1974.

Brown, Margaret W. *The Dead Bird*. Reading, MA: Addison Wesley, 1958.

Carrick, Carol. *Accident*. Boston: Houghton Mifflin, 1976.

Keeping, Charles. *Nanny Goat and the Fierce Dog*. New York: S. G. Phillips, 1974.

Uchida, Yoshiko. *Birthday Visitor*. New York: Scribner, 1975.

Viorst, Judith. *The Tenth Good Thing About Barney*. New York: Atheneum, 1975.

Warburg, Sandols. *Growing Time*. Boston: Houghton Mifflin, 1969.

Books on Death—Humans

Bartoli, Jennifer. *Nonna*. New York: Harvey, 1975.

Bernstein, Joann E. and Stephen V. Gullo. *When People Die*. New York: Dutton, 1977.

De Paola, Tomie. *Nana Upstairs, Nana Downstairs*. New York: Puffin, 1978.

Fassler, Joan. *My Grandpa Died Today*. New York: Human Sciences Press, 1971.

Miles, Miska. *Annie and the Old One*. Boston: Little, 1971.

Ness, Evaline. *Sam, Bangs, and Moonshine*. New York: Holt, Rinehart and Winston, 1966.

Stein, Sarah B. *About Dying*. New York: Walker and Company, 1974.

Zolotow, Charlotte. *My Grandson Lew*. New York: Harper and Row, 1974.

Part II

PUPPETMAKING

A rich source of materials as well as challenging projects encourage creativity.

PUPPETMAKING FOR CHILDREN

Puppetmaking with young children must be viewed in the duality of both philosophical and practical terms. What you hope to accomplish aesthetically must invariably be balanced with what the children are physically capable of doing.

In general, all Puppetmaking experiences should encompass these premises:

- **Allow for Individual Expression**. A puppet activity, even one that includes a pattern, should never be so rigid in its structuring that it excludes the opportunity for individual interpretation. Always make sure that some aspect of the activity, however small, allows sufficient leeway for personal expression.

- **Be Challenging**. Always aim to present projects that reach slightly above, rather than below, the ability level of the child or group. It is here that challenge is incarnated and new skills can be mastered.

- **Stretch the Imagination**. A rich source of materials as well as challenging projects encourage creativity. In addition, a child's imagination can be vastly stimulated by asking thought-provoking questions that offer alternate solutions such as "What kind of eyes should a mouse have? Wide, small, round or large?" or "If you walked into a dark, deep cave, what kind of creature would *you* see?"

- **Be Positive**. Much of this criteria depends on how you, as a teacher, guide the children

into the activity and offer individual recognition as well as group encouragement. Children require not only the physical rewards of creating the puppet but also the emotional rewards of knowing that their creations have the quality of "special-ness."

Many secondary benefits of a more specific nature can be derived from Puppetmaking activities in order to:

- Develop problem-solving skills
- Encourage fine motor skills and manual control
- Synchronize hand/eye coordination
- Promote conceptual awareness
- Provide opportunities to work alone or in group situations
- Permit messing in a controlled way
- Express feelings through character creation
- Build relationships between *what* is created and *how* it is used

Puppetmaking experiences with young children generally consist of five categories that reflect the philosophical view and individual activity goals of the teacher: namely, *free form, sensorial, copying, patterns* and *fine motor skills*. Inherent in each of these approaches is the power to develop specific skills at varying levels in both the affective and cognitive domains of the child. Thus, a mixture of *all* these approaches is recommended to constitute maximum learning experiences in the classoom.

Free Form

Children need freedom to express themselves through line and form. When restraints placed on the Puppetmaking activity are kept to a minimum, the children can "open up" and take liberties to explore and experiment independently so that spontaneity becomes a dominant factor. In the Free Form approach, the teacher merely presents an idea and provides the materials while the children decide "how" the idea is to be executed. Using this method it is important to:

- Focus on the art (interpretation of the materials) rather than the craft (workmanship) of the Puppetmaking activity
- Avoid using patterns and models
- Encourage the children to accomplish the project in their own way
- Be genuinely supportive of their creative efforts
- Always ask "Tell me about it" instead of "What is it?"

Large work surfaces lend themselves well to Free Form projects such as the construction of paper bag and paper plate puppets.

Sensorial

Children derive great satisfaction in touching and manipulating unusual textures. By selecting a rich assortment of materials and encouraging the children to verbalize their sensorial awareness of these materials, Puppetmaking activities can provide excellent opportunities for exploring the sense of touch. To make this objective as enriching as possible:

- Select materials with contrasting tactile appeal such as cotton balls, sandpaper, foil, plastic, carpeting and velvet.
- Encourage the use of descriptive vocabulary with the children in describing the materials as soft, furry, rough, bumpy, smooth and cold.
- Invite the children to label their tactile experiences by asking "How does this feel to you?" or "Can you think of a word to describe what it sounds like?"
- Help the children to develop concepts through comparison with questions such as "What else have you touched that feels like cotton?" or "If you close your eyes, can you

tell—just by touching—which is foil and which is sandpaper? What's the difference?"

Puppetmaking projects that rely on materials in the Free Form approach are suitable also for Sensorial exploration. Additional ideas can be found on page 112 (Shape/Texture) and on Page 112 (Sensorial).

Pattern approach

When time and materials are limited, patterns can provide an invaluable tool for the teacher. This approach is the antithesis of Free Form techniques but has value in teaching children cutting skills and hand/eye coordination. It also serves to be less messy than other procedures.

Patterns help answer a child's query as to what an animal "should" look like. There are many instances when a child wants the bunny's ears to stand up like that of the rabbit he saw in a storybook or he wants the cat's face to look like that of his pet cat at home. Children frequently express this desire for "look alikes" when they ask an adult to "Please draw me a ___ ." You might want to draw a picture of the re-

quested character as the children look on and explain to them its special features as you add ears, eyes, mouth and such. When drawn with a black marker pen, the picture can then be reproduced so that each child has a copy of the teacher's drawing to color.

Patterns throughout this book provide excellent models for reproducing so that the children may color them in and construct finished puppets. Even many of the illustrations found in the drawings in the Teacher's Puppetmaking section and other chapters make suitable drawings for use as simple puppets when attached to rods for manipulation.

Copying

The Copying approach emphasizes the craft aspect of Puppetmaking in which the teacher offers an image for the children to copy. This may be merely a pattern for the children to trace or a model to stimulate ideas. The benefit of this approach is to aid the children in creating a puppet that functions properly, especially in making puppets with moving parts. This method is of further value to children entering kindergarten or first grade who may need practice

Pattern activity using Paper Bag Puppet

in following verbal directions and making visual judgments. It also presents a fine exercise for developing hand/eye coordination.

To encourage individual artistic expression even within the Copying method, urge the children to choose colors and designs that are different from those in the model. For example, you may comment "I like red. That's why I painted my puppet red. What's your favorite color? Perhaps you would prefer making your puppet that color."

Many patterns in this book can be converted into master copies by reinforcing the pattern copy with lightweight cardboard. These can then be used by the children themselves in tracing exercises. For older children, you may wish to construct a finished puppet for the children to view with step-by-step instructions to be followed in the construction process.

Fine Motor Skills

Both the making and manipulation of puppets offer an excellent way to develop a child's fine motor skills. Construction techniques and the operation of tools reinforce hand/eye coordination, as well as dexterity in fingers, wrists and hands. With minimal planning, puppetmaking can provide practice for such activities as: pasting, cutting, inserting brass fasteners, manipulating crayons or paintbrushes and holepunching.

Several of the puppet projects included in this book were designed specifically to integrate these activities, particularly the "Multiple Shape" puppets in this chapter.

Copying activity using Envelope Puppets

142

It is preferable to accept the child's creations totally and feel comfortable with the young child's concept of art.

Constructing Puppets with Children

Because Puppetmaking is both an art and a craft, a delicate balance must be maintained between allowing the children sufficient freedom to explore their own ideas and providing directions that are adequate for making puppets that function properly. In so doing, the teacher must be cognizant of his/her own expectations, sensitive to the expectations of the child and know not only *when* to help the child but moreover *how much* aid to provide.

Teacher Expectation

As preschool teachers, we often desire that children's puppets reflect a certain charm so frequently associated with children's art. Yet, we forget that the ability to represent objects in line, color and form does not develop in children until around the age of five. As a result, we as teachers must be careful not to impose our own personal artistic criteria upon the children. Instead, it is preferable to accept the children's creations totally and feel comfortable with the young child's concept of art. To the three-year-old, a few purple scribbles on a paper bag may adequately represent a fox. Hence, in creative puppetry it is extremely important to focus on *process* rather than *product*. The respect that we show for the child's ideas, feelings and internal growth as expressed during the Puppetmaking process will aid the child to achieve a greater sense of individuality and confidence as a creator.

Children's Expectations

Every teacher has seen young children frustrated because something does not turn out as expected. They crumple up the project with anger, throw it to

143

the floor and moan that "It doesn't look right!" The root of this frustration is the discrepancy between the finished product and someone's expectation of what the puppet "should" look like. If the child is trying to meet an arbitrary standard—for example, the teacher's expectation—then the activity needs to be re-evaluated in terms of the approach and how it was presented. On the other hand, if the conflict develops because the child is unable to meet his own expectations, then the teacher should help the child to identify the difficulty and determine how it may be resolved.

In determining how much help to give a child, remember: *Never do for a child what she can do for herself.* Too often, well-intentioned adults underestimate the child's natural abilities and therefore give a child too much assistance. In so doing, the child is denied valuable learning opportunities to grow and blossom as independent thinkers. It is healthy for a child

to feel some degree of frustration in her struggle to find new solutions in artistic endeavors. However, the teacher needs to monitor how little or how much frustration should be allowed to occur. When a child approaches the teacher and says "I can't do this," respond first with a statement of confidence in the child's abilities by noting "I'm sure you can find a way if you try again." If the child returns repeatedly with unsuccessful attempts, gently guide her toward a solution by asking, for example, "What else besides glue do we have that would hold your puppet together?" or "Perhaps the Monster's mouth is not angry enough. How would your mouth look if you were very angry?" Regardless of the nature of the problem or how persistent the child may be, avoid answering the question directly or showing *exactly* how to do something. Instead, concentrate on furnishing the child with the means for finding answers on her own.

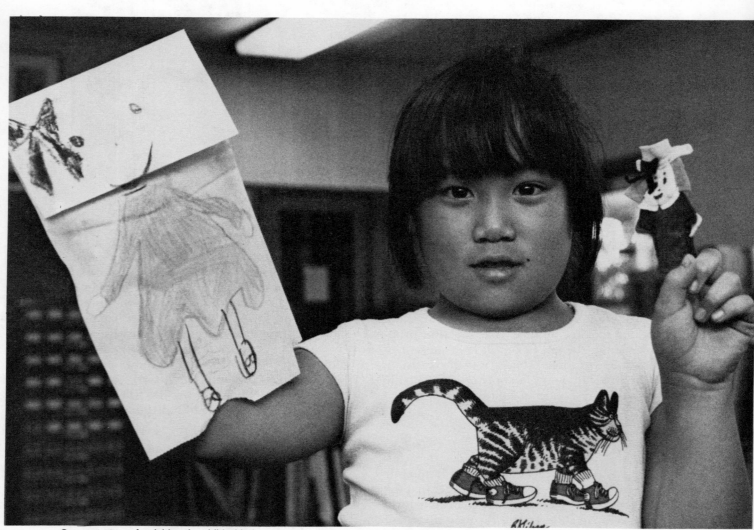

Concentrate on furnishing the child with the means for finding answers on her own.

Puppetmaking Tips

Here are some hints that may be helpful in choosing the type of project best suited to your overall objectives.

- **How Much Mess?** Decide in advance how much messiness you can tolerate. Some teachers prefer a work environment that is super neat and tidy while others are comfortable with a degree of chaos and messiness. Arrange the Puppetmaking activity in such a way that it will be a relaxing and enjoyable experience for you.

- **Adopt Familiar Procedures.** By employing the same work procedures you use in other arts and crafts activities, the children will know what to expect. This will avoid unnecessary confusion in adjusting to new work patterns.

- **Design "Failproof" Activities.** Remember that young children have limited motor skills and are easily frustrated with difficult feats or something they cannot achieve. Whatever challenge is presented, be sure it is in line with the children's capabilities.

- **Strive For Simplicity.** The younger the child, the simpler the construction procedures should be. Reduce material selections to a minimum as too broad a "smorgasbord" from which to choose can be confusing.

- **Use Tables For Construction.** Frequently used materials such as glue, crayons, tape and scissors should be within arm's reach, while secondary materials and tools, if necessary, are better kept on a separate table or counter. For example, if the final step of the construction involves taping a rod to a paper plate, then locate that "station" on another table. Or, if the teacher's task is to perform a specific function, such as stapling, you may wish to sit at a designated place where the children can come to you. Particularly with large groups of children, a division of steps that allows for separate locations for particular jobs will aid in diminishing congestion and pave the way for a comfortable work environment.

  Before you begin, cover the tables with newspaper or butcher paper to protect the surface and allow for easy clean-up. Children also enjoy having their own plastic "workmats" (perhaps featuring their own drawings laminated in plastic). These mats,

Arrange the puppetmaking activity in such a way that it will be a relaxing and enjoyable experience for you.

similar to placemats, offer each child a sense of working at his own "art center."

- **Work In Small Groups.** Remember that the younger the child, the more individual attention and guidance he will require, especially for projects that demand unfamiliar skills. Groups arranged according to skill-levels may facilitate construction projects.

- **Clean-Up Cooperation.** It is extremely important that young children learn that as an integral part of the Puppetmaking activity they are expected to share the responsibility of clean-up. Each child should make some contribution, no matter how small the effort. These positive work habits will carry over as the children progress to upper levels. Be sure to provide a sufficient number of trash cans—one at each table, if possible. Several "Mr. Trash-Grabber" puppets, as described in the Daily Routine chapter, are handy.

145

- **Post Sign-Up Lists**. When placed near work areas, these lists aid in minimizing chaos among large groups. Young children can draw a symbol or use a rubber stamp while older children can write their names. Plan related activities to fill the time when the children are waiting turns.

Safety Precautions

In selecting materials and tools for use with young children, be cognizant of possible hazards.

- Avoid tools or scissors with sharp points.

- Be sure rods for puppets have blunt ends or, if pointed, wrapped in tape.

- Avoid using metallic glitter as it can get into a child's eye.

Construction Methods

Various procedures are listed in order of increasing difficulty.

Easy
- **Gluing and Pasting**. Children delight in the "icky-sticky" glue on their fingers. Use small lids or containers with Q-tips for application.

- **Tearing**. An excellent substitute for children who do not yet know how to cut. An assortment of torn paper such as newspapers and construction paper can be pasted onto a puppet form.

Medium
- **Taping**. A heavy desk dispenser, besides being convenient, offers young children the opportunity to master the task of pulling the tape forward and tearing it off. The teacher may need to assist in demonstrating how to tape projects together properly.

- **Punching Holes**. Two- and three-year-olds may lack sufficient strength in their hand muscles to operate a hole punch. However, this method is extremely useful for making paper puppets with movable joints, also for creating unusual designs. When the child is incapable of handling a hole-punch, the teacher should assist and then allow the child to thread a brad fastener or string (for a marionette) through the hole.

- **Stapling**. Choose a sturdy desk-type stapler that will permit the children to operate by pressing down with both palms "with all their

might." A few small hand-staplers should be kept handy for difficult to reach places and for older children to operate.

Difficult
- **Brass Paper-Fasteners**. Although often frustrating at the outset, this activity is excellent for developing small motor skills. It also provides useful hand/finger coordination exercises when used in conjunction with a hole-punch.

- **Scissor-Cutting**. Young children need repeated experiences in using scissors. Select blunt scissors for safety. Yet choose ones with good cutting edges to avoid frustration. Free-form cutting is easiest for children to master. Pattern-cutting, on the other hand, helps children to develop hand/eye coordination and manual control. When patterns are used, select those that match the agility level of the children. Younger children will require simple shapes with minimal projections while older children enjoy more complex contours.

- **Sewing**. Although sometimes difficult for four- and five-year-olds, sewing activities are feasible when large, blunt needles with oversized eyes and thick thread or yard are used. Soft, pliable fabrics or burlap should be considered for the basic puppet or costume to assure ease in stitching. A line drawn on the fabric will provide a guide to follow. Concentrate on sewing activities that join basic pattern pieces together or apply decorations rather than on activities for attaching buttons or other small objects.

- **Tying**. Knots and bows require a great deal of supervision and moral support in their proper execution yet offer to the young child a great sense of satisfaction in their accomplishment. By incorporating into a puppet project a simple tying task such as a single knot in a string puppet or a ribbon with a bow tied around a puppet's neck, the children will have another opportunity to learn this important skill.

- **Lacing.** This basic activity can easily be integrated into large puppets such as when piecing together sections of paper plates or Multiple Shape Puppets.

Primary Tools and Materials

Brushes—small, medium, large sizes
Cardboard—posterboard, oak-tag
Coloring Media—pencils, crayons, felt-tipped
    pens, tempera paint, latex wall-paint
Construction Paper—assorted colors
Fabrics—assorted textures and types
Felt—many colors
Glue—white glue, glue sticks, rubber cement,
    paste
Scissors—blunt tipped
Stapler—desk and hand types
Tape—masking, cellophane

Secondary Tools and Materials

Compass
Ink and ink pad
Paper brad fasteners
Polyester fiberfil
Paper—mural, crepe, tissue, party wrapping,
    wallpaper
Rods—skewers, dowels, popsicle sticks, plastic
    drinking straws
Rubber bands—assorted sizes

Materials "Wish List"

Corks
Cotton
Cups—styrofoam or paper
Beads—sequins, jewelry
Boxes—cereal, spaghetti, pudding, cake,
    cosmetic
Buttons
Egg cartons
Envelopes—small letter size
Feathers
Foils—aluminum and colored
Gloves and mittens
Hair curlers
Handkerchiefs
Macaroni (dry)
Nature forms—pine cones, stones, shells, seed
    pods
Paper bags—all sizes
Paper plates—all sizes
Pipe cleaners
Plastic food wrap
Socks—all sizes
Sponges
Spools

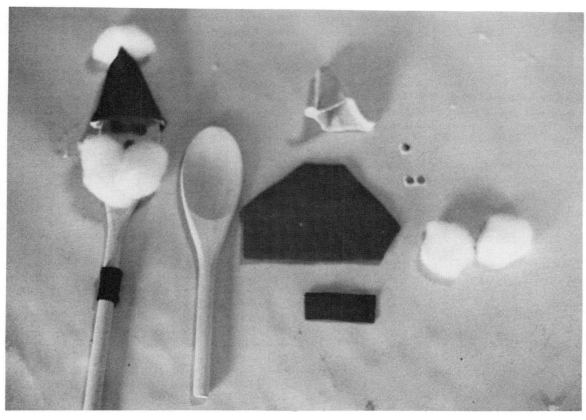

Basic materials for a Santa Spoon puppet

147

Spoons—wood and plastic
Stars—gummed
Stick-ons—contact paper, gummed dots and
    reinforcements
Styrofoam balls
Tinsel
Trims and ribbons
Tubes—cardboard
Yarns—assorted colors

Decorating the Puppets

There are several popular types of coloring media that may be considered as standard material for classroom use.

- **Crayons**—Economical and simple to use with little mess, crayons are particularly useful for blocking out color on large surfaces such as paper bags and paper plates.

- **Felt-Tipped Pens**. Vibrant colors (that delight children) can be created with these pens enabling the children to see more clearly small details and features. An olfactory element to the Puppetmaking process can be added by using markers with scents that correspond to fragrances such as orange, cherry, lime and grape. Be sure to remind the children to replace the caps when finished to assure long-lasting usage.

- **Painting**. Although rather messy, painting offers an extraordinarily satisfying experience for young children to dabble and swirl their brushes into the "wetness" of paint and blend together new color combinations. All paper-based puppets adapt well to painting. To dry, simply clip productions (with clips or clothespins) onto an easel or clothesline.

- **Stamps**. Sliced sections of fruits and vegetables, thumb-prints, sponges cut into shapes and office rubber stamps all provide exciting tools for puppet decorations. A quick-drying quality can be achieved by dipping the form into a thin layer of paint or onto an inked stamp pad.

- **Stick-Ons**. Contact paper, self-adhesive labels, dots and gummed reinforcements are well-suited for facial features and for giving the illusion of buttons and jewelry.

Evaluating The Children's Work

In the beginning, young children usually seek approval from adults for their creative efforts. It is important to discover ways to grant such approval in a non-judgmental manner. Remember that children perceive a teacher's response through the tone of voice as well as choice of words. Hence, your voice should convey wholehearted enthusiasm as well as sincere interest. Moreover, the teacher should seek to communicate to the child that there is no right or wrong way to create a puppet and that one child's puppet is neither better nor worse than that of another—only different. Therefore, instead of using words such as good, right and best, strive to develop a constructive vocabulary of descriptive adjectives such as:

Visual: Colorful, Interesting, Imaginative
Tactile: Soft, Rough, Smooth
Audio: Jingly, Rustling, Snappy
Emotional: Happy, Sad, Funny

In addition, search for sentences that are both comfortable for you and helpful to the child in learning to discriminate in his choices of materials. For example "What a *colorful* puppet you've made!" "Your puppet's hair is so *soft*." "I like the *rustling* sound of your puppet." "Your puppet makes me feel *happy* when I look at it."

Eventually the children will proceed beyond the need for your approval and, instead, will rely on their own instincts and feelings about what *they* like. This will indicate a noteworthy level of achievement that you have reached in your creature puppetry program.

Books on Puppet Making for Children

Armstrong, Beverly, *Pint Size Puppets*—A "reproducible" workbook with innumerous finger puppet patterns, well illustrated, of community workers and animals. Learning Works, Santa Barbara, California. (1978)

Hopper, Grisella, *Puppet Making Through the Grades*—Shows many simple and basic puppet making ideas from paper bags, balloons, socks and everyday items. Worcester, Massachusetts, Davis Publications, Inc., 1966

Renfro, Nancy and Armstrong, Bev, *Make Amazing Puppets*—A superb resource book on many "easy-to-make" puppets. Also includes ideas for special effects, sound effects and characterization. Learning Works, Santa Barbara, California. (1979)

Sims, Judy, *Puppets for Dreaming and Scheming*—One of the best resource books for curriculum application and puppet making ideas. Though geared to elementary grades, ideas are applicable to preschool level. Walnut Creek, California, 1978

Williams, De Atna, *Paper Bag Puppets*—Contains patterns for faces of animals, holiday and fairy tale characters to apply to paper bag puppets. Order from: Fearon-Pitman Publishers, Inc., 6 Davis Drive, Belmont, California 94002. (1966)

Wilt, Joy, and Hurn, Gwen and John, *Puppets With Pizazz*—Fifty two finger and hand puppets from throw aways, paper and felt. Waco, Texas, Creative Resources, 1977

"I like the rustling" sound of your puppet.

Rainbow Puppet

Box Puppets

MATERIALS

Box for body—cereal, pudding, spaghetti, cake, oatmeal, perfume, etc.; decorations from "Wish List" at beginning of this chapter.

PROCEDURE

Cut off one end of box so hand can easily slip inside.

Use paint, paper and other materials from the "Wish List" to decorate boxes.

Lightning Bug

lipstick box

Pudding Box Mouse

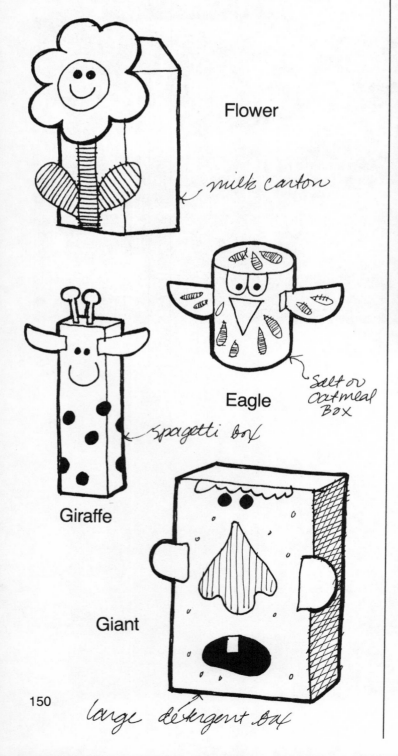

Flower

milk carton

Eagle

salt or oatmeal box

Giraffe

spagetti box

Giant

large detergent box

pudding box

Owl

Panda

cereal box

150

Bracelet Puppets

Bird

Car

MATERIALS

9-inch length of ribbon; picture or felt-shape.

PROCEDURE

Staple any picture (drawing, magazine, greeting card, etc.) or felt shape onto center of ribbon; tie ribbon around child's wrist.

Note: Though all young children enjoy wearing these puppets, they are particularly well-suited to handicapped children with limited motor control.

Sew ribbon onto back of puppet

Idea by Joann Click

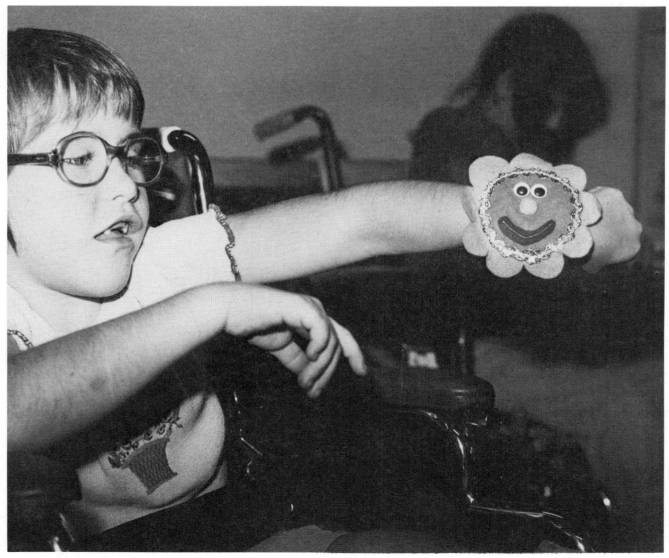

Felt Sun puppet

Outer Space

Clothesline Puppets

MATERIALS

Spring clothespins; a clothesline; construction or mural paper.

PROCEDURE

Draw and cut out large characters from paper.

Simply clip each character onto a clothesline as they appear in the song or story.

Halloween

Lady Bug

Bee

Clothespin Puppets
"Bitty Biting Bugs"

MATERIALS

Spring clothespins.

PROCEDURE

Make copies of bug patterns, below, for children to color with marker pens or crayons.

Cut out and glue to flat side of clothespin; dry thoroughly.

Pinch clothespin together at tail-end for "biting" bugs.

Basic Patterns

Ant

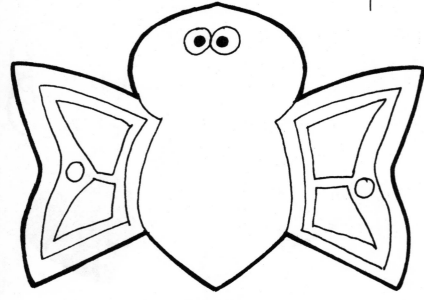

Butterfly

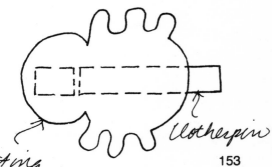

Biting Bug

Clothespin

Gingerbread Man

Cookie Cutter Gingerbread Men on rods

Cookie Cutter Puppets

MATERIALS

Cookie cutters; drinking straw or popsicle stick for rod control; construction paper.

PROCEDURE

Let each child choose a cookie cutter shape and trace around outer edges onto construction paper.

Decorate drawn shape and cut out puppet; tape puppet onto rod control.

cookie shapes

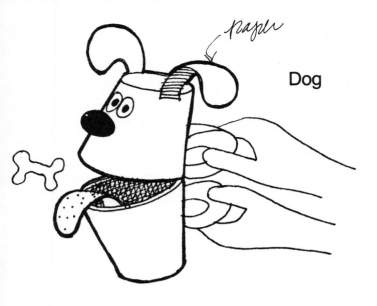

Dog

Clown

Double-Cup Puppets: Use cups with handles. Tape cups together along center backs of cups with masking tape; fold out handles and operate, as shown.

Basic Hand Puppets: Cut hole for "finger nose" in center of cup; place cup over hand, as shown. Add paper ears, hair, hats and other features.

Paper Cup Puppets

MATERIALS

Non-waxy surfaced cups, such as styrofoam or hot beverage; construction paper; string.

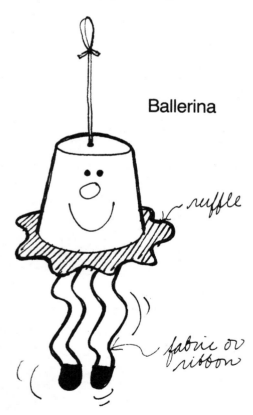

Ballerina

ruffle

fabric or ribbon

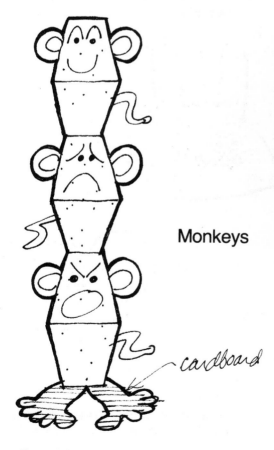

Monkeys

cardboard

String Puppets: Thread a length of string through center bottom of cup and tie a knot (or tape a string down) inside of cup to secure; tie a loop at end of string for fingers. Add pleated paper legs.

Stacking Cup Puppets: Stack and glue or tape cups together. Add paper features and funny feet.

155

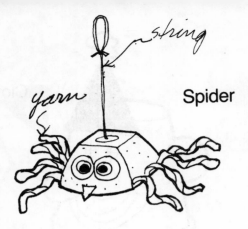

Spider

String Puppets: Thread a length of string through top center of carton cup and make a knot inside so it will not pull out; tie a loop at the opposite end for finger control.

Egg Carton Puppets

MATERIALS

Egg carton; paper features; pom-poms and yarn; string (for marionette), or popsicle stick (for rod puppet).

PROCEDURE

Dissect an egg carton into individual "cups."

Decide which type of puppet to make:

Rabbit

Elephant

Tabletop Puppets: Create characters by adding paper features, pom-pom noses and yarn whiskers.

156

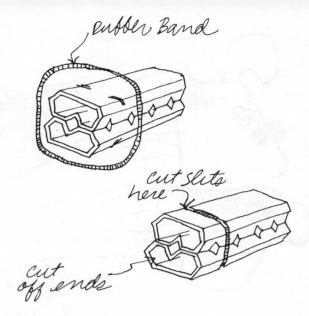

Egg Carton Crocodile/Wolf

MATERIALS

Two egg cartons; one large rubber band; construction paper and fabric.

PROCEDURE

Cut back ends off egg cartons then cut slits into four rear corners of cartons, approximately two inches from backs.

Line up egg cartons with cut-away ends together and wrap rubber band around both egg cartons, sliding down into slits (slits keep rubber band from slipping off).

Decorate cartons with egg carton cup eyes, paint and scrap materials.

To Operate: Hold bottom egg carton with one hand, firmly on bottom; put other hand into hold in top egg carton and move hand up and down.

One egg carton cut in half makes a shorter mouth for a dog, rabbit or donkey.

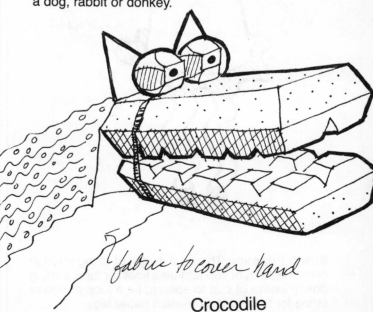

Crocodile

Pig

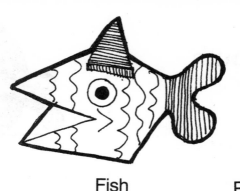
Fish

Parrot

Envelope Frog Puppet

Envelope Puppets

MATERIALS

6½ x 3½ inch letter envelope; construction paper.

PROCEDURE

Tuck flap of envelope inside envelope.

Place hand inside envelope as shown.

Genty "bite" finger of other hand to form mouth. Straighten out mouth if wrinkled.

Note: Avoid envelopes with overly large "V" cut-outs in back. If this is the case, seal envelope as normally and cut away one long edge of envelope. Proceed with above instructions.

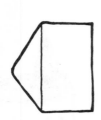

Tuck flap inside

press here

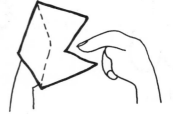

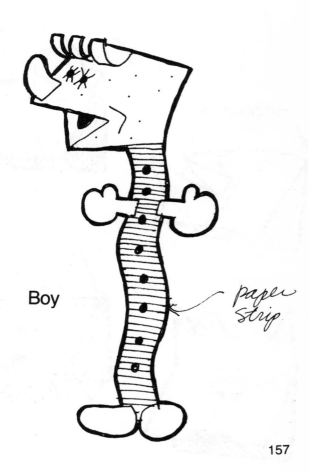
Boy

paper strip

157

Envelope Flat-Mouth Puppets

MATERIALS

6½ x 3½ inch letter envelope; paper features.

PROCEDURE

Seal envelope.

Fold in half, crosswise, with sealed side underneath; crease fold.

Slit creased line on outside only.

Add features with paper and coloring medium.

To operate, slip fingers in upper part of envelope and thumb in lower part; open and close hand.

Bird

Finger Tube Puppets

MATERIALS

Rectangle of 2 by 3-inch construction paper; paper features or magazine pictures.

PROCEDURE

Curl the paper into a cylinder shape to fit around the fingers; glue or tape together.

Decorate facial features directly onto the tube, or glue on colored patterns (below), magazine, cartoon or greeting card pictures.

Rhinoceros

Duck

Queen

Fox

Spider

Child

Santa

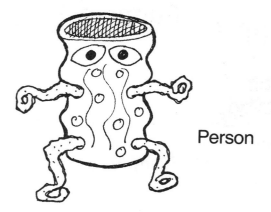

Person

Fruit and Vegetable Puppets

MATERIALS

Firm, fresh and clean vegetables and fruits; cloves; tongue depressors or popsicle sticks; paper features.

PROCEDURE

Poke tongue depressor or popsicle stick into the fruit.

Cut out simple paper features and tack to food with cloves or rubber cement.

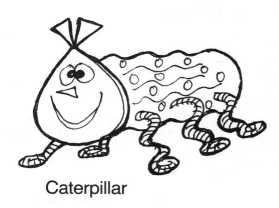

Caterpillar

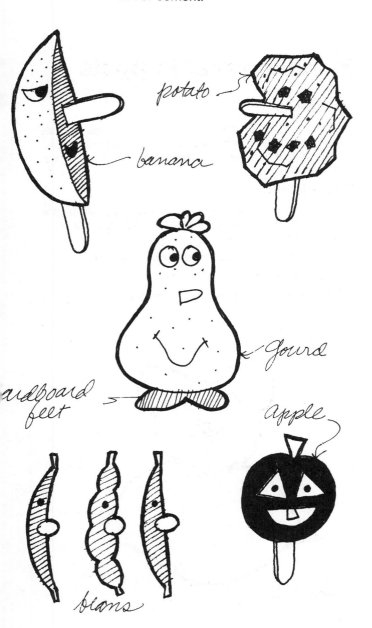

potato

banana

gourd

cardboard feet

apple

beans

Hair Curler Puppets

MATERIALS

Plastic hair curlers; pipe cleaners; paper features.

PROCEDURE

Cut out basic face or features and tape or glue onto curler.

Insert pipe cleaners through holes of curler for arms and legs. (Be sure to bend ends of pipe cleaners into blunted loops for safety.)

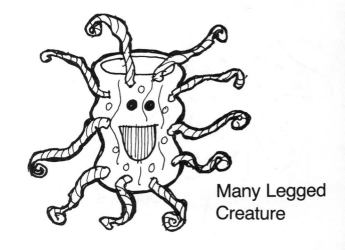

Many Legged Creature

Hand and Feet Puppets

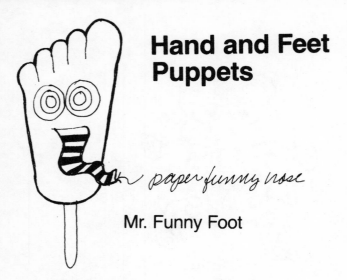

paper funny nose

Mr. Funny Foot

MATERIALS

Construction paper; skewers or drinking straw for rod control.

PROCEDURE

Trace around child's hand or foot onto paper and cut out.

Decorate the character capitalizing on the characteristics of the hand or foot shape; attach to a rod control.

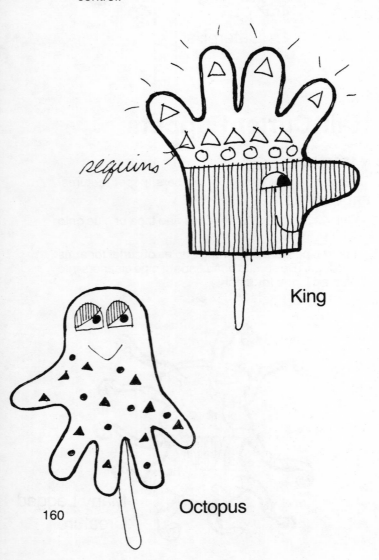

sequins

King

Octopus

160

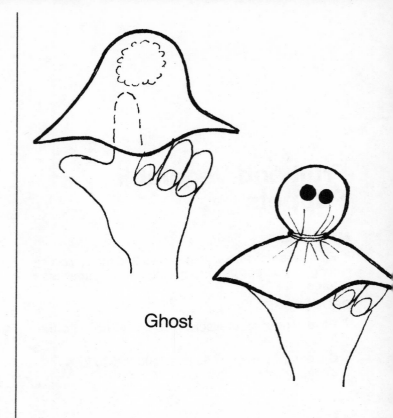

Ghost

Handkerchief Puppets

MATERIALS

Handkerchief or soft fabric 6 by 6 inches square (minimum size); small rubber band; polyester fibre-fill or paper tissues for stuffing; paper features; yarn for hair.

PROCEDURE

Stuff center of handkerchief or fabric square with a wadded paper tissue or piece of polyester fibre to form a head.

Slip stuffed cloth over index finger, as shown.

Wrap rubber band around neck.

Glue on paper features and yarn hair.

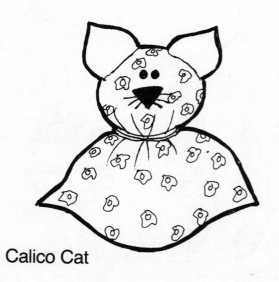

Calico Cat

Instant Puppets

MATERIALS

Lipstick and eyeliner or water soluable colored marking pens; double-backed masking or scotch tape.

PROCEDURE

Put hand in position as shown; move thumb joint up and down for moving mouth. Add features with colored medium specified above.

Variations: Paper ears, teeth and eyes can be added by using small pieces of double-backed tape.

Complete characters with "mouth holes" can be cut from paper using pattern below and secured to hand with double-backed tape. Or use the mouth hole measurements from samples, to create any character desired.

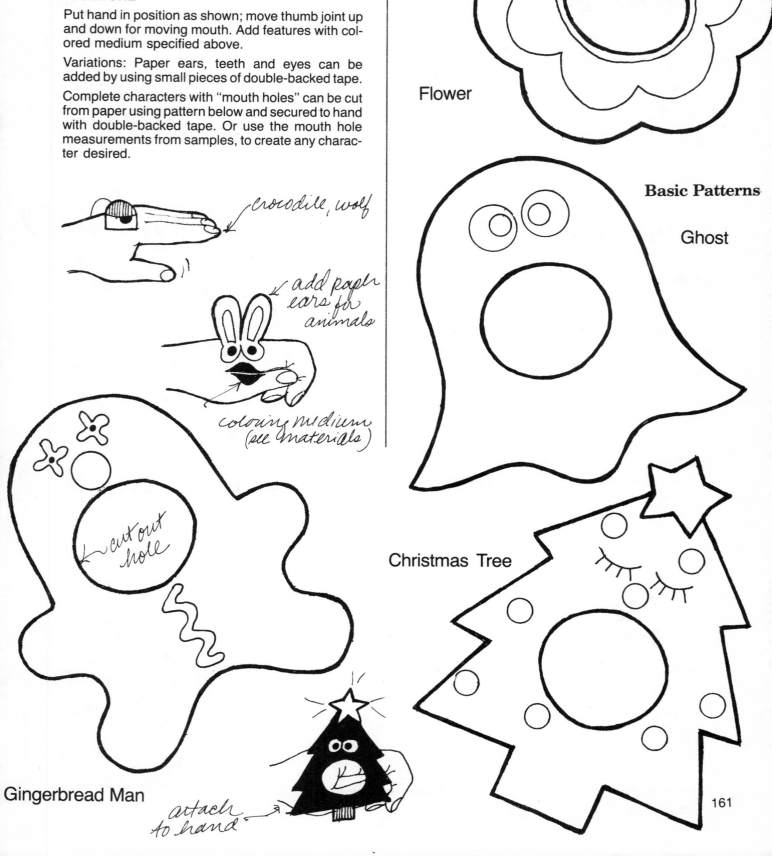

crocodile, wolf

add paper ears for animals

coloring medium (see materials)

Flower

Basic Patterns

Ghost

cut out hole

Christmas Tree

Gingerbread Man

attach to hand

161

Penguin

Creature

Farmer

Mitt Puppets

MATERIALS

Two pieces of 8 by 9-inch paper bag, mural paper or fabric; trim.

PROCEDURE

Make a master pattern on lightweight cardboard of mitt puppet for children to trace on desired materials; cut out.

Run a thin line of glue around border edges of one body piece, but leave bottom edge unglued.

Lay second body piece over glued edge of bottom piece; press flat and dry thoroughly. (Pieces may also be stapled or sewn together.)

Create features and costumes with crayons, marker pens, scrap fabric and trims.

Sheep

cut out 2 pieces

Person

Kangaroo

Tiger

162

hand position

Basic Pattern

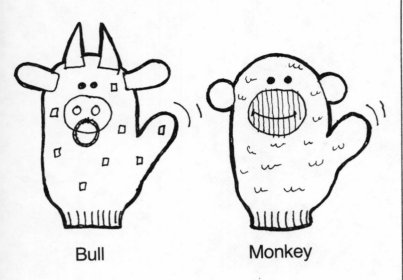

Bull

Monkey

Mitten Puppets

MATERIALS

Mittens; felt or paper; trim.

PROCEDURE

Glue or sew on felt or paper features. Pom-poms and plastic wiggle eyes as well as fabric trim may be used to complete characters.

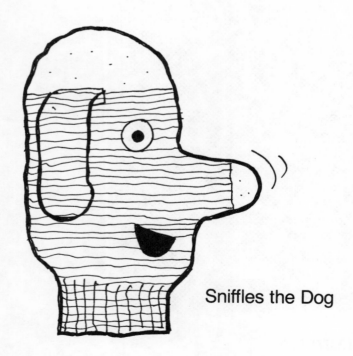

Sniffles the Dog

Leaf—With Chenille Worm

Nature Puppets

MATERIALS

Shells, twigs, pine cones, seed pods, leaves, roots, stones or other Nature forms for body.

PROCEDURE

Affix features onto nature forms with sticky-backed tape or glue. Stones and shells may have painted features as well.

Happy Walnut-
With Paper Circle Face Inside

Stone

Owl —Pine Cone

Snail—With Paper Face

Nerf or Styrofoam Puppets

MATERIALS

Styrofoam ball; dowel or skewer for rod control; 8 by 8-inch fabric square; cloves; cardboard for features or felt or construction paper.

PROCEDURE

Place fabric square on top of rod and poke rod and fabric together into ball halfway through diameter.

Stiff cardboard ears and noses can be pressed into ball. Poke tips of cloves into styrofoam for eyes. Other features, made from felt or construction paper, can be secured to ball with sticky-backed tape or cloves. Search for additional safe items to insert as features such as paper clips, clothespins, etc.

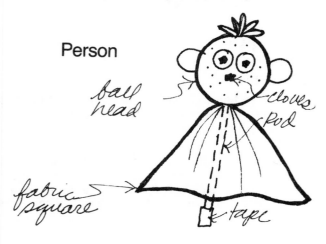

Person

ball head

cloves

rod

fabric square

tape

Bear

Pilgrim

Superhero

Robot

Paper Bag Puppets (Flap Mouth)

MATERIALS

Small or medium sized paper bag; paper features; assorted fabric scraps.

PROCEDURE

Children may make their own features for paper bag puppets or cut out and color the basic features illustrated in the earlier part of this chapter.

Provide assorted scrap fabric and coloring medium to decorate the bags; the bag surfaces lend themselves well to gluing and painting activities.

To operate, place fingers inside flap of bag as shown; move up and down.

Baby Chick—Very small bag

The Gobbler—Large Grocery Bag

hand position

165

Panda

slippers

Paper-Bag Body Puppets

MATERIALS

Large grocery bag; two medium rubber bands; two 3-inch wide fabric strips (length of the child's arm); a 2½-foot long fabric strip or ribbon for securing around neck; items from "Wish List" at beginning of this chapter.

PROCEDURE

Arms: Fold over the end of each fabric-strip and slip a rubber band in each hem; staple hems to secure rubber bands. Staple other end of each arm strip to paper bag, just below flap.

Neck Ribbon: Staple center of ribbon to top center of bag.

Decoration: Use a rich assortment of materials and coloring medium to add character, pattern and texture to the bag.

To Wear: Tie neck ribbon around the child's neck and slip rubber bands over wrists. The child then "becomes" the puppet and can dance or pantomime actions using his own legs and the fabric-strip arms.

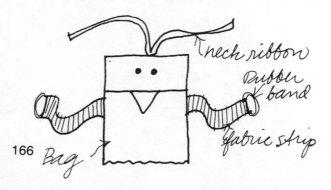

neck ribbon

rubber band

fabric strip

166   Bag

Rudolph's House   Duck Pond   Tree

Paper-Bag Homes and Habitats

MATERIALS

Large grocery bags; paint; paper.

PROCEDURE

Lay bag flat on table and use paint and paper to create special homes and habitats in which puppets may reside. When first side is dry, decorate the other.

Open up bag and stand on the table top or floor to serve as a puppet-home (see Page 57 for additional ideas). A cluster of individual bags, arranged in a grouping, can represent a "forest," "ocean," "village" or "universe."

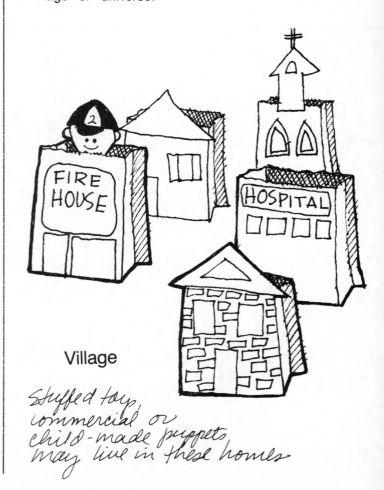

Village

stuffed toy, commercial or child-made puppets, may live in these homes

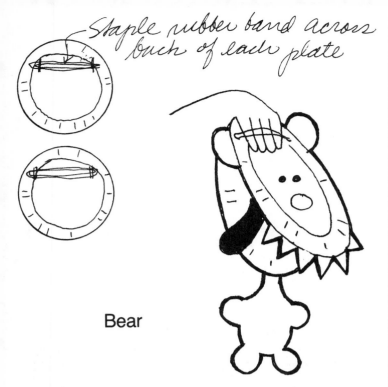

Staple rubber band across back of each plate

Bear

Paper Plate Talking Mouth Puppets

MATERIALS

Two small or large paper plates; two medium rubber bands; paper features; materials from "Wish List" at the beginning of this chapter.

PROCEDURE

Staple a rubber band across the back of each paper plate, about two-inches down from top, as shown.

Put both paper plates together with rubber band ends facing top and staple plates secure, as indicated.

Children can use features illustrated at the beginning of this chapter to color and glue onto the plates or create their own. A paper or fabric body can be attached to the bottom plate.

To Operate: Slip fingers under rubber band on top plate and thumb under rubber band on bottom plate; open and close hand.

small paper plates

Apple and Worm

paper worm on string

Paper Plate Hand Puppets

MATERIALS

One paper plate; half a paper plate; paper features; fabric or paper body.

PROCEDURE

Staple the half-plate along the edges onto the back of the whole plate.

Add facial features to whole plate and attach a fabric or paper body to bottom.

To Operate: Slip fingers behind half-plate to hold and move puppet about.

Owl

To hold slip hand up back half plate

Paper Plate Fish

MATERIALS

Two and a half paper plates.

PROCEDURE

Attach two plates together by stapling around the circumference, leaving end open so that hand may slip through. Cut a tail from half a plate and staple to end of fish. Decorate with paint or coloring medium.

Staple plates together around edges

add plate tail

Fish

Paper-Plate Rod Puppets and Masks

MATERIALS

Paper plate; skewer or cardboard tube for rod control; paper features.

PROCEDURE

Tape rod control onto back of paper plate. Children can make their own features or use those in early part of this chapter to glue onto the plate. By cutting out eye holes, puppets can be converted into masks.

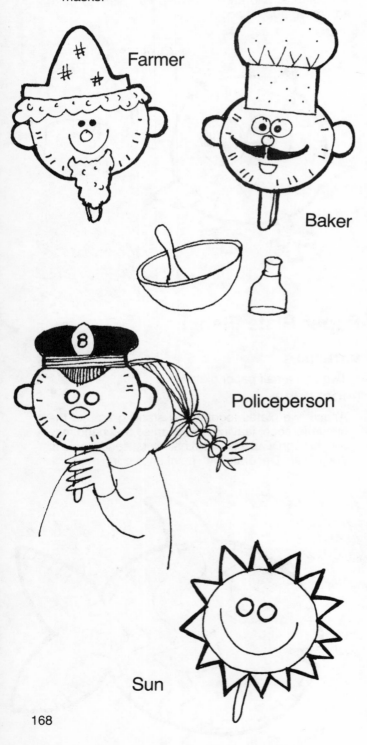

Farmer

Baker

Policeperson

Sun

Rod Puppets

MATERIALS

Small toys such as plastic cars, stuffed animals, little dolls, monsters, holiday characters and similar novelties, or a drawing or picture from coloring book, greeting card or magazine; dowel, drinking straw or blunt skewer for rod control.

PROCEDURE

Attach any small, lightweight two or three dimensional character (picture or toy described above) to rod control with glue or tape. Two dimensional material may be laminated or covered with clear contact paper.

Note: Any pattern or even illustration from this book may be converted into a rod puppet.

Banana—magazine picture with wiggle eyes on rod

168

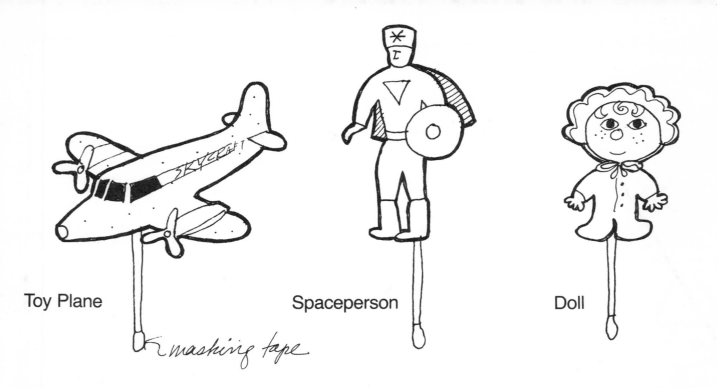

Toy Plane   *masking tape*   Spaceperson   Doll

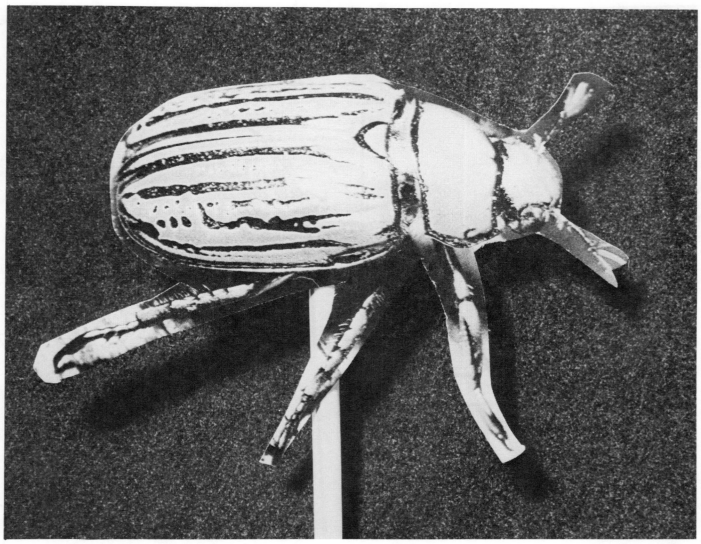

Insect from Nature magazine on rod

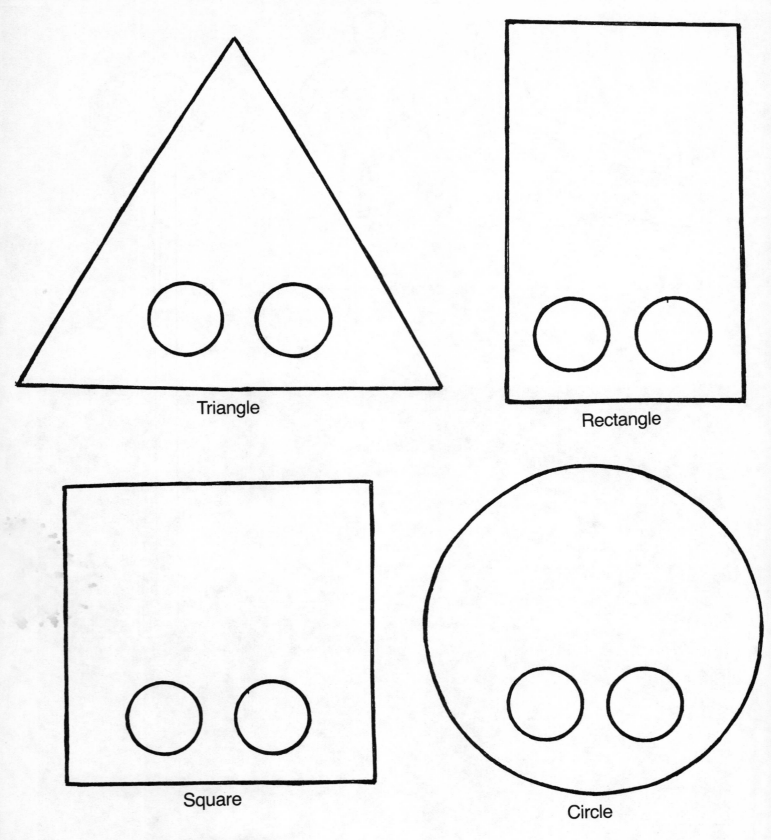

Triangle

Rectangle

Square

Circle

Basic Patterns

Shape Puppets

MATERIALS

Construction paper, oak tag or other stiff paper.

PROCEDURE

Make a master set of shape patterns, from stiff paper, for children to use throughout the year.

Children can trace around the master shapes onto stiff paper, to cut out. Use small thread scissors to help children cut out finger holes.

Use crayons or marker pens to create "funny faces" for shape monsters, animals and other characters.

Caterpillar Multiple Shape Puppet

Multiple Shape Puppets

MATERIALS

Poster board, oak tag or construction paper; paper fastener brads; string and cardboard tube (for marionette) or rod control (for rod puppet).

PROCEDURE

Using a master set of shape patterns of varied sizes and shapes, let the children trace a combination of shapes to cut out. If desired, all the children may make duplicate shapes for a specific character such as a snowman, train or caterpillar. Alternately, the children may be asked to design special characters of their own, combining a variety of different shapes.

With a hole punch and brad fasteners, link body parts together; attach strings or rods for maneuverability. Strings of a marionette can be tied onto a cardboard tube or dowel handle.

Create features with colored media or construction paper.

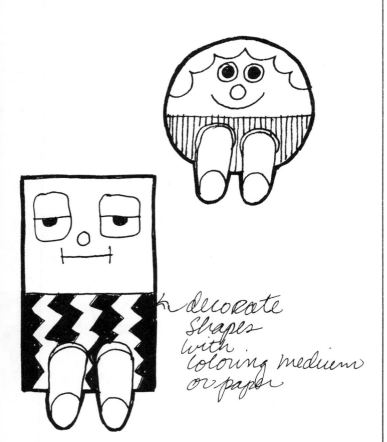

decorate shapes with coloring medium or paper

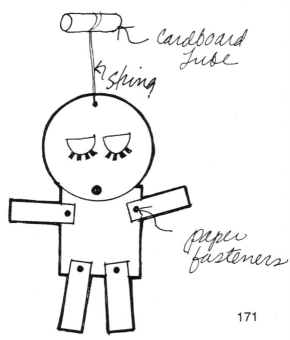

cardboard tube

string

paper fasteners

171

Small Paper Puppets

MATERIALS

Choose one of the following for manipulating the puppet: pudding or other small box; small rubber band; popsicle stick or drinking straw.

Construction paper or oak tag.

PROCEDURE

Make copy of puppet; color and cut out character.

Decide which form of manipulation you wish to use.

Stand-Up Puppets: Paint or cover a pudding box with paper, if desired (or it may be left with printing visible); glue puppet onto flat side of box.

Fingerpuppets: Glue puppet onto a piece of construction paper, oak tag or other stiff paper for strength. Staple a rubber band across lower back of puppet, as shown, through which first and second fingers may slip to act as walking legs.

Rod Puppets: Attach a popsicle stick or other rod to back of puppet, as shown; manipulate from below.

Rod Theater Puppets: Attach rod, upside-down, to back of puppet; manipulate from above.

stand-up puppet
pudding box

finger puppet
rubber band

Rod Theater puppet

Cut out window and top of box

grocery box

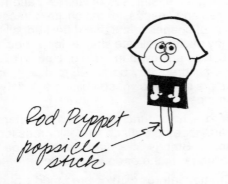

Rod Puppet
popsicle stick

Girl

Boy

172

Grandmother

Grandfather

Mother

Father

Baby

Basic Patterns

Alphabet

make many tab rings
with letters above
for children to use
to spell words.

174

The Three Pigs

Soda Tab Puppets

MATERIALS

Soda tab ring; pictures of animals, flowers, hearts, or other illustrations found on greeting cards; drawing or pattern below.

PROCEDURE

Cut out and decorate small-scale character from the above list. Tape flat surface of soda tab ring onto back of character. (Be sure tape completely covers any sharp edges.)

tape shape to back of tab ring

If tab rings are not available make your own rings from lengths of pipe cleaners

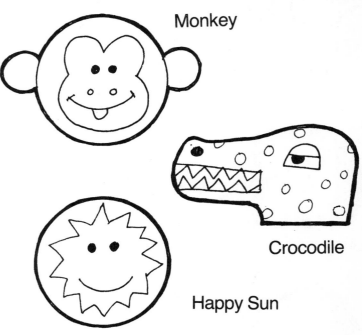

Monkey

Crocodile

Happy Sun

BAT

Idea inspired by Shirley Burgess

Basic Patterns

Goldilocks and the Three Bears

Creature

Baby Bear

Prince

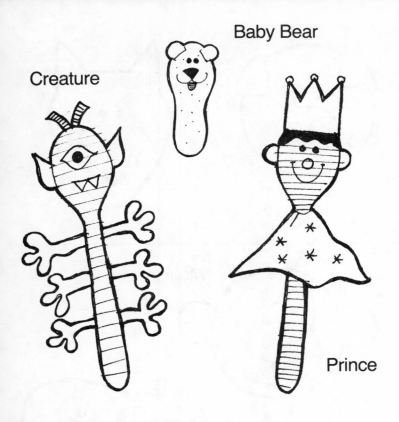

Spoon Puppets

MATERIALS

Wooden spoon or ice cream spoon; fabric; pipe cleaner; paper features.

PROCEDURE

Paint or glue basic paper or felt features onto spoon.

Make a simple costume from a circle of fabric with a hole cut in the middle for the spoon to slip through; add pipe cleaner or paper arms.

Provide a "home" for the spoon family in a teapot, flower pot or other vessel.

Family in Teapot

Santa

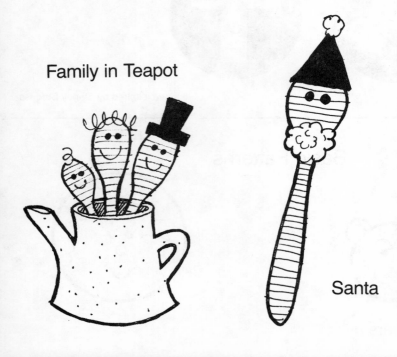

Stand-Up Puppets

MATERIALS

Milk carton (small or large), box (food or other type) or cardboard tube for body; cardboard for feet; construction paper or fabric.

PROCEDURE

Paint or cover body container with paper or fabric; add paper features. Children can create their own features or use color and cut out features shown at the beginning of this chapter.

Oversized cardboard or paper feet can be added to the base of the bodies to insure standing.

Ms. Happy

Mr. Sad

Mr. Short

Ms. Tall

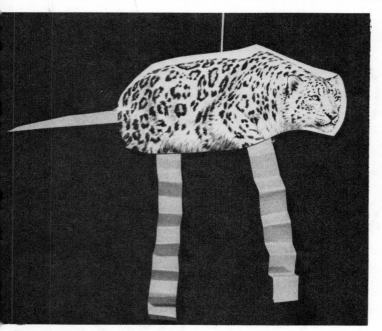

Tiger picture from Nature Magazine

String Puppets

MATERIALS

Small box or pint sized milk carton, or magazine picture; string or heavy thread; cardboard tube or dowel rod control; construction paper.

PROCEDURE

Thread a length of string through top of box or magazine picture and secure a knot.

Attach cardboard tube or dowel to other end of string for handle.

Add pleated legs and decorate with flair! A ruffle added to bottom of box makes an excellent skirt; cotton glued on surface a fuzzy sheep.

Note: When cutting out magazine pictures, omit legs and arms of character and replace with pleated ones instead.

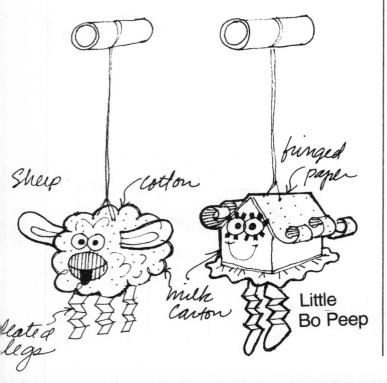

Thumbprint Puppets

MATERIALS

Ink pad with black or colored ink; paper; popsicle stick for rod control.

PROCEDURE

Make copies of incomplete characters below and let children fill in missing parts of animals such as ears, tail and body with their thumbprints.

Cut out characters and tape onto rod control. Ask children to make up their own characters by adding features to one or several thumbprints.

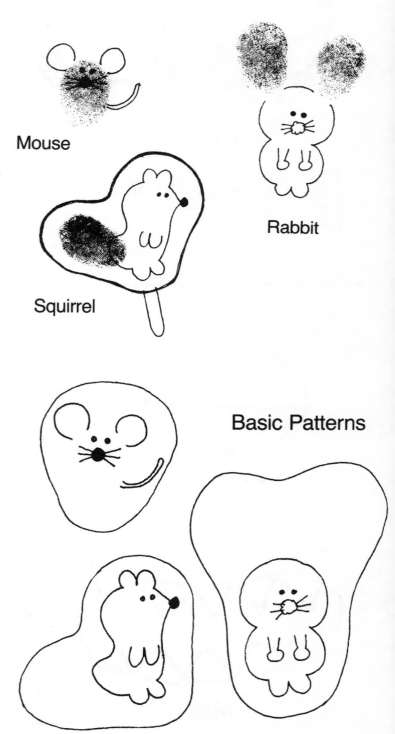

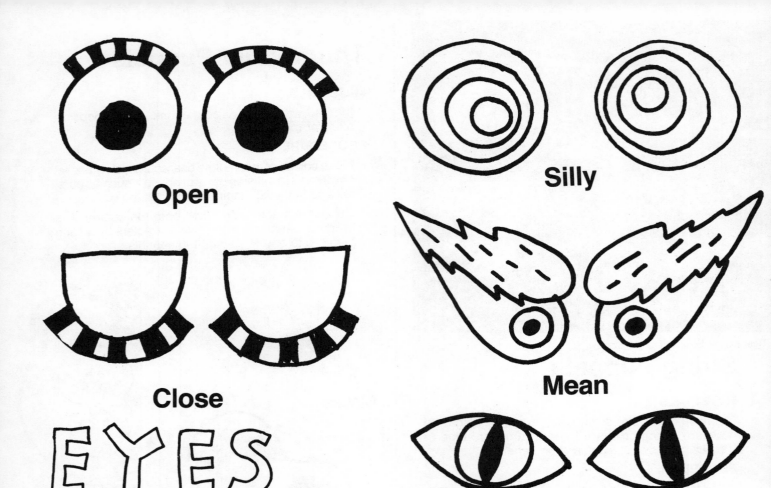

Open

Silly

Close

Mean

EYES

Wide

Pretty

Happy

Sad

Mean

Silly

MOUTHS

178

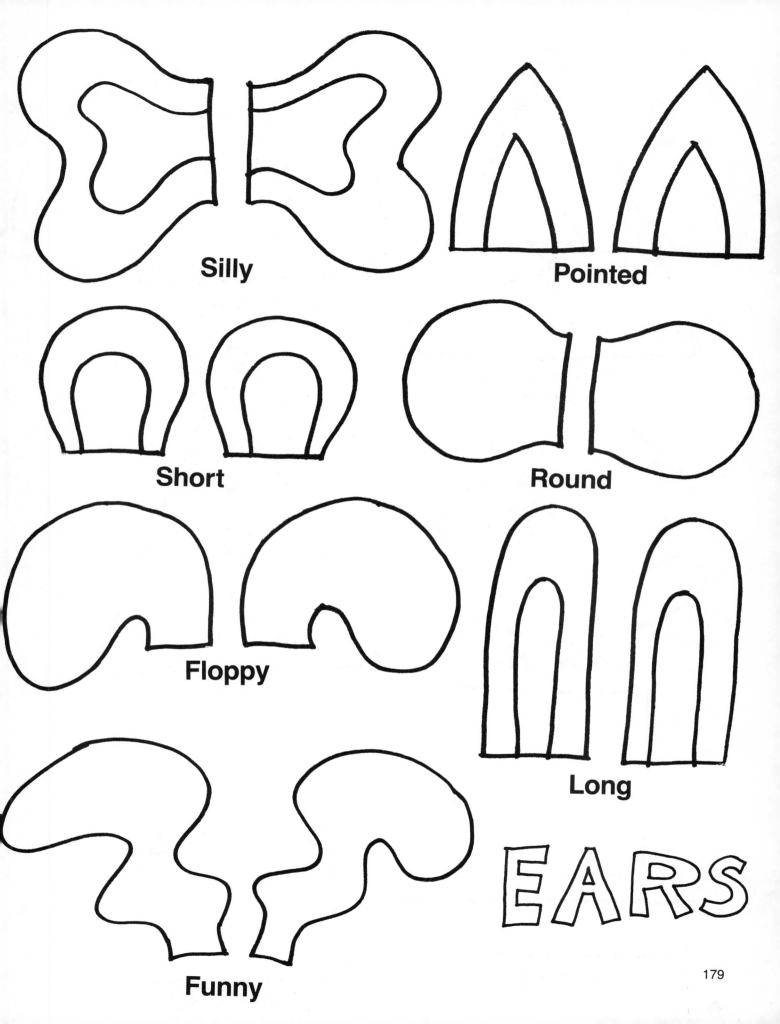

Silly

Pointed

Short

Round

Floppy

Long

Funny

EARS

Witch's Hat

Santa's Hat

HATS

Silly Hat

Party Hat

Top Hat

Baker's Hat

180

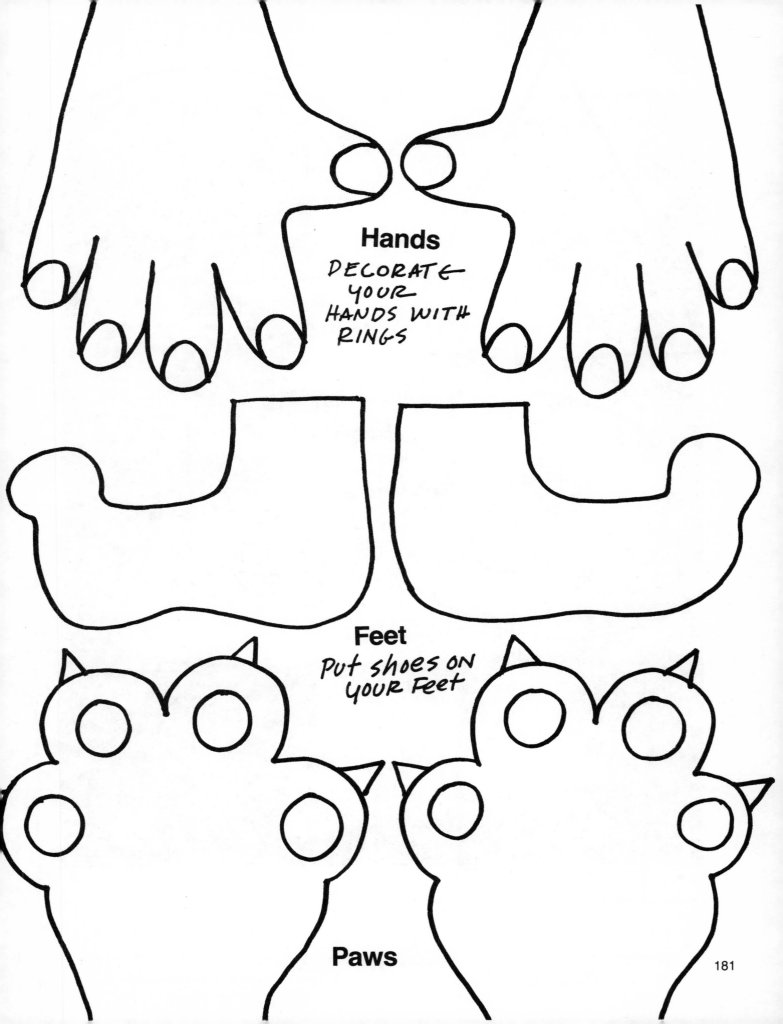

Hands
DECORATE YOUR HANDS WITH RINGS

Feet
PUT SHOES ON YOUR FEET

Paws

181

Pussy Cat—Hand Puppet (Pattern page 200)

PUPPETMAKING FOR TEACHERS

Getting Started

Acquiring a puppet collection is a bit like expanding a family constellation in that puppets provide new personalities, new relationships, and new types of interactions to incorporate into your existing structure. Therefore it is worth taking the time to carefully plan the kinds of puppets to be used which will best service the needs of the anticipated audience and accompanying activities.

Consider first, *who* will use the puppets, the adult or the children? If the children will be the primary users, puppets should be exceptionally durable, washable and devoid of sharp objects or pins which can scratch or cut. If the adult will be the primary user, then more flexibility is possible in terms of construction types and requirements for durability.

Next decide *how* the puppets will be used, which will determine the character types needed. If free play in a Puppet Corner is to be the primary activity, then a variety of familiar animals and people is best for child-puppet interaction. If story Puppetization is going to be the main thrust of puppet activity, then it would be worth investing in specific groupings, such as "Royalty," "Farm" or other related character themes commonly found in children's literature. Perhaps the puppets are to be used exclusively for Puppetelling purposes, in this case, acquire those which correspond to your favorite stories, poems, and fingerplays.

The next consideration is whether the puppets will be purchased or hand-made. time is limited, it is advisable to plan to buy puppets. A trip to a department or novelty store will produce a variety of puppet characters. In addition, stuffed toys and soft sculpture can also be converted into puppets (see Teacher's Puppet-Making chapter). A much wider selection of puppets, however, is available through the mail order houses listed in the appendix of this book. Addresses are listed to facilitate writing for catalogues and/or ordering information.

If you have an inclination towards adventure and want to create your own puppets, you will find puppetmaking a rich and rewarding experience when translating your "puppet visions" and efforts into works of art. You will discover hidden artistic talents in yourself, as well as new methods for applying the basic craft skills to future teaching situations. Puppet-making also provides the flexibility of being able to have the proper puppet for any activity, especially true when a specific character such as *Madeline* or a *Cat in the Hat* is desired. Once made or bought, the basic puppet "family" should be separated into those designated for child-use and those reserved for adult-use. Store these puppets in areas around the room out of children's reach, so that their presence may be felt even when not in use. It is important *not* to let the children play freely with your own puppets in order to retain the special aura they deserve.

Tools and Supplies

Puppetmaking can be made easier if the right tools and supplies are selected. Construction methods basically include cutting, copying, sewing, painting and gluing. *The methods described below are intended for adult use and are not designed for children.* Remember that quality work and quality tools often go hand-in-hand. Even the most skillful artist cannot do superior work with inferior tools!

Cutting

The avid puppet-maker should consider investing in several pairs of scissors. It is worth the extra expense in terms of making preliminary cutting a pleasurable part of Puppetmaking activities, while eliminating any potential frustrations that might arise due to trying to accomplish a cutting feat with an improper tool. It is recommended to have on hand at least three types of scissors:

- **Basic all-purpose scissors.** For general work to cut paper, cardboard, extra heavy fabric and fake fur. This scissors can be of any medium grade type that will withstand rugged service.

- **Fabric scissors.** Fabric cutting can be a joy with the purchase of a high-quality scissors, such as a "Gingher" name brand found in better fabric shops. Reserve this scissors to function exclusively in the capacity of fabric cutting since paper or cardboard will dull the edges.

- **Small thread or manicure scissors.** With their sharp points these scissors are excellent for cutting out small holes, intricate designs and slits in fabric or paper.

A long slender scissors, while optional, is a bonus for one who works continuously in paper. It is a wiz at making long sweeping curves as well as short zigzag cuttings.

Other cutting tools include a serrated bread knife for rigid styrofoam and an electric kitchen knife for spongy polyurethane foam materials.

Copying

Permission is granted by the authors and publisher to reproduce patterns in this book for *nonprofit* purposes.

Several methods of reproducing may be considered:

- **Duplication.** The quickest and easiest method for copying patterns is to photocopy or duplicate the pattern page by other similar means. Then by simply pinning or tracing the pattern directly onto the fabric the piece can then be cut.

- **Graph method.** For enlarging or reducing a pattern from a book, transfer the pattern picture to a graph chart which then is reduced or increased proportionately by redrawing the picture, grid by grid. Grid paper can be purchased at a local stationery store or supplier of architectural materials.

- **Tracing.** Any reproduced pattern can easily be transferred to fabric or paper by means of carbon tracing paper or dressmaker's tracing tools found in fabric shops. An excellent idea is to build up a collection of *master patterns* that can be used continuously. These should be constructed from stiff, flexible paper such as poster board or oak tag. Lay the master pattern piece flat onto the fabric and hold the pattern firmly down with one hand, while tracing around the edges with the other, using a felt tipped marker pen or dressmaker's pencil. The addition of small holes on the master pattern can aid in locating such features as eyes, nose and waistline.

Sewing

Puppets that need to withstand the "wear and tear" test of young children should be sewn (rather than glued or stapled) and will mean less work later in both repairs and general upkeep.

If you are planning to purchase a sewing machine, select a model with a free arm since it will make sewing small items much easier. Fancy stitches, available in many machines today, can add a professional as well as decorative touch for hemming, trimming costumes or finishing off seams.

When selecting straight pins for pinning fabrics together, choose longer ones with extra large heads to facilitate ease in working with all types of fabric.

Painting

In any project that requires painting, it is advisable to purchase two or three quality brushes. Your brush collection might include: a small, pointed brush for fine detailing; a medium, rounded brush for general work; and a broad, flat brush for surface painting.

There are several paint mediums to choose from:

- **Flat latex wall paint.** Available at local paint stores, latex paints are by far the best medium for paper, cardboard, paper maché and even plastic puppets. This water soluble paint is cheaper, thicker and adheres better than standard tempera paints. The store's color chart has an array of beautiful colors from which to choose. Simplify your color selection by choosing basic colors of red, blue, yellow, black and white; secondary colors can then be mixed from these basic ones. Eventually treat yourself to some special shades that are frequently used

184

such as a flesh tone. Be sure to ask for *flat* latex wall paint. To cut costs watch for local paint sales.

● **Tempera.** A standard paint in schools, tempera is easily accessible to the classroom. Spend time comparing paints to find the best quality. A paint that is too thin may be cheaper but can be a nuisance to manage, will cause excess buckling in paper products, and often require two layers to coat materials, causing waste in both time and expense. A small quantity of liquid dishwashing detergent or acrylic floor wax (such as "Future" name brand), when added to the paint will help it to adhere to surfaces that are waxy.

● **Acrylics.** Though expensive, acrylics in tubes are useful to the puppetmaker. Reserve this extra-thick paint for such things as facial features and fine details.

Gluing

Modern glues are a salvation to the craft profession. There are so many types to choose from that it is often difficult and confusing to know exactly which glue to use for each specific material. Usually one type of glue is not sufficient for the puppetmaker and several types should be kept in stock:

● **White liquid glue.** Is a universal all-around glue that is especially useful for gluing: felt to felt; felt to paper; and paper to paper. It is not waterproof nor does it adhere well to plastic.

● **Tacky glue.** Comes in a tube or jar and has the benefit of being waterproof. It may be used on fabrics and some plastics, and is ideally suitable for constructing pom-pom finger puppets.

● **Rubber cement.** For gluing flat surfaces of paper together, rubber cement serves to prevent these surfaces from buckling. Apply the cement to both surfaces, allow it to dry and then stick the two sides together.

● **Contact cement.** This extremely strong glue is highly suitable for spongy materials, such as polyurethane foam. Apply in the same method as rubber cement. If a mistake is made, surfaces glued with contact cement can be separated by blowing hot air on the seam with the blow dryer.

● **Electric glue gun.** Available at most hardware stores, this indispensable tool is a must for anyone who works regularly in crafts. By plugging it in, the glue gun melts a small nylon pellet inside which is then applied to the surfaces to be glued, forming a high strength joint. It has invaluable uses as a substitute for sewing chores as well as general gluing. This tool requires handling with care to avoid contact of the hot material on the fingers.

Staplers

One of the most worthwhile investments to add to your basic tool collection is a sturdy hand-grip type stapler, similar to those used in check-out counters at stores. An excellent model is the "Arrow" name brand #P-22 found in most hardware stores. This stapler manages hard to reach areas and has extra long staples for superior stapling of heavyweight papers and cardboards.

Fabrics

A good working knowledge of fabric types can be a great benefit to you in your puppetmaking endeavors:

● **Cotton/polyester blends.** Offer a tremendously broad range of patterns and textures from which to choose. Fabric shops abound with a selection of plaids, calicos, ginghams and stripes.

● **Double knits (polyester).** Come in a rich array of patterns and solids to match with a broad selection of character types: a woven tweed for a dignified crocodile; a striped design for a sneaky tiger; or a dotted one for a playful giraffe. These fabrics have added benefits of great durability, washability and non-wrinkling qualities. The "stretchiness" of the fabric will enable it to mold easily to the hand and arm as the puppet is manipulated. However, to get the best results, choose a fabric with minimal stretch for puppets to better retain their shapes.

● **Fake furs.** Can bring softness and "cuddleness" to your puppet collection. Shag furs are wonderful for wigs or creatures such as gorillas, monsters and wolves. They also make excellent birds (giving a "feathered" effect), shaggy dogs or raccoons. Short furs are good for short-haired animals like seals and penguins. When cutting fake fur, turn the fabrics upside-down and cut the backing only, *not the fur.*

● **Felt (wool).** Should be used predominantly for facial features and decorations. Because this fabric is "pressed", rather than woven, it lacks strength and should not be used for basic bodies, bird beaks, mouths or other features which require constant manipulation and handling, causing the fabric to wear or puncture. Also, wool felt is not washable (it runs and shrinks) and therefore not the ideal fabric for general purposes.

● **Felts (polyester).** Is a recent arrival in modern technology and a boon to the puppet maker. This felt substitute has superior qualities of traits in both strength and washability. Inquire at your local fabric shop about these fabrics some of which come under the brand name of "Phun Phelt" and "Poly Felt."

● **Foils and dotted nets.** Make excellent costumes for achieving an ethereal effect as found in such characters as angels, princesses and ballerinas. A unique application of these fabrics would be in representational puppets depicting Nature's elements, such as rain, wind and snow.

● **Glitter fabrics.** Often give the illusion of scales and adapts well to fish and reptiles. It is also an excellent choice for royalty, angels or fairies. Glitter fabrics always add a special enchantment to any puppet collection.

● **Velours.** Make soft appealing basic bodies and faces. Their lovely color tones also adapt well to animal skins, such as a pig or hippopotamus. They are finely suited to royalty costuming as well. Be sure to select non-stretching velours such as a robe fleece for bodies. Fancier velours may be selected for costumes.

Summary List of
Tools and Materials:
- scissors (all-purpose, fabric and thread or manicure)
- glue (white liquid, rubber cement, contact cement, tacky glue, electric glue gun)
- needle and thread
- tape (masking, scotch, double and carpet tape)
- hole puncher
- sewing machine
- stapler and staples

Paper Products:
- construction paper—assorted colors
- poster board or other lightweight cardboard
- grocery carton cardboard
- oak tag paper
- nerf balls

Fabrics:
- pellon
- muslin
- fake fur
- felt
- double knit
- cotton

Coloring Medium:
- permanent marker pens
- paint (tempera, acrylic in tube, flat-latex wall paint)
- fabric coloring medium (fabric crayons, embroidery in a tube, textile paint)

(additional materials can be found on page 147 under the children's materials "wish list".)

Washing the Puppets

Always consider washability when making puppets. If strength and long-lasting qualities are desired then all materials, including fabrics and glue need to be evaluated. It is always wise to test wash samples of these materials before proceeding in constructing the finished puppets. Here are some general washing instructions:

Soak puppet, *individually*, in basin of cold water with a small amount of cold water detergent, for 3 to 5 minutes. Gently squeeze puppet all over (never twist!) Rinse in clear water and gently squeeze out water. Let puppet dry on clean towel in warm place; turning puppet over from time to time for faster drying.

Puppets made from predominantly felt material should be dry cleaned.

186

Designing the puppets

Designing the puppet is the most creative and fulfilling part of puppet making. Perhaps the puppet's every detail has been drawn before construction is actually begun. On the other hand, you may decide to shape the character as you go, adding features here and there until it "looks right." Whatever the preferred approach, putting on the finishing touches is a totally satisfying aspect in the culmination of the puppetmaking activity.

Keep a scrapbook of ideas gathered from magazines, newspaper cartoons, greeting cards, posters and comic books which capture features and expressions you find appealing and will aid in the duplication of puppet characters, both animals and people (young/old, man/woman, baby, etc.).

Make simplicity in construction a basic rule in all puppet making. Young children will show far greater appreciation for a puppet's "inner" qualities as opposed to the external elements as found in fine stitchery or artistic detailing. Allow yourself less time for puppet construction and more time to shaping its personality (described in the Puppetelling chapter).

The puppet will begin to take on its own personality as the head and face is defined. Facial features such as eyebrows, eyes, eyelashes, noses, ears, mouths, teeth and tongues give expression through their shape, placement and color. General features can be made from robe fleece velours, heavy-weight cottons and Pellons (decorated with permanent marker pens). Felt, of course, remains one of the most versatile materials for glue-on features, provided washability is not a criteria.

Material suggestions for various features are:

- **Wigs.** Yarn, shag fur, fringed paper or fabric, straw, upholstery fringe, mop (can be dyed), commercial hair wig.

- **Eyes.** Plastic craft eyes, buttons, flower lace trim, drapery pom-poms, beads.

- **Eyelashes.** Upholstery fringe, feathers, yarn, fringed felt.

- **Noses.** Drapery pom-pom, bottlecap covered with fabric, button, plastic animal nose (craft shop), stuffed fabric shape.

- **Mouths.** Yarn, vinyl plastic, acrylic paint.

- **Teeth.** Rick rack, Pellon, plastic from plastic bottles, felt.

- **Cheeks and eye areas.** Powdered blusher, eye shadow, permanent marker pen.

- **Ears.** Felt, stuffed fabric shape.

Costumes and accessories also add a great deal of interest to a puppet's personality. Depending on the size of your puppet, doll's clothes or infant/toddler clothing make instant wardrobes when readily available.

Don't forget to accessorize with hats, eyeglasses, and jewelry pieces.

Books on Puppet Making for Teachers

Chesse, Bruce, *Spongees*—A short handbook with clear instructions on making a basic movable mouth puppet from polyfoam. Especially of value are the pages of facial features that can be applied to all hand puppets. Walnut Creek, California, Early Stages, 1977

Marshall, Kerry, *Pom Pom Storybook*—Contains charming ideas for constructing basic pom pom glove characters, many of which are fairy tales and nursery rhymes. Order from: Zim's, PO Box 7620, Salt Lake City, Utah 84107, Order Number PP-178, (Cost $2.50)

Paludan, Liz, *Playing With Puppets*—One of the best books on varied and colorful sewn puppets. Well illustrated with colored photographs. Includes many patterns and construction techniques. (See Puppetry Store for ordering in back of book). Copenhagen, Denmark. Mills and Boon, 1974

Philpott, Violet and McNeil, Mary Jean, *The Funcraft of Puppets*—Contains a rich variety of simple puppets from assorted materials, found objects, paper maché, paper and fabric. New York, Scholastic Books, 1975

Rottman, Fran, *Easy to Make Puppets and How to Use Them: Early Childhood*—A superb book for preschool teachers filled with activities, ideas and puppet patterns. A special focus on religious puppetry is woven through book. Ventura, California G/L Publications, 1978

Scholz, Claire E., *Patterns & Stuff*—Instructions and Patterns are shown of a basic movable mouth puppet that can be expanded into other characters. Order from: Dragon's Puppets, 649 Main, Deadwood, North Dakota, 57732.

Wilt, Joy and Hurn, Gwen and John, *Puppets With Pizazz*—Fifty two finger and hand puppets from throw aways, paper and felt. Waco, Texas. Creative Resources, 1977

See Puppet Store in bibliography for additional patterns and books.

187

Character List

The following is a compiled listing of characters to serve as a reference for building a permanent puppet collection. One group is arranged according to classifications, the other, alphabetically:

Birds
Bird
Bluebird
Cardinal
Eagle
Hummingbird
Owl
Parrot
Peacock
Pelican
Penguin
Pigeon
Robin
Seagull

Fantasy
Dragon
King
Monster
Prince
Princess
Queen
Superhero

Farm Animals
Chicken
Cow
Donkey
Duck
Goat
Goose
Horse
Lamb
Pig
Turkey

Fruits
Apple
Banana
Grapes
Orange
Pears

Halloween
Bat
Ghost
Pumpkin
Scarecrow
Skeleton
Witch

Christmas
Christmas Tree
Elf
Mr. and Mrs. Santa Claus
Rudolph
Snowman

Thanksgiving
Indians
Pilgrims
Turkey

Easter
Bunny
Duck
Egg

Celebrations
Birthday Cake
Firecracker
Leprechaun
Menorah
Uncle Sam
Valentine

Insects
Ant
Bee
Butterfly
Caterpillar
Grasshopper
Lady Bug
Lightning Bug
Spider
Worm

Meteorological Characters
Cloud
Day
Moon
Night
Ocean
Rain
Snow
Star
Sun
Wind

People
Baby
Boy
Girl
Father
Grandfather
Grandmother
Mother

People in My Neighborhood
Dentist
Doctor
Fireperson
Grocer
Mailperson
Nurse
Policeperson

Mailperson
Policeperson

Pets
Bird
Cat
Dog
Gerbil
Goldfish
Mouse
Snake

Plants
Cactus
Flower
Tree

Sealife
Crab
Fish
Octopus
Shark
Starfish
Turtle
Whale

Special
Astronaut
Clown
Dinosaur
Dragon
Monster
Superhero

Woodland Animals
Badger
Beaver
Chipmunk
Deer
Fox
Frog
Hedgehog
Lizard
Mole
Opossum
Porcupine
Rabbit
Raccoon
Skunk
Squirrel
Wolf

Vegetables
Carrots
Celery

Tomato
Potato

Zoo Animals
Alligator
Bear
Boa Constrictor
Camel
Elephant
Giraffe
Hippo
Kangaroo
Leopard
Lion
Monkey
Rhinoceros
Seal
Tiger
Zebra

188

A: Acrobat, Actor, Alligator, Angel, Astronaut, Artist, Ant

B: Baker, Brother, Boy, Batman, "Bert," Baby, Baseball Player, Bunny, Bird, Bear, Bee, Butterfly, Big Bird, Birthday Cake, Bookworm, Bambi, Bluebird, Badger, Bat, Beaver, Buffalo, Boa Constrictor, Bull

C: Cowboy, Clown, Captain, Cookie Monster, Cow, Cat, Caterpillar, Camel, Chicken, Crocodile, Crow, Cockatoo, Cardinal, Crab, Cactus, Cloud, Chipmunk, Coyote, Cinderella, Christmas Tree, Chef

D: Doctor, Daddy, Dancer, Detective, Donkey, Dinosaur, Duck, Dog, Deer, Dove, Dragon, Devil

E: Engineer, Eskimo, Elf, "Ernie," Elephant, Eagle, Eel

F: Fireman, Farmer, Father, Fairy, Fish, Frog, Fly, Fox, Flower

G: Girl, Grandma, Grandpa, Gardener, "Grover," Giant, Ghost, Gentleman, Goblin, Gypsy, Guard, Goat, Goose, Giraffe, Gorilla, Gekko, Gerbil, Goldfish, Guinea Pig, Grasshopper, Gila Monster, Gnome, Goldilocks, Gingerbread Boy

H: Humpty Dumpty, Helper, Husband, Human, Hero, Harlequin, Horse, Hog, Hummingbird, Hedgehog, Hippo

I: Indian, Iguana, Insect

J: Judge, Janitor, Juggler, Jogger, Jockey, Jack-in-the-Box, Jellyfish

K: King, Knight, Kitten, Koala Bear, Kangaroo

L: Librarian, Lady, Lion, Lamb, Lizard, Lobster, Lady Bug, Lightning Bug, Little Red Riding Hood, Leopard, Llama

M: Man, Mother, Mommy, Monster, Mailman, Magician, Mother Goose, Mouse, Mule, Moose, Monkey, Mosquito, Mole, Mongoose

N: Nurse, Nun, Nightingale, Nightmare

O: Operator, Owl, Ox, Octopus, Ostrich, Opposum, Otter

P: Policeman, Priest, Prince, Pinocchio, Principal, Punch, Pony, Pig, Parrot, Pigeon, Penguin, Pelican, Peacock, Panda, Polar Bear, Panther, Platypus, Prairie Dog, Python, Princess, Pilgrim

Q: Queen, Quail

R: Rabbit, Raggedy Ann and Andy, Rudolph the Red Nosed Reindeer, Rabbi, Rooster, Robin, Raccoon, Rattlesnake, Rhinoceros

S: Superman, Sister, Skeleton, Mr. & Mrs. Santa Claus, Snowman, Soldier, Snail, Sheep, Squirrel, Snake, Shark, Seagull, Starfish, Spider, Sun, Seal, Shrew, Skunk, Swan, Snow White, Scarecrow

T: Teacher, Tree, Teddy Bear, Tadpole, Troll, Tiger, Turkey, Turtle, Toad, Termite, Tarantula

U: Uncle, Uncle Sam, Unicorn

V: Vampire, Veterinarian, Vulture, Valentine

W: Wonderwoman, Woman, Wife, Wizard, Water, Witch, Worm, Whale, Woodpecker, Wasp, Wolf

X: X-Ray Fish

Y: Yak, Yankee Doodle

Z: Zebra

Jellyfish, Octopus, Starfish and Fish
Puppets by Nancy Renfro Studios

189

Three Little Rabbits

Fingerpuppets—
Basic Felt

MATERIALS

Assorted pieces of colored felt for body and features; yarn for hair; miniature pom-pom for nose.

PROCEDURE

Using pattern, cut out front and back body pieces from fabric.

Sew body pieces, right sides together, with ears and arms sewn between pieces to secure in seams; turn right sides out. Alternate method; simply top-stitch the puppets entirely to avoid turning right sides out.

Glue or sew features and eyes onto body. Miniature pom-poms make good noses; yarn is suitable for beards and hair. Hem bottom edges.

For Durability: Features can be machine-stitched (with small stitches) onto body pieces prior to sewing the pieces together. For body, consider lining pieces with iron-on Pellon before cutting out.

190

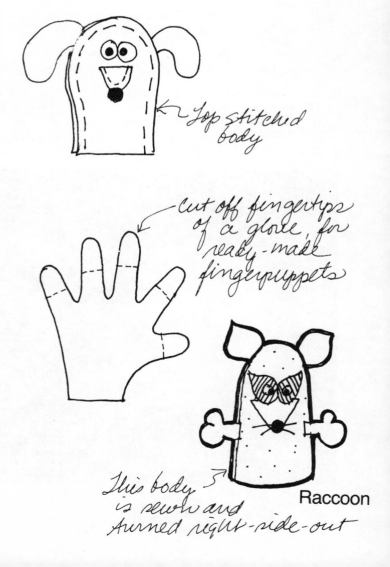

Top stitched body

cut off fingertips of a glove, for ready-made fingerpuppets

This body is sewn and turned right-side-out

Raccoon

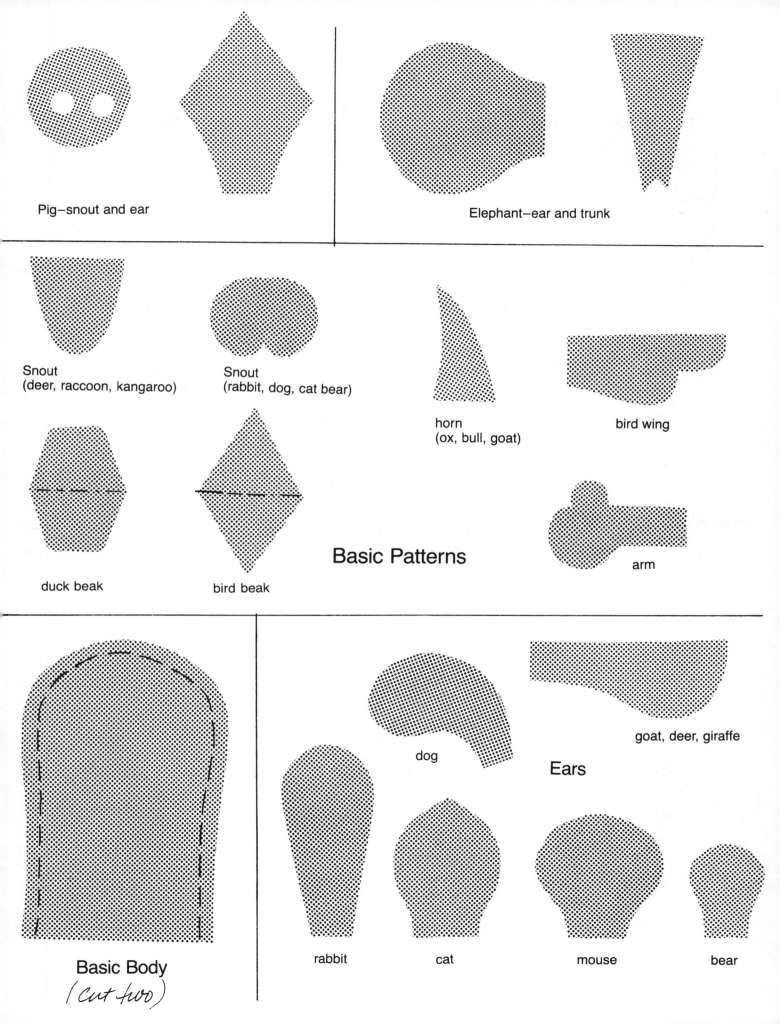

Pig—snout and ear

Elephant—ear and trunk

Snout
(deer, raccoon, kangaroo)

Snout
(rabbit, dog, cat bear)

horn
(ox, bull, goat)

bird wing

duck beak

bird beak

Basic Patterns

arm

Basic Body

(Cut two)

dog

goat, deer, giraffe

Ears

rabbit

cat

mouse

bear

Rabbit

Goat

Pig

Duck

Elephant

Mouse

192 Dog

Boy

Hen

A Mother Hen hand puppet with five baby chicks

Characters from basic finger puppet pattern

fringed felt

felt beak

a side view of pattern
can be converted into
a chicken or bird

Glove Puppets— with Pom Pom Characters

MATERIALS

Garden or other type glove; pom poms of assorted sizes and colors; velcro pieces; felt scrap; small wiggle eyes.

PROCEDURE

Build character by gluing together pom poms to create basic body.

Add a small pom pom nose, felt features and wiggle eyes. Glue or sew velcro pieces to pom pom character's back and to fingertips of glove, for interchangeability.

Note: An electric glue gun is superb for building pom pom puppets.

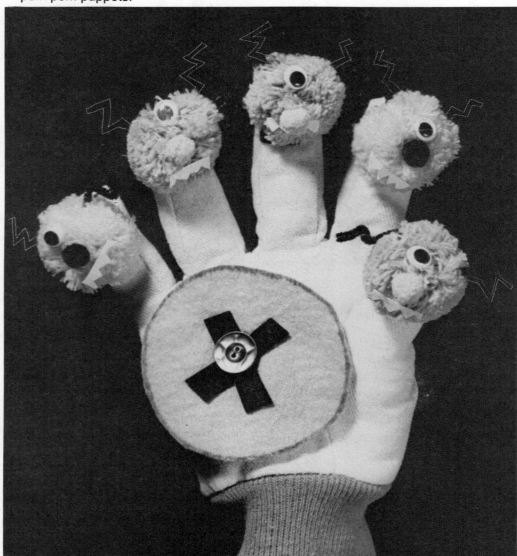

Five Little Martians Sitting on a Planet (to same rhythm as *Five Little Monkeys Sitting in a Tree*). Features a button on planet.

Lion (drapery fringe)

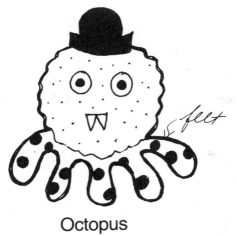

Octopus (felt)

Flower (felt)

Granny (ruffle)

Magician

Walrus (pom pom body and head)

Baby (yarn)

Princess (felt hats and body) (small pom-pom)

Doctor

Leaves, Snowflakes, Blossoms and nuts can all be used on a Tree glove

Seasonal

Five Little Ducks

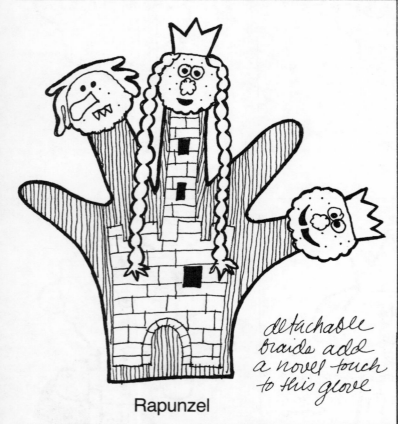

detachable braids add a novel touch to this glove

Rapunzel

Make a fist with fingers and slowly open up hand

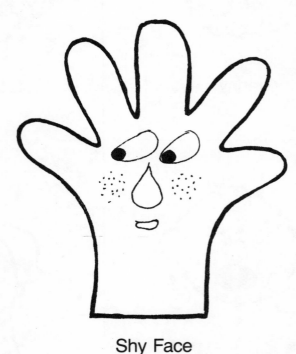

Shy Face

Decorated Muslin Gloves: Make basic glove from heavyweight muslin fabric or Pellon using pattern that follows. Use coloring medium (paint, permanent marker pens or fabric crayons as described in Puppetelling chapter under story aprons) to draw pictures onto the palm depicting "growing things" such as a carrot, tree or flower. Or, make a more general scenery background to complement stories such as a bridge and river for *Little Red Riding Hood* or *The Three Billy Goats Gruff* or a rising sun for a "Morning Greeter" puppet.

196

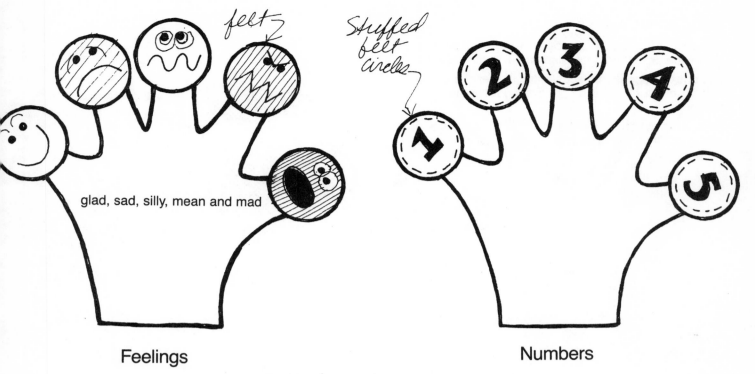

felt

stuffed felt circles

glad, sad, silly, mean and mad

Feelings

Numbers

Curriculum Glove: Teach numbers, letters, colors and shapes with felt symbols.

Ocean Voyage

Hickory Dickory Dock

Gloves With Scene Changes: Sew a button onto the center palm of a glove. Use this mechanism to attach simple scenery shapes such as a clock, flower, moon, house, space ship or geometrical shape.

197

BASIC GLOVE PATTERN

Use a sturdy material for gloves—heavyweight muslin, Pellon or cotton, double knits are ideally suited.

Cut out two opposite pieces, using pattern, and sew right sides together; turn right sides out and hem bottom edge.

Note: This pattern has extra short finger lengths to fit young children and allows for maximum palm area for scenery placement.

198

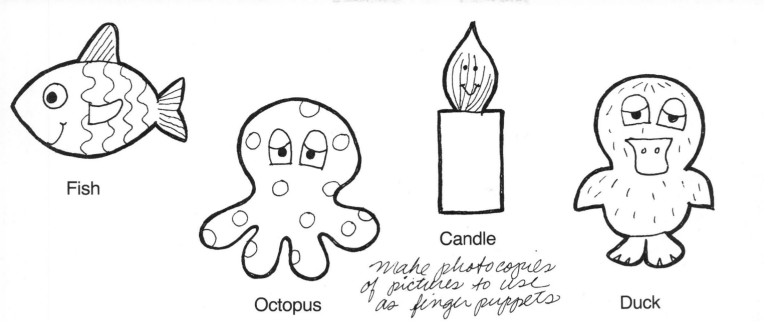

Fish

Octopus

Candle

make photocopies of pictures to use as finger puppets

Duck

MATERIALS

Rubber Cleaning Gloves: A simple and clever idea is to use rubber housecleaning gloves to take advantage of the smooth surface to "stick-on" pictures from magazines and greeting cards, drawings and so forth. Simply cut out the picture or figure and affix to the rubber glove with small pieces of double-backed tape. Consider permanency with your stick-ons by laminating them between plastic or clear contact paper. These puppets may also be used with a velcro glove, as well (use contact cement to adhere velcro to paper or plastic laminate).

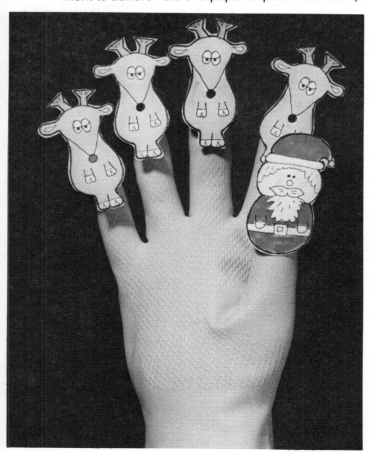

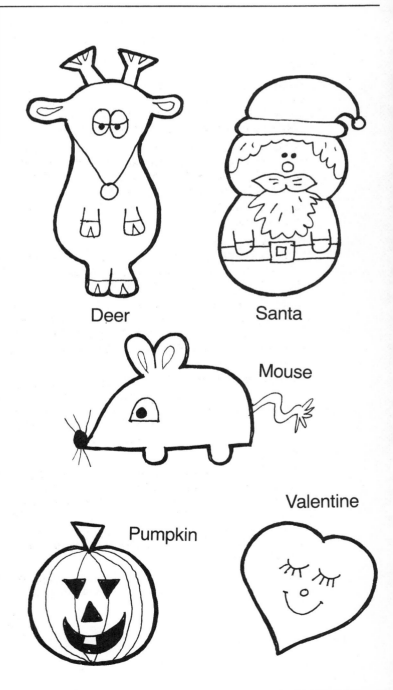

Deer

Santa

Mouse

Pumpkin

Valentine

Hand Fabric Puppets-Basic

This all-purpose basic hand puppet pattern was designed for versatility in characterization and costuming. A wardrobe of costumes offers sufficient interchangeability for a puppet to play many roles, ranging from a simple peasant to a regal king. For quick character changes, a collection of felt hats comes in handy.

MATERIALS

For basic body and head—felt, velour or double knit for people; fake fur for animals; assorted fabrics and trims for costumes; yarn or fake fur for wigs.

PROCEDURE

Body: Cut out front and back body pieces following pattern. Sew front and back pieces, right sides together, around entire body, leaving bottom edge open. Turn right side out and hem bottom.

Head: Cut out front and back head pieces, following pattern. Sew front and back pieces, right sides together, around sides and upper portion of head, between two dots. Turn right side out.

Assembling: Slip head over neck of body and glue or sew in place.

Hair: A wig can be made from shag fur. Cut out front and back wig pieces and sew, right sides together; turn right side out and tack to head (refer to beginning of chapter for cutting shag fur).

Nose: Glue or sew a pom-pom nose onto face. To make a custom nose, use pattern and sew together two nose pieces, right sides together. Turn right side out and stuff with fiber-fil. Blind stitch nose to face.

Costumes and Hats: Refer to beginning of chapter for fabric suggestions for costumes. Cut out a front and back piece for each costume or hat and sew seam lines, right sides together; turn right side out. Hem and decorate to match with particular role.

Animals With Ears: Prepare ears before sewing head pieces together. Ears with fur backs to match body and lined with a pink or tan felt are attractive. Cut out a front and back ear piece and sew, right sides together; turn right side out. Pin ears between head pieces and follow procedure under "Head" section.

Tails: Pom-poms, braid trims, braided yarn or stuffed fabric tails to match body can be chosen for an animal puppet.

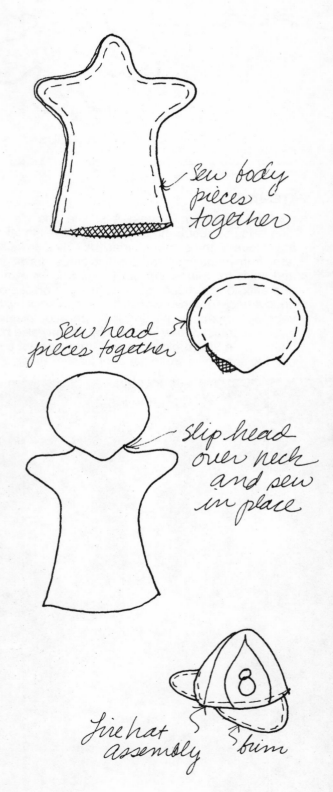

sew body pieces together

sew head pieces together

slip head over neck and sew in place

fire hat assembly   trim

200

Chef

Hen

Lion

King

Witch

Clown

Hats

chef

police person

witch

fire person

crown

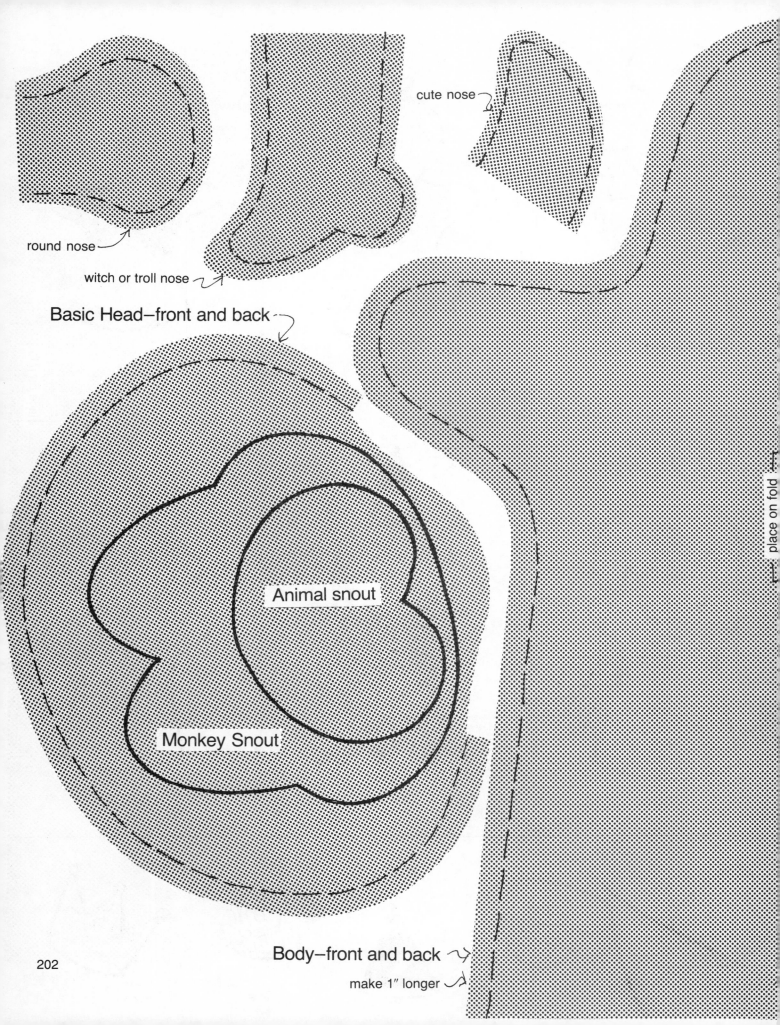

round nose

witch or troll nose

cute nose

Basic Head—front and back

Animal snout

Monkey Snout

place on fold

Body—front and back

make 1" longer

202

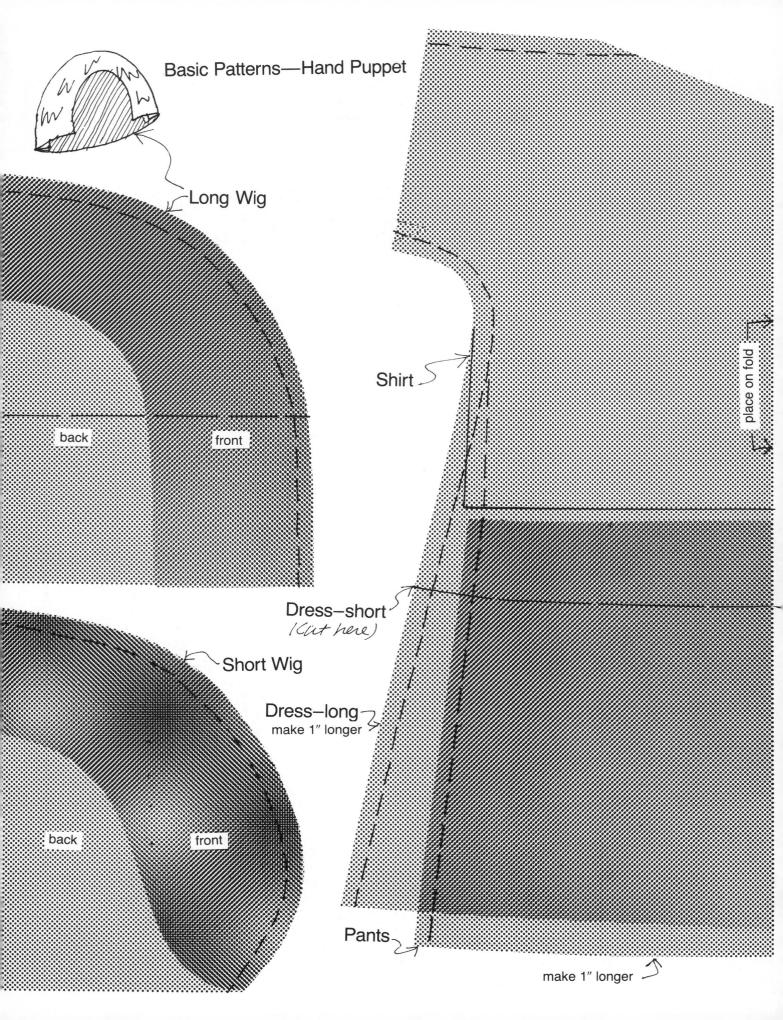

Basic Patterns—Hand Puppet

Long Wig

back

front

Short Wig

back

front

Shirt

place on fold

Dress—short
(Cut here)

Dress—long
make 1″ longer

Pants

make 1″ longer

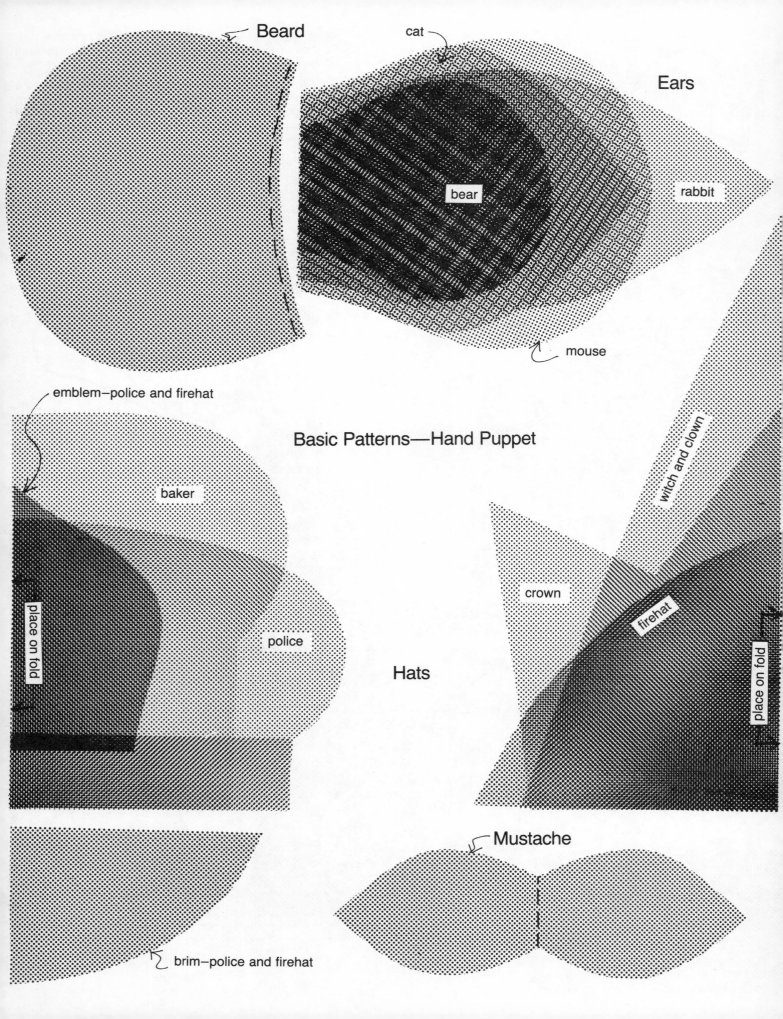

Beard

cat

Ears

bear

rabbit

mouse

emblem—police and firehat

Basic Patterns—Hand Puppet

witch and clown

baker

crown

firehat

place on fold

police

Hats

place on fold

Mustache

brim—police and firehat

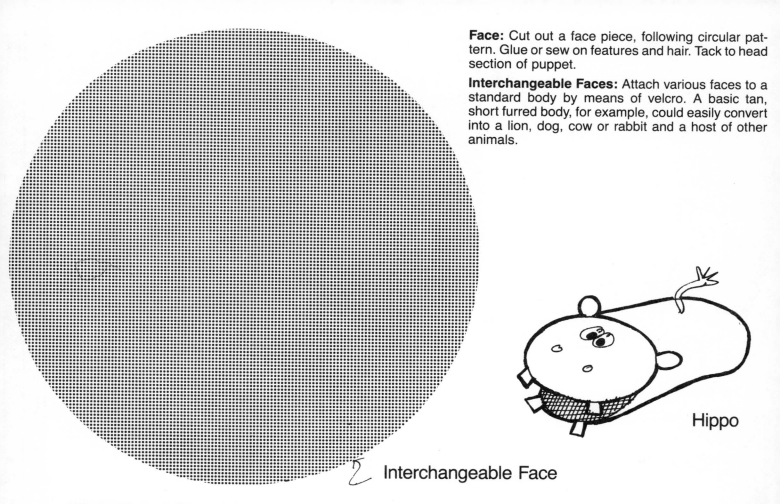

Face: Cut out a face piece, following circular pattern. Glue or sew on features and hair. Tack to head section of puppet.

Interchangeable Faces: Attach various faces to a standard body by means of velcro. A basic tan, short furred body, for example, could easily convert into a lion, dog, cow or rabbit and a host of other animals.

Hippo

Interchangeable Face

Talking Mouth Fabric Puppets

MATERIALS

Felt, polyester double-knit, fake fur, velour or other sturdy fabric for body and face; red or pink double-knit, velour or felt for mouth; assorted felt and fabric for features.

PROCEDURE

Basic Body: Cut out front and back body pieces, extending pattern length 4 inches or more (even longer for a caterpillar or snake) depending on desired finished length.

Basic Talking Mouth: Place pattern on fold and cut out mouth piece from red or pink fabric.

Assembling: Sew front and back body pieces, right sides together, along side seams up to dots.

Pin and fit mouth, right sides together, to match body pieces, lining up fold line of mouth with dots of body, as shown. Sew together and turn entire puppet right side out.

Tiger

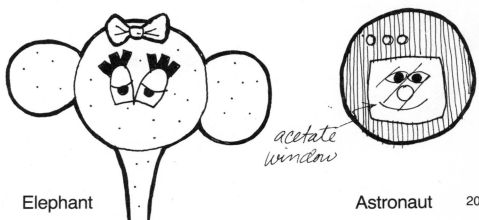

Elephant

acetate window

Astronaut

205

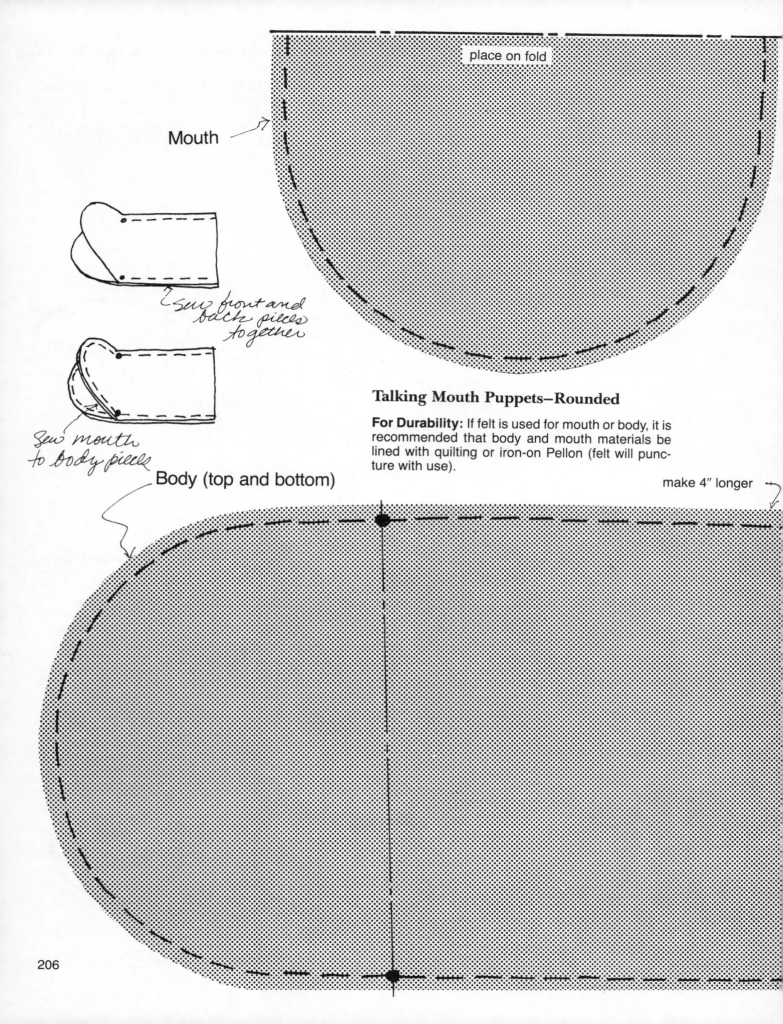

Mouth

sew front and
both pieces
together

sew mouth
to body pieces

Body (top and bottom)

place on fold

Talking Mouth Puppets—Rounded

For Durability: If felt is used for mouth or body, it is recommended that body and mouth materials be lined with quilting or iron-on Pellon (felt will puncture with use).

make 4″ longer

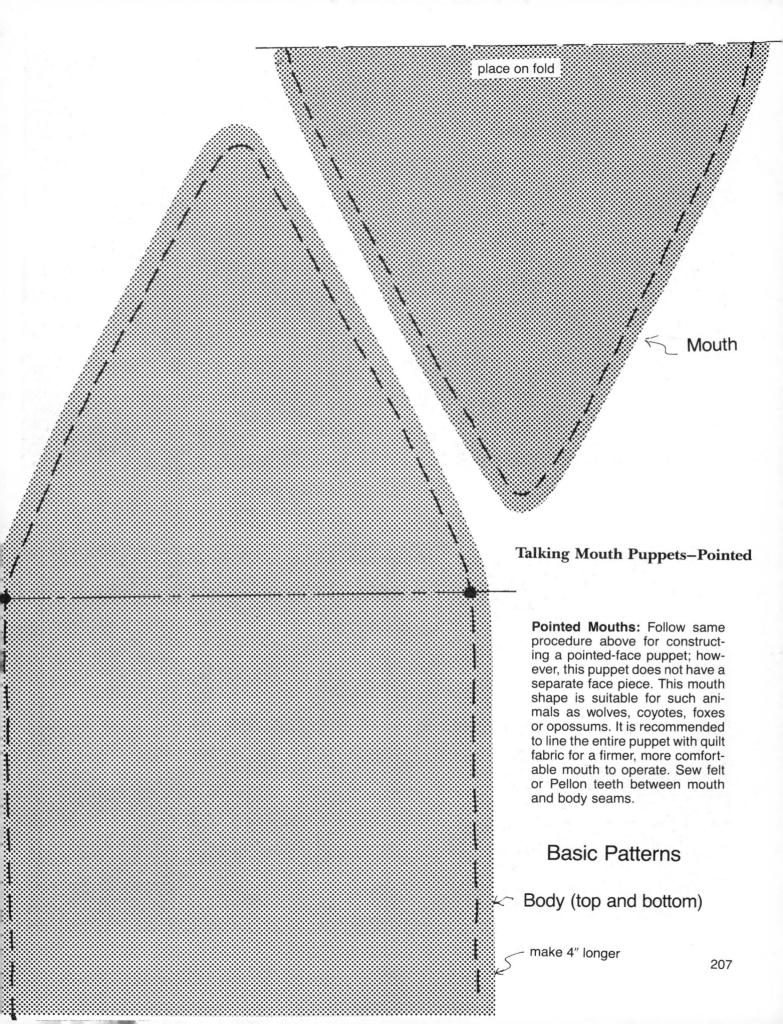

place on fold

Mouth

Talking Mouth Puppets—Pointed

Pointed Mouths: Follow same procedure above for constructing a pointed-face puppet; however, this puppet does not have a separate face piece. This mouth shape is suitable for such animals as wolves, coyotes, foxes or opossums. It is recommended to line the entire puppet with quilt fabric for a firmer, more comfortable mouth to operate. Sew felt or Pellon teeth between mouth and body seams.

Basic Patterns

Body (top and bottom)

make 4″ longer

207

Paper Envelope Kangaroo

Paper Envelope Sheep
has cotton glued to a stiff paper body.

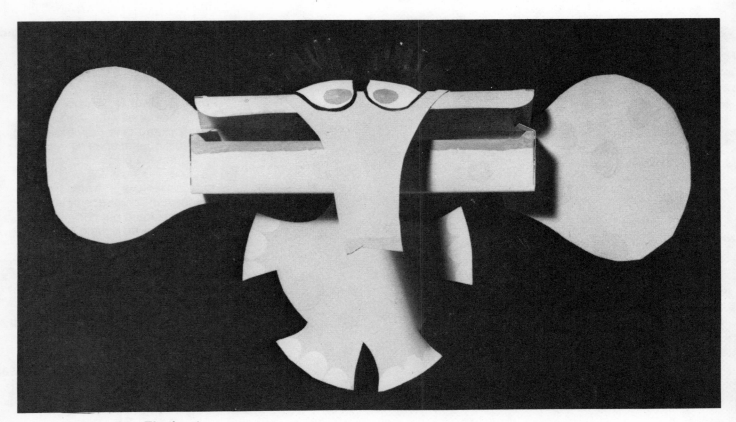

Baggy Box Elephant

Staple a rubber band across top of box for placing
fingers under and operating

Paper Puppets

Many of the puppets found in the Children's Puppet Making chapter are highly suitable to serve the teacher as visuals for classroom application. By adding details as shown on these pages they can be particularly appealing. Do not let the children play freely with them and they will be assured a long life span. Instead hang them for display on puppet clothesline.

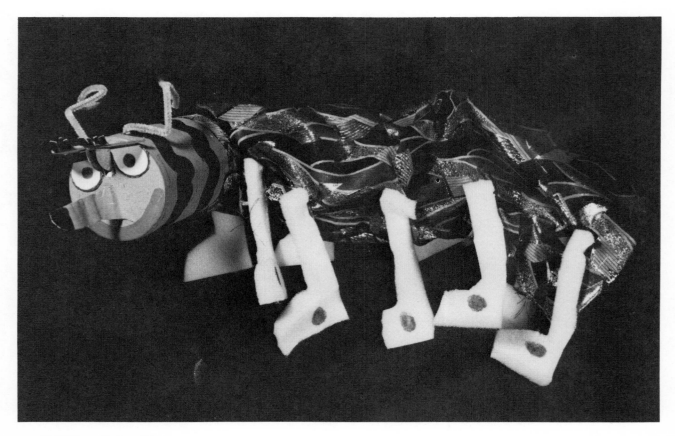

Salt Box Caterpillar

Cut off end of box and insert hand inside to maneuver metal "salt pour" device with attached "fluttering eyelashes." Attach a tube of fabric for long body and add cut foam bouncy legs.

Potholder Pattern

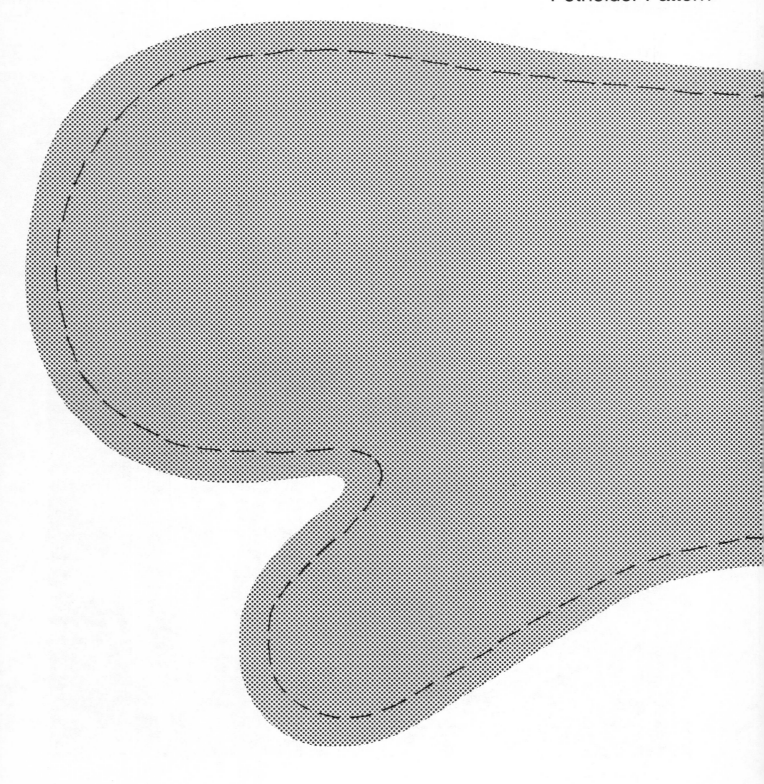

Turtle

Snail

Potholder Puppets

MATERIALS

Heavyweight Pellon or muslin fabric; quilt lining (optional); felt, trim or yarn.

PROCEDURE

For making your own potholder, cut out two opposite pieces of fabric, following the pattern. Sew two pieces, right sides together, all around, leaving bottom open. Turn right sides out; line with quilted fabric for extra comfort, if desired.

Use a coloring medium or glue on felt, trim and yarn to decorate and individualize the puppet characters.

Note: This is an excellent pattern for children to make their own puppets from mural paper or grocery bags. Glue or staple edges together and let them create their own special characters.

Ready made pot holders may also be used with glue-on felt features.

Hi!

Camel

Stork

211

Rod Puppets

MATERIALS

Small toys such as plastic cars, stuffed animals, little dolls, monsters, holiday characters and similar novelties, or a drawing or picture from coloring book, greeting card or magazine; dowel, drinking straw or blunt skewer for rod control.

PROCEDURE

Attach any small, lightweight two or three dimensional character (picture or toy described above) to rod control with glue or tape. Two dimensional material may be laminated or covered with clear contact paper.

Bird from nature magazine with wiggly eye

Gingerbread Men rod puppets

Toy Car

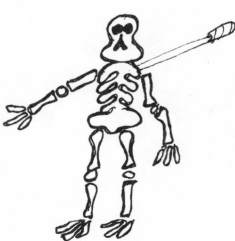

Novelty Skeleton

Doll

212

Sock, Slipper and Sleeper Puppets

MATERIALS

Sock; plastic milk carton; fabric, felt or fake fur.

PROCEDURE

Using pattern, cut out mouth piece from plastic milk carton and insert inside sock as shown.

To secure insert, machine stitch $1/8$ to $1/4$-inch in on both sides of center of plastic insert.

To operate: Put hand inside sock entirely, fold insert in half with thumb against bottom half; move hand up and down.

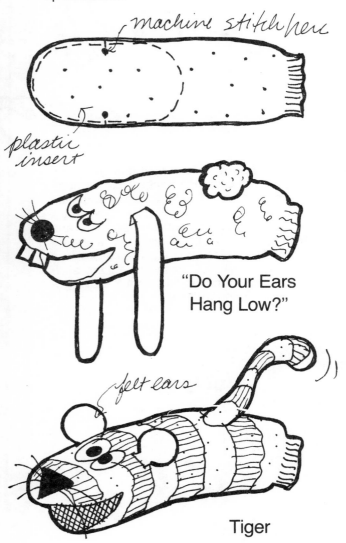

"Do Your Ears Hang Low?"

Tiger

Tiger: Add a stuffed tail and ears made from a piece of matching sock (line ears with felt). Fake fur or felt also make good ears.

Plastic Insert Pattern

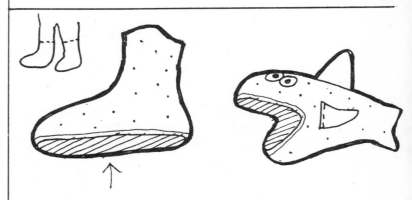

Folded Slipper or Sleeper sock: simply fold the sole of a slipper-sock in half or cut off the feet sections of a child's sleeper garment; add basic features.

To operate: Place thumb in lower half of sock, and fingers in upper, open and close hand.

213

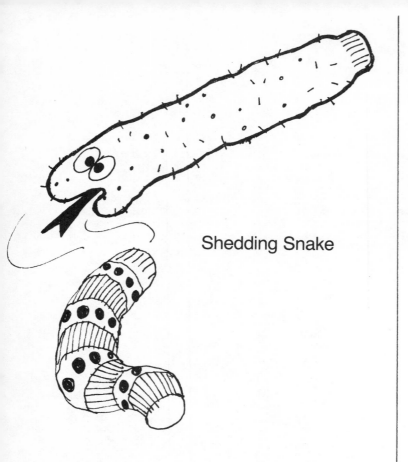

Shedding Snake

Shedding Snake: Use a knee-length tube sock for a basic snake body. For a "shedding skin," cut off the toe of a contrasting sock of the same size as the snake; slip on and off the snake sock.

Snail Shell Back: Cut two 3¾ by 12-inch strips of fabric (striped, dotted or other appropriate pattern). Sew sides and one end seam, right sides together, turn and stuff lightly, stitch close the end and roll into a "jellyroll." Attach jellyroll into back of snail sock body.

Variation of Snail with rolled up foam back

Tennis Sock Puppet: This puppet has an intriguing stretch mouth for eating things such as numbers, colors, shapes, beginning sounds, health foods and so forth. It also comes with a ready-made pom-pom nose; simply add felt arms and legs and some eyes. Cut out a miniature cardboard menu to feed the finished puppet. The children will enjoy a whole "family" of these characters, each serving a particular function and identified by symbols glued to the puppet's front.

214

Stuffed Toys

MATERIALS

Commercial stuffed animals, soft-sculpture and novelty characters; string and cardboard tube or dowel, (for marionette).

PROCEDURE

String Puppets: Attach strings to body parts to be animated; attach the other ends of the strings to a cardboard tube or wooden dowel control. Puppets can be manipulated in front of an inverted table top to which scenery has been taped.

Hand Puppets: For toys large enough to fit over the hand, cut a slit or hole in or near the bottom of the toy. Remove all stuffing and insert hand inside. An alternate method for handling the puppet is to sew an inverted pocket on the back of the toy in which to tuck the hand for holding. Arms of toy may need to be readjusted in order to be manipulated comfortably; cut off and re-sew in appropriate places. Perhaps the stuffed toy arms may be long enough to attach dowels for rod type controls, instead.

Raggedy Ann Doll

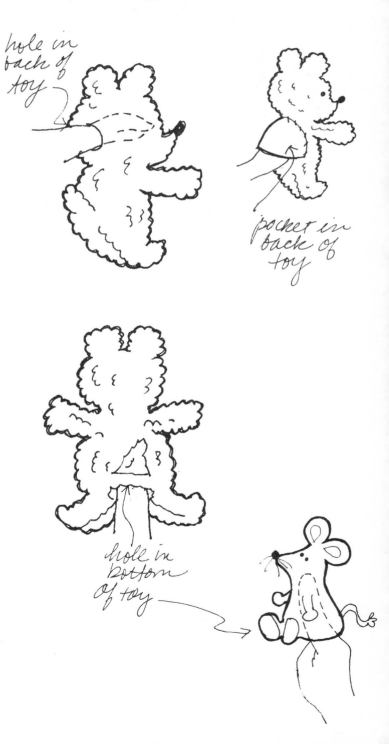

hole in back of toy

pocket in back of toy

hole in bottom of toy

Parent Power at work!

PUPPETS AND PARENTS
Building a Puppet Collection

Does the idea of having fifty new puppets appear in your classroom overnight sound like magic? Better than magic, it is Parent Power! A simple and effective way to increase your puppet collection is through a parent workshop. In an evening or weekend session, parents can construct numerous finger and hand puppets with little effort and at almost no expense.

The keys to success are enthusiasm on the part of the parents and good organization from you. First, decide what kinds of puppets you want. The puppets should be quick and easy to make, durable and suitable for use by you as well as the children. (For ideas, see the teacher's Puppetmaking section.) Next, plan to send out an appealing flyer announcing the workshop and encouraging parents to come.

The workshop should be about two to three hours in length and divided in two parts: demonstration and construction. Spend half an hour to one hour showing how to make the puppets. If no one in the school feels comfortable explaining puppet construction, invite a student or professor of puppetry from a nearby university or contact a local puppetry guild to see if a professional puppeteer might be available to demonstrate.

The construction period can last anywhere from one to two hours and should be carefully planned. The following suggestions will help make maximal use of your time for product output.

Consider first where the puppets will be made. A large room with work tables and chairs to accommodate everyone is the most satisfactory. Try to locate in the same area where the children work every day! Place one large table in a central location for community items like patterns, fabric, trims and glue.

Another table (or bulletin board area) should be cleared for drying or displaying puppets.

Have one or more portable sewing machines at the workshop session and designate one person to operate each machine or electric glue gun. This saves the hassle of every person needing instructions on how to run the equipment. Sewing machines and electric glue guns are not mandatory but they will make construction speedier and sturdier.

Have patterns for basic finger and hand puppets pre-cut from poster or cardboard to facilitate tracing, or make photocopies for each participant of the patterns in the Puppetmaking chapter this saves time and eliminates the possibility of the puppets fitting improperly. At this session, it would be useful to make a tabletop theatre as well.

Have pictures and books available for easy reference. If, for example, a puppet of a character from Dr. Seuss' *The Cat in the Hat* is desired, give the book to the parent for appraisal. If community helpers are desired, provide pictures or photographs that depict proper uniforms so parents will not waste time puzzling over graphic details. Do likewise if parents are making animals, insects, people or things; they need something visual for stimulation.

Be sure to have a good supply of robe fleece velour and heavy textured doubleknit or polyester fabric for basic puppet bodies. These fibers are the easiest to work with and often require no hemming. Costumers at local theaters have wonderful assortments of unusual fabric scraps they may be willing to donate. Such scraps are excellent for those detailed features that will make the puppets extra-special.

You may wish to approach, also, other local businesses for scrap materials such as fabric from a seamstress, fur scraps from a furrier, foam pieces from an upholstery shop and yarn from a knitter.

Parent Participation

Ask parents to bring a needle, thread, scissors, a sock, buttons (for eyes) and any scraps of felt, also trims, ribbons or other fabrics. This information can be written on the flyer advertising the program.

Start by auctioning off the puppet characters to be made! "Who wants to make five barnyard animal finger puppets?" "Who wants to make Curious George?" If there are no takers, specific puppets can always be assigned to participants.

Have handy more ideas than you think you will use. The parents may be faster than you anticipate. On the next school day, display the puppets on a class bulletin board or a clothes line. Just as parents love to see their children's art work, so too will the children enjoy seeing what their parents create.

If parent participation workshops are held as an annual event, the scope and depth of the puppet collection will increase proportionately. The classroom will soon claim proud ownership of a growing family of puppet characters to complement every aspect of daily activities.

Local Puppet Guilds
To obtain information about your local puppet guild, write to: Gayle Schulter, #5 Cricklewood Path, Pasadena, CA 91107.

Showing off some Potholder Puppets

218

Parent Puppet Power

Please Join Us
in a session of Puppetmaking Fun to help us build our Puppet Collection

If you can:

- Cut
- Sew
- Glue
- Comment
- Praise!

At _____

Time _____

Date _____

Bring _____

_____

This flyer reproduced courtesy of **Nancy Renfro Studios**

Part III

Daily Routine
Holiday
Language Arts

Morning Greeter Puppet designed by Mary Olsen and Anna Viggiano   Photo by Arman Kitapci

DAILY ROUTINE

Puppets can weave in and out of a daily preschool routine with minimal effort and maximal effectiveness. As much as it may hurt one's ego, the truth is that children would rather listen to a puppet than hear the same information from an adult! Yet puppets should not be used for everything and should never be a substitute for the teacher. One or two well-chosen puppets who regularly visit the classroom can enliven an activity and add a light touch to the curriculum for teacher and children alike. (See Page 52 for Buddy Puppets.)

A word of caution: *Do not use puppets as a means to avoid direct dialogue between teacher and child.* (There are some things the children need to hear directly from the teacher.) Puppets should be employed only when the activity can be enhanced or made more effective by use of a puppet. To make that determination, ask yourself these questions: "What do I say every day that the children would rather hear from a puppet?" "What do I do every day that a puppet can do better?" "What interactions occur regularly that a puppet could make more interesting and meaningful?"

Morning Greeter

A "Morning Greeter" puppet can welcome children every morning and join in saying goodbye to mom or dad. Especially for young children and newcomers, the puppet can ease the sometimes difficult ordeal of separation from parents. In schools where circle-time is the first structured activity of the day, the "Greeter" puppet may encourage punctuality by giving a morning hug to those who arrive early. The puppet may also bid farewell at the end of the day.

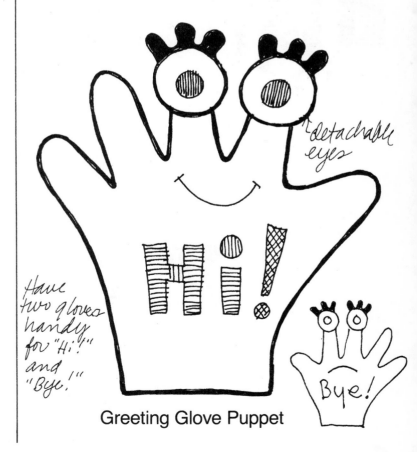

Greeting Glove Puppet

Rest or Nap-time

A "sleepy" puppet who is always yawning, nodding off to sleep or snoring is a great way to introduce nap-time. If the puppet is large enough to have a functional hand, he can squeeze toothpaste onto toothbrushes or supervise placement of sleep mats. The puppet might also awaken the children at the end of their naps. Be sure the puppet has its own special sleeping place: a miniature mat, a blanket in a desk drawer or shoe box serve equally well.

A turn a-round puppet depicting a sleepy expression on one side and a wide-awake one on the other is ideal to hint to the children that it is naptime. Use pattern on page 200 make a basic hand puppet for your permanent collection. Or consider coloring two faces on paper plates and staple together, back to back, with a tube-neck inserted up between the plates.

Awake

Basic fabric hand puppet pattern on page 200

Turn a round puppet - create a face on both sides may also be made from two paper plates with neck tube - see page 103

Sleepy

Snack and Lunch Time

Morning and afternoon snack periods as well as lunch-time offer favorable opportunities to discuss nutrition. A "Snack-a-Roo" kangaroo puppet who carries healthful snacks in its pouch can move around the table enabling the children, individually or in small groups, to talk about what tasty foods are in its pouch. A Nutrient puppet in the form of a person, animal or food item (such as a carrot, milk carton, apple) might also visit the children occasionally. Puppet-motivated conversations will prompt the introduction of new words and concepts such as food groups, proteins, vitamins, nutrients and calories.

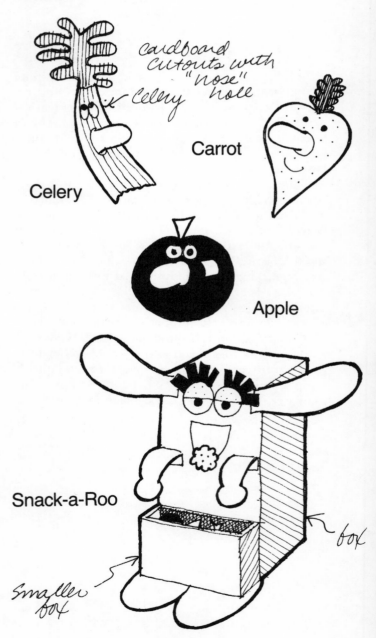

cardboard cutouts with "nose" hole

Celery

Carrot

Apple

Snack-a-Roo

smaller box

box

224

Clean-Up Time

The "Clean-Up" puppet is an effectual "live-in" helper for preschools and elementary levels. He can announce clean-up times by ringing a bell or calling out a magic word (invented by the children). He can issue instructions and enjoy "checking up" on the thoroughness of the children's jobs. With comic joy, he can also search for misplaced legos or scraps of paper on the floor that someone has overlooked! In these activities, the "Clean-Up" puppet can provide an ideal substitute for the teacher.

A related "Mr. Sweeper-Upper" puppet is simple to construct by adding facial features onto a brush or a broom.

A garden glove (or any other type) may be converted into a "Trash Grabber" by gluing on felt features. You will want to have several available since the children will vie to take turns wearing it!

Mr. Trash Grabber

Show and Tell

If your circle time offers an occasion for children to share something special from home, like a new book or a story about the family, let the puppet invite the children to "show and tell." The puppet can ask lots of questions, encourage the sharing child to speak louder and, if necessary, bring to an end a tale that rambles unnecessarily.

225

Christmas

HOLIDAY PROJECTS

Puppets can bring pomp and year-round fun for helping children to celebrate holidays. Celebrations of these special occasions punctuate the routine of everyday life and represent some of the most impressionable events of a young child's life, serving as noteworthy references for marking the child's own seasonal calendar. Puppets can help to instill in the minds of young children the meanings of these holidays and even serve to define the changing of seasons. For example:

● A Bunny puppet can teach the children to sing *Here Comes Peter Cottontail*.

● A Santa puppet may distribute greeting cards and gifts.

● A puppet in a nightshirt and cap may read *The Night Before Christmas*.

● A simple Jack-O-Lantern on a stick may emcee your favorite spooky Halloween tale.

By elaborating on the various traditions, familiar "buddy" puppets may join the children in the spirit of the festivities. By adding simple props or costumes you may easily adapt these puppets, for example:

● *Valentine-St. Patrick's Day.* Pin a heart or shamrock onto the puppet's lapel.

● *Easter.* Fill a small basket with lavender, yellow and pink eggs, baby chicks and bunnies for the puppet to carry.

● *May Day.* Place a flower lei around the puppet's neck.

● *July 4th.* Let the puppet hold a miniature flag.

● *Halloween.* Don a black cape on a puppet, add a pointed hat and it will instantly become a wonderful witch! For a ghost puppet, merely drape a white cloth, handkerchief or diaper over a puppet and tape on two black circles for eyes.

● *Christmas.* The colors of green, red, white, gold and silver are usually sufficient to suggest the Yuletide in the form of a hat, vest, scarf or apron.

A clever way to transform a puppet for a holiday theme is to allow a squirrel or mouse puppet to undergo an "identity crisis." He may appear with paper bunny ears at Easter, a Santa's beard at Christmas and a pleated paper turkey tail at Thanksgiving. Build up anticipation among the children as they await the appearance of their favorite character in yet another surprise holiday costume.!

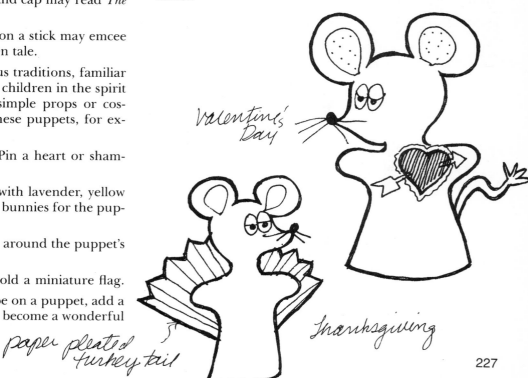

Valentine's Day

paper pleated turkey tail

Thanksgiving

227

Birthday—The Big Birthday "Fake"

Motivation: In a "surprise" box keep a Big Birthday "Fake" puppet and crown. This box can be a gift box decorated with birthday wrapping paper and a big bow on top, or a hatbox made to look like a Birthday cake, as shown below (make a hole in cake to pop out puppet). When you bring out the box, ask the children "What do you like best about birthdays?" "Whose birthday is it today?"

Puppetelling: Invite the birthday child to open the surprise box that contains the Big Birthday "Fake" wearing the birthday crown. (He's called a "Fake" because he always thinks it is *his* birthday!) When the "Fake" puppet is unable to convince the birthday child that it is his birthday, let the birthday child remove the puppet crown and place it on the child's own head. The "Fake" may then gleefully lead the class in singing "Happy Birthday" and invite everyone to join him in granting best wishes to the birthday child and make a special wish.

decorated hatbox

The Birthday "Fake"

Halloween

Motivation: Open up discussion about pumpkins with the children by asking "What color is a pumpkin?" "How do you turn a pumpkin into a Jack-O-Lantern?" Ask them to transform their own faces into expressions like those found on Jack-O-Lanterns by frowning, smiling, looking sad or afraid.

Puppetelling: Sing the song below using a bright orange nerf ball with a green patch of leaves on top (see page 50). Leave one side of the ball plain; on the other, glue black felt pieces to represent a Jack-O-Lantern face. (For a changeable face, affix the felt pieces on with straight pins.) Wear a black glove and poke your first finger up into the center of the ball. As you sing the song, turn the plain side of the ball towards the children then during the second verse turn the ball around to reveal the Jack-O-Lantern face.

This is the Way the Pumpkin Grows
by Tamara Hunt
(to the tune of "This is the Way We Wash Our Clothes")

This is the Way the Pumpkin Grows,
    The Pumpkin Grows,
    The Pumpkin Grows.
This is the Way the Pumpkin Grows,
So early Halloween morning.

This is the Way the Jack-O-Lantern shines,
    The Jack-O-Lantern shines,
    The Jack-O-Lantern shines,
This is the Way the Jack-O-Lantern shines,
So late on Halloween evening.

Puppetmaking: Have the children draw a picture of a large pumpkin on a piece of orange construction paper using shape forms, see Page 170. Glue each pumpkin shape onto the front of an individual cereal box. Cut out holes in the boxes for features and a hole in the back of the box large enough to insert a flashlight.

Puppetizing: Invite the children to the playing circle. Place all the "pumpkins" on a table top, darken the room and take turns inserting the flashlight into each "pumpkin" creation while the children sing the song in unison.

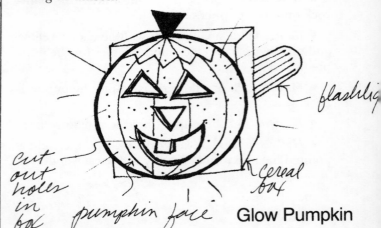

cut out holes in box

pumpkin face

flashlight

cereal box

Glow Pumpkin

228

Thanksgiving

Motivation: Discuss the Thanksgiving celebration. Ask "What are the traditional foods your family usually prepares for Thanksgiving dinner?" "What are some of the ways you can help?" "What features make turkeys distinctive from other birds?"

Puppetelling: Hide a Turkey puppet or a puppet with a turkey tail pinned onto its back as described on page 227. behind your back or inside a grocery sack that has been decorated to look like a barn. Recite the poem below and for each "gobble" pop your turkey puppet up into view. At the end of the poem, let it "run away" out of sight behind your back or inside the "barn" bag.

Popping Turkey Poem
By Tamara Hunt

"Gobble, gobble, gobble", I heard the turkey say.
"Gobble, gobble, gobble", It is Thanksgiving Day!
"Gobble, gobble, gobble", Come closer this-a-way.
"Gobble, gobble, gluck!" Why did you run away?

Puppetmaking: Have the children make turkey rod puppets by using their hands as the outline for a turkey shape as described on Page 160. Attach each turkey puppet to a skewer or popsicle stick for rod control.

Puppetizing: As the children stand around the playing circle, ask them to hide their turkey puppets behind their backs. As you recite the poem all the turkey puppets may pop out and "gobble" in unison. At the end of the poem, the children may make their turkeys "run away" behind their backs.

Turkey

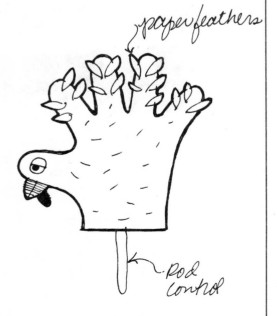

paper feathers

Rod control

Chanukah—Happy Candles

Motivation: Talk about the meaning of Chanukah. If you have a Jewish child at your school, invite a parent to visit and explain the meaning of the occasion. Show a picture of a Menorah and, if possible, bring a Menorah to school and light the candles for the children to see.

Puppetelling: Introduce a "helper candle" puppet who is searching for eight candles to light on its own Menorah. Let the puppet invite the children to make their own candle puppets.

Puppetmaking: Ask the children to make candle puppets by covering toilet tissues tubes with foil or by painting them different colors. Attach a flame cut-out to a rod (popsicle stick or dowel) and draw a face on the flame. Animate the flame up and down inside the tube as each candle is "lighted."

Puppetizing: Invite eight puppeteers to be the Menorah. As the "Helper Candle" puppet "lights" each of the eight candle-puppets, ask the remaining children to think of a gift they would like to give someone on Chanukah evening. Although the ceremony actually takes eight days to perform, the children will enjoy lighting all the candle-puppets at once.

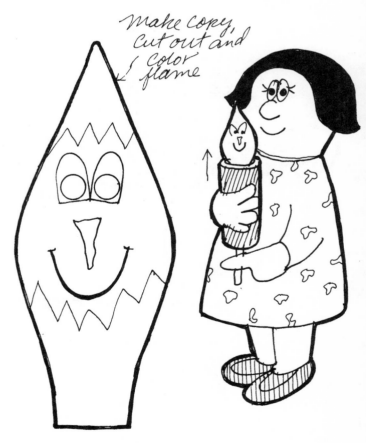

make copy, cut out and color flame

Happy Flame Pattern
Idea by Mary Craven

229

Christmas—Rudolph Puppet

Motivation: Bring up for discussion the topic of reindeer with the children. Show them a picture of a reindeer and talk about where these animals live and what they eat. Tell them about an imaginary reindeer named Rudolph and ask "What does Rudolph do every year?"

Puppetelling: Use a Rudolph puppet or another puppet in a Santa costume to lead the children in singing *Rudolph the Red-Nosed Reindeer*.

Puppetmaking: Ask the children to make "regular" reindeer puppets (*not* Rudolph) by cutting out and coloring a reindeer face. Tape twig antlers onto the face to complete reindeer.

Puppetizing: In the playing circle, ask one child to allow her puppet to become Rudolph by adhering onto the child-made puppet (with sticky back tape) a shiny red paper nose or pom-pom. Review with the children those segments in the song when the remaining reindeer puppets tease Rudolph and then shout with glee. You, as the teacher, play the Santa-puppet and invite "Rudolph" to guide your sleigh appropriate time in the song. At first, it may be desirable to sing the song alone. Later, when the children know when you will stop for action, they can join you in singing. By switching the nose around, the puppets of the other children may assume the role of "Rudolph."

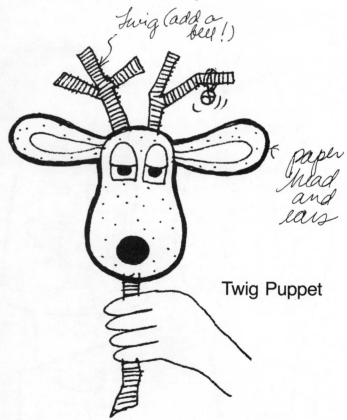

Twig Puppet

Valentine's Day —Five Heart Rings

Motivation: Inquire of the children "What is Valentine's Day?" "What do you give on Valentine's Day and why?" Help the children understand that Valentines offer a means to tell others we care about them. Emphasize the concept of friendship.

Puppetelling: Velcro five small red valentine heart-shapes of felt onto your glove. As you recite the poem below, remove the hearts one-by-one and give to the children. Let them replace the hearts when you are finished. Repeat until everyone has had a turn to receive a valentine.

Five Red Valentines
By Tamara Hunt

Five red valentines I take from my drawer,
I'll give one to (*child's name*), now there are four.
Four red valentines, pretty as can be,
I'll give one to _____, now there are three.
Three red valentines, can you guess for who?
I'll give one to _____, now there are two.
Two red valentines, sharing them is fun.
I'll give one to _____, now there is one.
One red valentine, lonely as can be.
I'm going to keep it for me, me, me!

Puppetmaking: Let the children make "Valentine Rings" by taping paper valentines onto soda pop tabs, see Page 175.

Puppetizing: Invite a child to wear five Valentine Rings and distribute them to other children while the group recites the poem. Let the other children have a turn.

Valentine Rings

230

St. Patrick's Day—Green Gobblers

Motivation: Request that the children look at one another to find if anyone is wearing green that day.

Puppetelling: Sesame Street's Kermit the Frog (or another green puppet) may suddenly pop out from a pocket on your Story Apron and announce: "Look at me, look at me! Nobody guessed me! I'm wearing green—green all over me!" Kermit may then lead a discussion in which the children seek to identify green-colored objects in the room. If the children are older, they may distinguish between shades of light and dark green. Later, Kermit can beckon the children outdoors to search for the green colors in nature—grass, leaves, stems and such.

Puppetmaking: Let the children make their own talking "green gobblers" from paper plates see Page 167. Decorate the "gobblers" with natural materials found outdoors (leaves, grass, etc.) as well as scraps of green paper and fabrics from the material "wish list."

Puppetizing: As an informal Puppet Play activity, the children with their puppets may discover additional green objects and pretend to gobble them up outdoors or in the Puppet Corner.

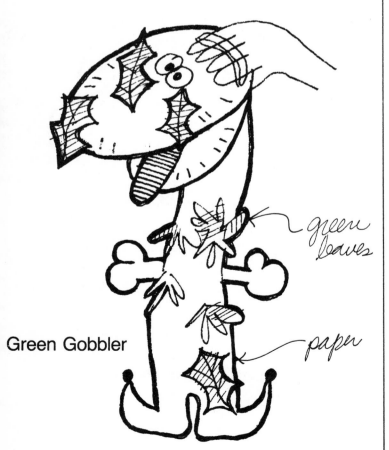

Green Gobbler

Easter—Bunny Puppets

Motivation: Open up discussion with the children about bunnies, asking "How can you tell when an animal is a bunny?" "What is another name for a bunny?" "Who is the Easter Bunny and why is it so special?" "How big would a bunny be if it were only the size of an elf?"

The Night Before Easter
by Anna Fleming

'Twas the night before Easter,
"Oh dear," said the Bunny.
"How can I buy eggs,
Without any money?"
This terrible problem,
Made Bunny so sad,
"No child will get eggs!
And they'll all feel bad!"
Just then an idea,
Popped into his mind,
"If I hurry," said Bunny,
I think I'll have time!"
He worked very hard,
With scissors he clipped.
And the clock ticked on,
While he trimmed and he snipped.
"At last," he cried out,
I am finally done!
And if I've counted right
There's enough for each one!"
And he left for each child,
A gift made of himself,
A bunny just like him—
The size of an elf.

Puppetmaking: Prior to reading the poem, ask the children to make tiny fingerpuppet bunnies using copies of the pattern below. Let them color and decorate the bunnies and write their names on the finished puppets. Roll each bunny into a tube to fit the child's finger and glue or tape together.

Elf Sized Bunny Pattern

Puppetelling: Place all the children's finger-puppets in an Easter basket and hide it under your Story Apron or behind your back. Using a soft, furry bunny puppet, recite the poem to the children (tape a copy onto the puppet's back so you can see it easily). At the end of the poem, surprise the children by bringing into view the basket full of their own fingerpuppets.

Puppetizing: Let each child find her puppet while pretending to be the Easter bunny. Let her tell you what special gift she will deliver to someone on Easter morning.

Mother's Day—"Ask Mr. Bear"

Literature: Marjorie Flack, *Ask Mr. Bear.* New York: MacMillan 1958.

Motivation: Ask the children, "If you could give your mom any present in the world what would it be?" "If you could do something for your mom that would make her very happy what would it be?"

Puppetelling: Read the book *Ask Mr. Bear*, to the children and at the very end, pop up a stuffed toy bear puppet. (see page 215). After finishing the story let each child come up one by one and join in giving the bear a big gentle hug.

Puppetmaking: Let each child select one character from the book and make a Flat Paper-Envelope puppet (page 158): Boy, Hen, Goose, Sheep, Cow, Bear or Mother.

Puppetizing: Invite the children back to the playing circle. Select specific puppeteers to play each part and puppetize the story with you playing the little Boy. If there are duplicates of certain animal characters, then these could act as units. On the other hand, if all the characters are not made then just have a child act out the part without a puppet.

Father's Day —My Father

Motivation: While the children close their eyes and think about their fathers, ask "What does your father look like? What color hair does he have? Does he have a beard? What color are his eyes? What does he wear that you like best?" Let the children compare fathers to determine *how* they differ. If possible, have the children bring to school their father's picture. (If a child's father is not in the home, suggest he substitute an uncle or male adult friend or neighbor.)

Puppetelling: Read a story to the children with a theme that evolves around fathers such as those listed at the end of this chapter.

Puppetmaking: Using the pattern below, ask the children to make paper puppets and personalize them by adding facial features and hair to match that of their fathers. (Or glue on a photograph of their father.) See Page 172 for ways to manipulate these puppets.

Puppetizing: The children may Puppet Play informally in the Puppet Corner with these puppets. Provide props such as play furniture, cars and other toys to aid the children in creating an environment in which the children usually interact with their fathers.

Basic Father Pattern

Independence Day

Motivation: Ask the children "What do you like best about the Fourth of July?" "What do you like and dislike about firecrackers?"

Puppetelling: Ask the children to close their eyes and imagine the sounds of firecrackers as you read the poem.

Five Little Firecrackers
by Tamara Hunt

See the little firecrackers all in a row.
Each getting ready for a great big show.
Line up the firecrackers, light them at the top.
Ready, set, go! Wizz, bang, pop!

Puppetmaking: Use short cardboard tissue tubes for firecrackers. Have the children add funny paper noses and other facial features. Attach some fringed, shiny red cellophane or tissue paper to the top of a skewer or dowel for hair. Insert the dowel through the tube so that the hair will pop up and down.

Puppetizing: Invite the children to the playing circle. In groups of three or four, line them up inside the circle. Recite the poem and let the children make different sounds to synchronize with the action of their "firecrackers" as they pop the hair up and down.

Popping Firecrackers

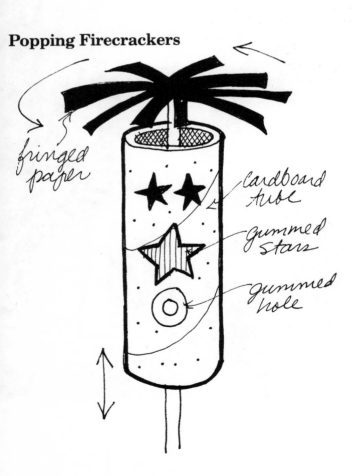

fringed paper

cardboard tube

gummed stars

gummed hole

Books on Birthdays

Anderson, Clarence W. *Billy and Blaze*. New York: Macmillan, 1962.
Annett, Cora. *The Dog Who Thought He Was A Boy*. Boston: Houghton Mifflin, 1965.
Averill, Esther. *Jenny's Birthday Book*. New York: Harper and Row, 1954.
Barrett, Judith. *Benjamin's Three Hundred Sixty Five Birthdays*. New York: Atheneum, 1974.
Carle, Eric. *Secret Birthday Message*. New York: T. Y. Crowell, 1972.
Clifton, Lucille. *Don't You Remember?* New York: Dutton, 1973.
Cole, William. *What's Good for a Five-Year Old?* New York: Holt, Rinehart and Winston, 1971.
Emberley, Ed. *Birthday Wish*. Boston: Little, Brown, 1977.
Fujikawa, Gyo. *Betty Bear's Birthday*. New York: Grosset and Dunlap, 1977.
Hoban, Russell. *A Birthday for Frances*. New York: Harper and Row, 1968.
Keats, Ezra J. *A Letter to Amy*. New York: Harper and Row, 1968.
Kellogg, Steven. *Won't Somebody Play With Me?* New York: Dial, 1972.
Reinach, Jacquelyn. *Happy Birthday Unicorn*. New York: Holt, Rinehart and Winston, 1978.
Seuss, Dr. *Happy Birthday to You*. New York: Random, 1959:

Books on Halloween

Alexander, Sue. *Witch, Goblin, and Sometimes Ghost: Six Read-Alone Stories*. New York: Pantheon, 1976.
Anderson, Lonzo. *The Halloween Party*. New York: Scribner, 1974.
Barton, Byron. *Hester*. New York: Greenwillow, 1975.
Bright, Robert. *Georgie's Halloween*. New York: Doubleday, 1971.
Embry, Margaret. *The Blue-Nosed Witch*. New York: Holiday, 1956.
Johnson, Hannah L. *From Seed to Jack-O-Lantern*. New York: Lothrop, 1974.
Kahl, Virginia. *Gunhilde and the Halloween Spell*. New York: Scribner, 1975.
Kraus, Robert. *How Spider Saved Halloween*. New York: Scholastic, 1980.
Massey, Jeanne. *Littlest Witch*. New York: Knopf, 1959.
Mooser, Stephen. *The Ghost with the Halloween Hiccups*. New York: Avon, 1978.
Prager, Annabelle. *The Spooky Halloween Party*. New York: Pantheon, 1981.
Prelutsky, Jack. *It's Halloween*. New York: Greenwillow, 1977.
Rockwell, Ann. *A Bear, A Bobcat, and Three Ghosts*. New York: Macmillan, 1977.
Varga, Judy. *Once-A-Year Witch*. New York: Morrow, 1973.
Wiseman, Bernard. *Halloween with Morris and Boris*. New York: Dodd, 1975.
Zolotow, Charlotte. *Tiger Called Thomas*. New York: Lothrop, 1963.

Books on Thanksgiving

Balian, Lorna. *Sometimes It's Turkey, Sometimes It's Feathers*. Nashville, TN: Abingdon, 1973.

Child, Lydia M. *Over the River and Through the Wood*. New York: Coward, 1974.

Dalgliesh, Alice. *Thanksgiving Story*. New York: Scribner, 1954.

Devlin, Wende and Harry Devlin. *Cranberry Thanksgiving*. New York: Scholastic, 1980 repro. of 1971 ed.

Janice. *Little Bear's Thanksgiving*. New York: Lothrop, 1967.

Lowitz, Sadyebeth and Anson Lowitz. *Pilgrim's Party*. New York: Dell, 1977.

Weisgard, Leonard. *Plymouth Thanksgiving*. New York: Doubleday, 1967.

Books on Jewish Holidays

Adler, David. *House on the Roof*. New York: Hebrew Publications, 1976.

Aleichem, Sholem. *Hanukah Money*. New York: Greenwillow, 1978.

Cone, Molly. *Purim*. New York: T. Y. Crowell, 1967.

Hirsh, Marilyn. *Hanukkah Story*. New York: Hebrew Publications, 1977.

Simon, Norma. *Hanukkah*. New York: T. Y. Crowell, 1966.

Simon, Norma. *Passover*. New York: T. Y. Crowell, 1965.

Shulevitz, Uri. *Magican*. New York: Macmillan, 1973.

Books on Christmas

Bright, Robert. *Georgie's Christmas Carol*. New York: Doubleday, 1975.

Domanska, Janina. *Din Dan Don It's Christmas*. New York: Greenwillow, 1975.

Duvoisin, Roger. *Petunia's Christmas*. New York: Knopf, 1952.

Ets, Marie and Aurora Labastida. *Nine Days to Christmas*. New York: Viking, 1959.

Frost, Frances. *Christmas in the Woods*. New York: Harper and Row, 1976.

Gregorowski, Christopher. *Why a Donkey Was Chosen*. New York: Doubleday, 1978.

Hoban, Russell. *Emmet Otter's Jug Band Christmas*. New York: Scholastic, 1978.

Hoban, Russell. *Mole Family's Christmas*. New York: Scholastic, 1980.

Hopkins, Lee Bennett. *Sing Hey for Christmas*. New York: Harcourt, Brace, Jovanovich, 1975.

Hutchins, Pat. *The Silver Christmas Tree*. New York: Macmillan, 1974.

Keats, Ezra J. *Little Drummer Boy*. New York: Macmillan, 1968.

Kent, Jack. *The Christmas Pinata*. New York: Scholastic, 1975.

Lobel, Adrianne. *A Small Sheep in a Pear Tree*. New York: Harper and Row, 1977.

Low, Joseph. *Christmas Grump*. New York: Atheneum, 1977.

Mack, Gail. *Yesterday's Snowman*. New York: Pantheon, 1979.

Miller, Edna. *Mousekin's Christmas Eve*. New York: Prentice-Hall, 1965.

Moore, Clement C. *The Night Before Christmas*. New York: Random, 1962.

Nyce, Vera. *Jolly Christmas at the Patterprints*. New York: Scholastic, 1971.

Seuss, Dr. *How the Grinch Stole Christmas*. New York: Random, 1957.

Thayer, Jane. *Puppy Who Wanted a Boy*. New York: Morrow, 1958.

Wells, Rosemary. *Morris's Disappearing Bag: A Christmas Story*. New York: Dial, 1975.

Zakhoder, Boris. *How a Piglet Crashed the Christmas Party*. New York: Lothrop, 1971.

Books on Valentine's Day

Adams, Adrienne. *The Great Valentine's Day Balloon Race*. New York: Scribner, 1980.

Bulla, Clyde R. *Valentine Cat*. New York: T. Y. Crowell, 1959.

Cohen, Miriam. *Bee My Valentine*. New York: Greenwillow, 1978.

De Paola, Tomie. *Things to Make and Do for Valentine's Day*. New York: Watts, 1976.

Kelley, True. *A Valentine for Fuzzboom*. Boston: Houghton Mifflin, 1981.

Mariana. *Miss Flora McFlimsey's Valentine*. New York: Lothrop, 1961.

Schweninger, Ann. *Hunt for Rabbit's Galosh*. New York: Doubleday, 1976.

Santa puppet being hugged

234

Books on St. Patrick's Day

Barth, Edna. *Shamrocks, Harps, and Shillelaghs: The Story of the St. Patrick's Day Symbols.* Boston: Houghton Mifflin, 1974.

Calhoun, Mary. *Hungry Leprechaun.* New York: Morrow, 1962.

Cantwell, Mary. *Saint Patrick's Day.* New York: T. Y. Crowell, 1967.

Janice. *Little Bear Marches in the Saint Patrick's Day Parade.* New York: Lothrop, 1967.

Books on Easter

Adams, Adruenne. *The Easter Egg Artists.* New York: Scribner, 1976.

Armour, Richard. *Adventures of Egbert the Easter Egg.* New York: McGraw-Hill, 1965.

Balian, Lorna. *Humbug Rabbit.* Nashville, TN: Abindgon, 1974.

Brown, Margaret W. *The Golden Egg Book.* New York: Western, 1947.

Coskey, Evelyn. *Easter Eggs for Everyone.* Nashville, TN: Abingdon, 1973.

Duvoisin, Roger. *Easter Treat.* New York: Knopf, 1954.

Friedrich, Priscilla and Otto Friedrich. *Easter Bunny That Overslept.* New York: Lothrop, 1957.

Heyward, Du Bose. *Country Bunny and the Little Gold Shoes.* Boston: Houghton Mifflin, 1974.

Hopkins, Lee B. *Easter Buds Are Springing: Poems for Easter.* New York: Harcourt, Brace, Jovanovich, 1979.

Milhouse, Katherine. *Egg Tree.* New York: Scribner, 1950.

Roser, Wiltrud. *Everything About Easter Rabbits.* New York: T. Y. Crowell, 1979.

Wahl, Jan. *Old Hippo's Easter Egg.* New York: Harcourt, Brace, Jovanovich, 1980.

Weil, Lisl. *The Candy Egg Bunny.* New York: Holiday, 1975.

Books on Mother's Day

Eastman, Philip D. *Are You My Mother?* New York: Beginner, 1960.

Flack, Marjorie. *Ask Mr. Bear.* New York: Macmillan, 1958.

Fisher, Aileen. *My Mother and I.* New York: T. Y. Crowell, 1967.

Mayer, Mercer. *Just for You.* New York: Western, 1975.

Phelan, Mary K. *Mother's Day.* New York: T. Y. Crowell, 1965.

Schlein, Miriam. *Way Mother's Are.* Chicago: A. Whitman, 1963.

Books on Father's Day

Mayer, Mercer. *Just Me and My Dad.* New York: Western, 1977.

Raynor, Dorka. *This Is My Father and Me.* Chicago: A. Whitman, 1973.

Zolotow, Charlotte. *Father Like That.* New York: Harper and Row, 1971.

Books on Fourth of July

Flora, James. *Great Green Turkey Creek Monster.* New York: Atheneum, 1979.

Graves, Charles P. *Fourth of July.* New Cannan, CT: Garrard, 1963.

Phelan, Mary K. *Fourth of July.* New York: T. Y. Crowell, 1966.

Imagine the children's pleasure when a favorite storybook character suddenly appears in the classroom.

Puppet by the Puppet Factory

LANGUAGE ARTS

Language Arts is one of the most expansive areas in which to apply puppets and appeal to their many attributes for Puppetization activities. Stories come to life, songs take on tangible rhythms and poems sound of new tempos as puppets are woven into such activities. Most of all something quite special occurs through the addition of puppets. Both children and teacher have the opportunity to share the experience of entering into the magic domain of the theater, bringing to language arts a multi-dimensional aspect that includes color, shape and form, as well as action and words.

Stories

Everyone loves a story and a storyteller. When puppetry accompanies the telling of a tale, the whole atmosphere becomes charged with a new dimension of excitement. As an adjunct to the teller, the lead character may simply introduce the story or even act out focal scenes as the tale unravels. Children delight in this extra attraction, regardless of how modest the effort.

These guidelines may prove helpful:

● Concentrate on learning only the sequencing of major events. There is no need to memorize the entire story. In fact, for the sake of variety, you might want to change the story a little each time it is told.

● Have fun with the puppets and the story. Your sense of enjoyment will be highly infectious with the children.

● Consider those stories with relatively few characters and minimal dialogue.

● Choose stories in which action is a primary factor. Avoid stories that dwell on dialogue and will not sustain young children's interest.

Poems

Poetry is a natural language for young children. Often, when alone, they relish in the sound of their own words, turning them into rhymed and unrhymed verses. Children also like to listen to the poetry of others. At the mere mention of A. A. Milne's "Has Anybody Seen My Mouse?" a child I know immediately transforms into a little mouse, hiding engagingly around the room.

Remember there is a sense of magic about poems that carries over to the person who recites them. Poetry has a quality that draws an adult undefinably closer to a child. The appearance of a puppet enhances that closeness, bringing the poem within a touchable context that captures the child's imagination.

Songs

The purest form of rhythm in motion is portrayed by children as they run and skip, jump and play. It is the same rhythm manifest in songs that children joyfully sing themselves or listen to enraptured as others sing to them. For Puppetization, songs offer an excellent medium because there is a definite beat plus a built-in time-frame that prevents a story from dragging. Many teachers use records rather than singing themselves oftentimes because they lack self-confidence in the quality of their own voices. In so doing, they fail to realize that no matter how wonderfully performed a record may be, it can never convey the warmth and spontaneity of the teacher's own voice in singing directly to the children. Actually, children care little about pitch and tones. Instead, what they seek is a pleasurable experience that can be shared only through the spirit of your own voice. So be fearless, unplug your record player and sing out from the bottom of your heart!

The Bear Went Over The Mountain

Motivation: Ask the children "What things do you see in this room that you can go *over*?" "What can you think of outside on the playground that you can go *over*?" "Is there anything special at home that you like to crawl, jump or climb *over*?"

Puppetelling: Introduce a stuffed-toy-bear puppet to the children. Invite one child to be a "mountain" by forming a hill shape with his body. Ask everyone else to sing the song while the bear puppet goes over the "mountain." Change the second verse of the song by using one of the suggested lines below or by letting the children make up their own versions.

The Bear Went Over The Mountain

The bear went over the mountain,
The bear went over the mountain,
The bear went over the mountain,
    To see what it could see.

The other side of the mountain,
The other side of the mountain,
The other side of the mountain,
    Was all that it could see!

Alternative lines for what the bear might see on the other side of the mountain:

The tree that grows in the meadow . . .
The flowers that bloom in the springtime . . .
The mice that run in the fields . . .
The cats that stretch in the sunshine . . .
The ducks that swim in the river . . .
The bears that eat lots of honey . . .
The bees that buzz in the hive . . .

Puppetmaking: Let the children make bear puppets from paper bags or flat envelopes (See pages 157 and 166).

Puppetizing: Invite the children to the playing circle. Working in teams of two's, let one child be the "mountain" with the other enacting the bear puppet. Sing the song in unison as the children Puppetize the actions. Repeat, letting the "mountains" switch places with the "bears." Encourage the children to make different kinds of "mountains" with their bodies to be "climbed" in different ways. You can Puppetize other lines in the song by letting the children act out "trees that grow" and "flowers that bloom" when the "bear" crosses to the other side of the "mountain."

Stuffed Toy Bear

The Itsy-Bitsy Spider

Motivation: Ask the children "What is a water spout?" "Where do you see water spouts?" "What comes down and out of a water spout?" "What do you suppose could go inside and up the spout?"

Puppetelling: Introduce your Itsy Bitsy Spider puppet by having it peek out of your Story Apron for it is far too shy to crawl out! Say to the Spider puppet "Don't be afraid, these children are your friends. They're very gentle." This type of introduction will alleviate possible fears among younger children; it will also discourage aggressive behavior toward the puppet. Invite the children to sing the song with you. Hold up your arm and let the spider puppet crawl up and down. Hold up your arm as a spout. Let the children imitate falling rain with downward motions of their fingers and the sunshine with their arms in a circular shape.

The Itsy Bitsy Spider

The Itsy Bitsy Spider
Went up the water spout.
Down came the rain
And washed the spider out.
Out came the sun
And dried up all the rain.
And the Itsy Bitsy Spider
Went up the spout again.

238

A Glove Spider Puppet

Puppetmaking: Have the children make spider puppets from paper tubes (see Page 00).

Puppetizing: Invite the children to the playing circle. Reverse roles and let the children make "spouts" for their "spiders" by holding up an arm while you imitate the falling rain and sun as the song is sung in unison.

Old MacDonald Had A Farm

Motivation: Ask the children to close their eyes and imagine a farm. "What does your farm look like?" "What animals live on your farm?"

Puppetelling: Introduce yourself as "Old MacDonald." (If you have a farmer's hat, wear it!) Sing the song with the children while you pop up finger-puppet animals as they occur in the song, one by one.

Old MacDonald Had A Farm

Old MacDonald had a farm
Eei, eei, O.
And on the farm he had a _____
Eei, eei, O.

Puppetmaking: Ask the children to choose a farm animal and make a corresponding clothesline puppet (see Page 158) Encourage the children to think about what sounds the different farm animals make. Let them add as many kinds of animals as they can think of.

Puppetizing: Invite the children to the playing circle. Sing the song again but substitute the names of those animal characters made by the children. As the song progresses, have each child, one at a time, come forward and clip an animal onto a clothesline.

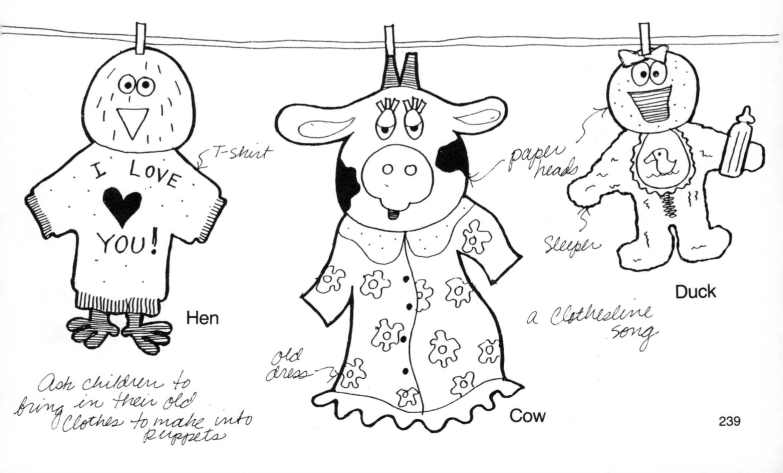

Hen

Cow

Duck

239

Variations: This song can be varied in many ways. For example:

Zoo Animals:
  Honolulu has a Zoo,
  Eei, eei, O.
  And in the Zoo there lives a _____ .
  Eei, eei, O.

Vehicles:
  Every city has a street,
  Eei, eei, O.
  And on the street I drive a _____
  Eei, eei, O.
  with a beep beep?
    toot toot?
    rum, rum?
    skid, skid?
    honk, honk?

Sing A Song of Sixpence

Motivation: Ask the children "What do you suppose a blackbird looks like?" Talk about blackbirds, kings, queens, maids and parlors so that the children will have a mental image of the meaning of the words in the song.

Puppetelling: Place your blackbird puppet in a pie pan and cover it with a circle of beige cloth. As you sing the song, have the blackbird puppet pop out of the pie "When the pie was opened." Let the blackbird puppet point to the king and queen on your Story Apron during appropriate times and snip off the maid's nose (put a velcro nose onto a hand or stand-up puppet). Or, a child can play the role of the "maid" and have her nose gently pulled.

Sing A Song Of Sixpence

Sing a song of sixpence
A pocket full of rye,
Four and twenty blackbirds
Baked in a pie.

When the pie was opened
The birds began to sing,
'Wasn't that a dainty dish
to put before the king!'

The king was in his counting house
Counting out the money;
The Queen was in the parlor
Eating bread and honey.

The maid was in the garden
Hanging out the clothes,
And along came a black bird
And pecked off her nose.

Royalty Story Apron

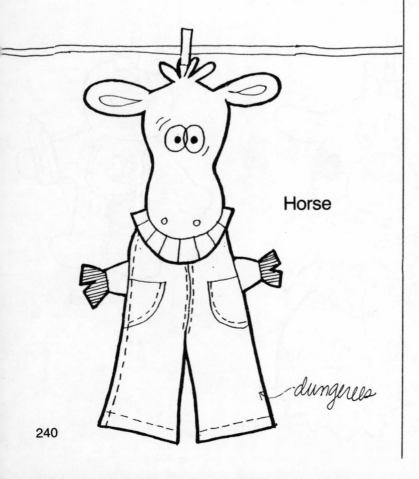

Horse

dungerees

240

Maid

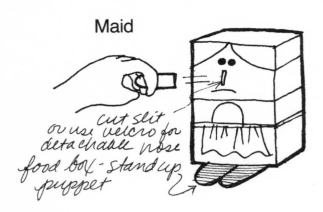

cut slit or use velcro for detachable nose
food box - stand up puppet

Puppetmaking: Have the children create Instant Puppets (see Page 161) by forming their hands into the shape of "blackbirds" and adhering eyes to the sides of their hands, using sticky-backed tape. Stick a real black feather or a paper feather on the top of their hands.

Puppetizing: As the group stands around a table, have each child put his hand in a super large pan covered with a large circle of beige cloth. Again sing the song and proceed with the same actions described above, choosing one child to be the "blackbird" that pecks off the "maid's" nose.

Six Little Ducks

Motivation: Encourage discussion about ducks with questions such as "Where do ducks live?" "Can you think of some words to describe how ducks walk?" "Why do you suppose ducks have feathers?"

Puppetelling: Using finger puppets let the children count the ducks on your glove then sing the song. When you come to the part in the song "But the one little duck with the feather on its back . . ." surprise the children by bringing out a large hand puppet duck with a big feather or plume on its back.

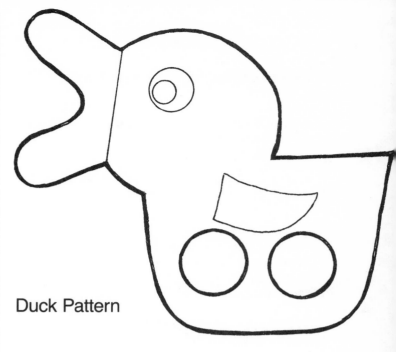

Duck Pattern

Six Little Ducks

Six little ducks that I once knew,
Fat ones, skinny ones, fair ones, too.
But the one little duck with the feather on its back
It leads the others with a Quack, Quack, Quack,
Quack, Quack, Quack
He leads the others with a Quack, Quack, Quack.

Down to the river they would go,
Widdle Waddle Widdle Waddle to and fro.
But the one little duck with the feather on its back
It leads the others with a Quack, Quack, Quack
Quack, Quack, Quack
It leads the others with a Quack, Quack, Quack.

Puppetmaking: Let the children make duck puppets using photo copies of the pattern.

Puppetizating: Place a low table in the middle of the playing circle. Drape a blue cloth over it or have the children paint a pond onto a piece of mural paper. While everyone sits around the playing circle, invite six puppeteers to come forward and sit around the table. Attach a feather to the tail of one of the duck puppets. Let everyone sing the song while the six puppeteers "waddle" their puppets around the table top pond.

The Beehive

Literature: Emilie Poulsson. *The Beehive*. New York: Lothrop, Lee and Shepard

Motivation: Ask the children "Do you like honey?" "How do you like to eat honey?" "Do you know what makes honey?" "Where do honey bees live and make their honey?"

Puppetelling: Velcro small felt "bees" to your glove. Make a fist "hive" and hide the bee puppets inside. Bring out your "hive" and Puppetell the rhyme. The children will be surprised when you open your fingers and one-by-one reveal the "bees."

The Beehive
By Emilie Poulsson

This is the beehive,
But where are the bees?
Hiding away where nobody sees.
Look they're coming out of the hive,
One, two, three, four, five.

Puppetmaking: Let the children make bee puppets with spring clothespins using pattern on Page 153.

Puppetizing: Ask the children to be seated around the playing circle. Invite five puppeteers to sit close together inside the circle. Give each puppeteer a number from one to five so they will know in what order to leave the "hive." Ask the remaining children to make a large "hive" with their bodies by embracing shoulders and forming a large circle to surround and cover the five "bee" puppeteers. Leave an opening for the puppeteers to get out.

Recite the poem and let the puppeteers "fly" their puppets out of the "hive" one-by-one while making buzzing sounds. Repeat this procedure until everyone has had a chance to be a puppeteer.

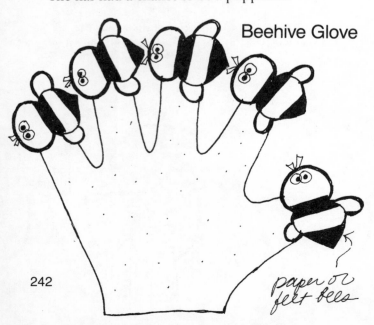

Beehive Glove

paper or felt bees

242

Five Little Monkeys

Motivation: Ask the children "What does teasing mean?" "Have you ever been teased?" "How does it make you feel?" "Is it sometimes fun to be teased?"

Puppetelling: Show the children your "tree" glove puppet with felt "monkey" faces velcroed onto the top part. Save your crocodile puppet for a surprise (see sock puppet pattern on Page 00). "These are my five monkey friends and I'd like to tell you what happened to them one day." Recite the rhyme with the "crocodile" biting a "monkey" off the tree each time. Drop each "monkey" face behind you or into the pocket of your Story Apron.

Five Little Monkeys

Five little monkeys sitting in a tree
Teasing Mr. Crocodile, "Can't catch me!"
(Crocodile enters quietly) "Snap!"

Four little monkeys sitting in a tree
Teasing Mr. Crocodile, "Can't catch me!"
(Crocodile enters quietly) "Snap!"

Three little monkeys sitting in a tree
Teasing Mr. Crocodile, "Can't catch me!"
(Crocodile enters quietly) "Snap!"

Two little monekys sitting in a tree
Teasing Mr. Crocodile, "Can't catch me!"
(Crocodile enters quietly) "Snap!"

One little monkey sitting in a tree
Teasing Mr. Crocodile, "Can't catch me!"
(Crocodile enters quietly) "Snap!"

No little monkeys sitting in a tree
I'd better watch out or he might get me!

Tree Mitt

velcro felt, paper or fur circle monkeys onto tree

felt Tree

arm

Idea by Loreen Yogi

Puppetmaking: Have the children make paper bag monkey puppets using the pattern below for faces. Let each child color and cut out a "monkey" face and attach to the flap of a bag.

Puppetizing; Ask a child to pose as a tree in the middle of the playing circle. Select five other children to be "monkeys" and pretend that they are up in the "tree" (they can cluster around). Invite the remaining children to repeat the rhyme while your crocodile puppet "eats" each "monkey" one-by-one. Return each child to her place in the playing circle as the monkey puppet is "eaten." Replay as long as interest is high.

Hey Diddle Diddle

Motivation: Ask the children "Can you think of something really silly that you would like to do? Something that nobody would believe?" or "Would you laugh if you ever saw a cow jump over the moon?"

Puppetelling: Recite the poem while making a cow puppet jump over a large yellow "moon" attached to your story Apron (see page 61). Or use a glove with a "moon" buttoned onto the palm and the "cat," "dog," "spoon" and "dish" as the fingerpuppet characters (see page 67).

Hey Diddle Diddle

Hey diddle diddle,
The Cat and the Fiddle,
The Cow jumped over the Moon.
The little Dog laughed,
To see such a sport,
And the dish ran away with the spoon.

Puppetmaking: For the cat, dog and dish characters, let the children construct Paper-Plate Rod Puppets (see Page 00). Use a real wooden spoon for the "spoon" character.

Puppetizing: Invite the children to the playing circle. Ask a child to form a round moon shape with his arms. Then ask the puppeteers to enact the poem with their puppets while you and the remaining children recite the verse. If the children construct duplicate puppets of the same character, simply repeat the poem until each child has had a turn using his puppet.

Two Little Blackbirds

Motivation: Use a word game in which you call out the names of animals, insects, birds and other creatures. Then ask the children to respond by describing how those creatures move. For example:

Kangaroos—Jump	Tigers—Run
Snakes—Slither	Spiders—Crawl
Horses—Gallop	Ducks—Waddle
Fish—Swim	Bunnies—Hop

This activity encourages the use of a broader, more precise vocabulary.

Puppetelling: Using your knees as the "hill," fly bird puppets (made of socks, envelopes or storebought birds on rods) behind your back and then out again, as you recite the poem.

Two Little Blackbirds

Two little blackbirds
Sitting on a hill,
One named Jack, One named Jill.
Fly away Jack, Fly away Jill,
Come back Jack, Come back Jill.

Puppetmaking: Divide the children into pairs and let each team decide what kind of creatures to make. Let them construct envelope puppets - see Page 157 and match the rhyme to their chosen puppets.

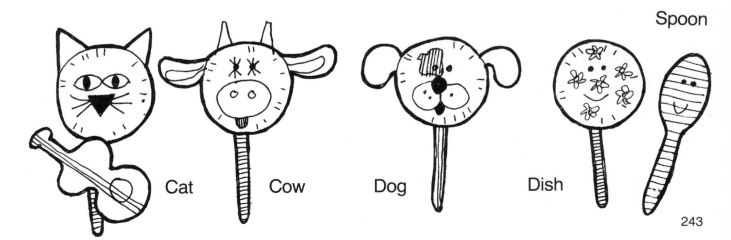

Cat   Cow   Dog   Dish   Spoon

243

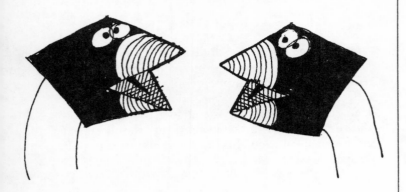

Puppetizing: Invite everyone to sit around the playing circle. Select someone to be the hill. Let the pairs of puppeteers say their rhyme while puppetizing their adapted rhymes and using the "hill" as the central prop. For example:

> Two little spiders sitting on a hill,
> One named Jack, One named Jill.
> Crawl away Jack, Crawl away Jill,
> Come back Jack, Come back Jill.

Other examples:

> Two little dogs jumping on a hill . . .
>
> Two little mice running up a hill . . .
>
> (and so forth)

The Gingerbread Boy

Motivation: Ask the children to describe their favorite cookies. "How do you make cookies?" "How do you decorate them?" "Close your eyes and imagine one right in front of you now. Smell it! Take a bite! Yummy!"

Puppetelling: Tell the story of *The Gingerbread Boy* using two hand puppets—a gingerbread boy and a fox. The remaining characters—the old man, old woman, cow, dog and cat—should be flat felt characters that you may velcro to your Story Apron as they occur in the tale (See page 61). Consider decorating your Apron with a "road" and "river."

Puppetmaking: Let the children make instant paper puppets. The Gingerbread Boy pattern is on page 161. An instant fix can be fashioned from the hand as shown below by adhering paper features with sticky-backed tape.

Puppetizing: Bring the children back to the playing circle; arrange each puppeteer around the perimeter. Ask the Gingerbread Boy to walk around the circle and have each character in turn chase him around the circle once. Finally the Fox gobbles him up!

Henny Penny

Motivation: Ask the children "If a little nut fell from a tree and hit you on the head and you didn't know it was a nut, what would you think? What would your imagination tell you it was?" Talk about things that can fall and hit you on the head such as leaves, pine cones, even coconuts!

Puppetelling: Tell the story using a Henny Penny hand-puppet and vecroed fingerpuppets for Ducky Lucky, Cocky Locky, Goosey Loosey, Turkey Lurkey and Foxy Loxy.

Puppetmaking: Let each child make one of the characters (except Henny Penny) using pointed Envelope Puppets- see Page 157.

Puppetizing: Invite the children to the playing circle. Select your cast of puppeteers and act out the story while you handle the Henny Penny puppet and lead the dialogue. Use the playing circle as the "road" with the puppeteers seated at intervals. The Henny Penny puppet should move from character to character as the story is told. Re-cast and repeat as long as interest remains high.

Gingerbread Boy

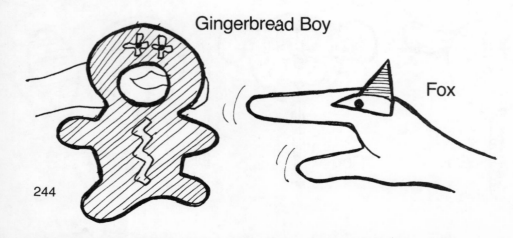

Fox

244

The Three Little Pigs

Motivation: Ask the children "Do you know what your house is made of?" "Can the wind blow it down?" "Why do you suppose your house is so strong?" (After hearing this story, some young children may fear their own houses may be easily destroyed. The motivation period is a good time to alleviate this possible fear.)

Puppetelling: Tell the story with pom-pom "pig" fingerpuppets velcroed onto your glove- see page 190, a "wolf" hand puppet of any type and three felt houses that can be velcroed onto your Story Apron (see page 61). Let the wolf "huff" and "puff" and "blow the house down" by taking each house, in turn, into his mouth and tucking it into the pocket of your Apron. Also, one of your pockets can be converted into a "big pot" (attach black felt pot shape to outside of pocket) for the "wolf" to fall into at the end of the story.

Puppetmaking: Let the children make string "pig" puppets from paper shapes(See page 170)or paper plates. Make three houses from boxes with tops cut off for the "pigs" to jump into as the story unravels.

Puppetizing: Invite the children to the playing circle. Let a little "pig" pretend to build a house and then climb inside before the "wolf" arrives. You should play the "wolf" in order to generate dialogue with the puppeteers and keep the story moving. Use a large pot for a cauldron for the "wolf" to fall into. After the children become familiar with the story, select one child to play the "wolf" using a string shape puppet.

The Little Red Hen

Motivation: Share with the group their various baking experiences. Did they ever share anything they or their parents baked before?

Puppetelling: Read the story *The Little Red Hen* while using a paper bag Red Hen (page 165) puppet character. Use a real piece of wheat, some flour, mixing bowl, spoon and loaf of bread for props. Other children can play the animal characters without puppets.

Puppetmaking: Direct the children to make their own body puppets (page 166) of the Red Hen and other characters.

Red Hen

paper feet

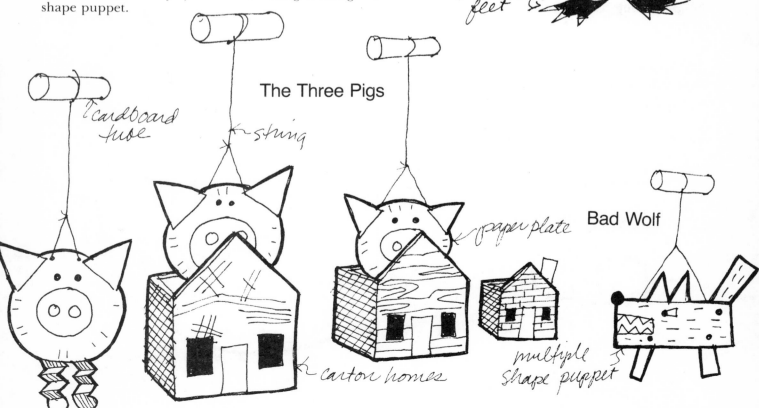

The Three Pigs

cardboard tube

string

paper plate

Bad Wolf

carton homes

multiple shape puppet

Puppetization: Invite the children to the playing circle and decide where to locate Max's room, the ocean and where the "wild things" live. Select one child to be Max and you play the role of his friend who comes to spend the night. In so doing, you can motivate dialogue and pace the sequencing of events. The addition of crowns made of construction paper to be worn by Max and his friend make the enactment even more exciting. Before the Puppetization begins, ask the remaining children to practice with their puppets "roaring terrible roars," rolling their eyes and showing ferocious claws. Because children love this story so much they may become overly-enthusiastic. Hence, you may wish to schedule its enactment just prior to recess or outdoor playtime.

Inch by Inch

Literature: Author/artist Leo Lionni. *Inch by Inch.* New York: Astor-Honor, 1960.

Motivation: Ask the children to use their hands and feet to measure various objects around the school. For example,

"How many feet long is the rug?"
"How many hands tall is the bookshelf?"
"How many hands wide is the window?"

Puppetelling: Using a green felt finger puppet or paper tube puppet, read the story, letting the children count the number of inches that the inchworm moves across the page.

Puppetmaking: Let the children make inch worms using a one by three inch piece of green construction paper. After decorating their puppets and taping them into tube shapes, encourage the children to wear them on their fingers and measure the many objects all over the school, both indoors and out.

Puppetization: Invite the children back to the playing circle. After putting on their Inchworm puppets encourage the children to measure their arms, legs, noses and other body parts. Then let them measure objects both in and outside the school environment. Work on the concept that things are measureable,

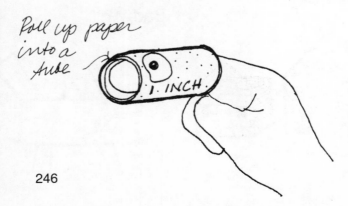

Roll up paper into a tube

Swimmy

Literature: Author/artist, Leo Lionni's. *Swimmy.* New York: Random House, 1963

Motivation: Begin the activity by asking: "Have you ever seen a large saltwater aquarium?" or "Did you ever swim in the ocean?" "What kinds of fish did you see there?" If possible, show pictures of various kinds of sealife and bring to the classroom shells for the children to touch.

Puppetelling: Introduce a black felt finger puppet of "Swimmy" and ask "What do you suppose might happen to a little fish like Swimmy in a great big ocean?" Read Leo Lionni's book *Swimmy* to the children and let your Swimmy puppet "swim" across the pages of the book.

Puppetmaking: Using both red and black construction paper, invite the children to cut out two identical fish puppets and glue them together with a straw rod between. By rotating their two-toned fish puppets they can take turns being "Swimmy" or part of the red fish.

Puppetization: Select one child to be "Swimmy." Repeat the story and at the end let all the puppeteers put their little fish together, red-sides out, to make the red fish. Each can take a turn being "Swimmy." If possible, snap a photograph of the children making the large red fish configuration so they may later see how their small fish contributed to the larger image. Or, let the children perform the Puppetization in front of a mirror.

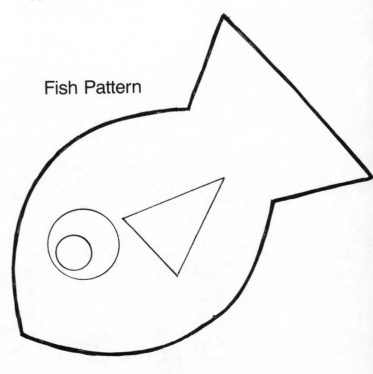

Fish Pattern

The Very Hungry Caterpillar

Literature: Author/artist, Eric Carle. *The Very Hungry Caterpillar*. New York: Philomel Books, 1969.

Motivation: If possible, bring a chrysalis to school to observe until the butterfly emerges. Or ask the children "Why do you suppose caterpillars eat so much?" "If you were a caterpillar what would you like to eat?" "If you could turn into a butterfly what colors would you like your wings to be?"

Puppetelling: Portray the story with a small chenille "caterpillar" and a larger sock "caterpillar-cocoon" with felt "butterfly" fingerpuppet surprise, tucked inside toe of sock. Hide this puppet in a pocket or other place. Begin story with chenille "caterpillar," and peek its head through the various holes of food depicted in book. Switch small "caterpillar" for larger caterpillar sock within story; as the story progresses turn the "caterpillar" sock slowly inside-out to form a "cocoon." Then pull out the "butterfly" fingerpuppet when it is time to appear in the story.

Puppetmaking:

Teacher Project:

(1) Use two different tube socks (without heels) of the same size, a decorative one striped or speckled for the caterpillar, and a plain white sock for the cocoon. Place the white sock inside the colored one and sew the cuff ends together by hand or with zig zag machine stitch. Decorate the colored sock to look like a friendly caterpillar,

(2) Make a butterfly fingerpuppet from two pieces of felt top-stitched together. Use felt strips for antennas; sew ¼ inch ribbon streamers to wings.

Child Project:
   Have children construct their own "butterfly" rod puppets using an array of colored construction paper, scrap fabric and trims. These puppets can be large and colorful and used later for a display.

Puppetizing: Ask the children to hide their butterfly puppets behind their backs. Repeat the story using the chenille and sock caterpillars as leads. When it is time for the "butterfly" to emerge, cue the children to hold up their butterflies. Extend this activity by letting the children move their butterflies about the room to graceful music.

Butterfly

Caterpillar

felt

pull butterfly out

turn sock inside out to create cocoon

247

Books on Nursery Rhymes

Alderson, Brian. (compiler) *Cakes and Custard: Children's Rhymes*. New York: Morrow, 1975.

Bailey, Nicola. *Nicola Bayley's Book of Nursery Rhymes*. New York: Knopf, 1977.

Briggs, Raymond. *The Mother Goose Treasury*. New York: Dell, 1980.

Chorao, Kay. (illus.) *The Baby's Lap Book*. New York: Dutton, 1977.

Gorsline, Douglas. (illus.) *Nursery Rhymes*. New York: Random, 1977.

Hillman, Priscilla. *A Merry-Mouse Book of Nursery Rhymes*. New York: Doubleday, 1981.

Himler, Ron. (illus.) *The Bedtime Mother Goose*. New York: Western, 1980.

Lobel, Arnold. *Gregory Griggs and Other Nursery Rhyme People*. New York: Greenwillow, 1978.

Marshall, James. (illus.) *James Marshall's Mother Goose*. New York: Farrar, Straus, and Giroux, 1979.

Mayer, Mercer. (illus.) *Little Monster's Mother Goose*. New York: Golden, 1971.

Opie, Iona and Peter Opie. *A Nursery Companion*. Oxford, ENG: Oxford Press, 1980.

Richardson, Frederick. (illus.) *Mother Goose*. New York: Rand McNally, 1981.

Rockwell, Anne. (illus.) *Gray Goose and Gander and Other Mother Goose Rhymes*. New York: T. Y. Crowell, 1980.

Scarry, Richard. (illus.) *Richard Scarry's Animal Nursery Tales*. New York: Golden, 1975.

Scarry, Richard. (illus.) *Richard Scarry's Best Mother Goose Ever*. New York: Western, 1970.

Sendak, Maurice. *Hector Protector and As I Went Over the Water*. New York: Harper, 1965.

Watson, Clyde. (illus.) *Father Fox's Pennyrhymes*. New York: Scholastic, 1971.

Wildsmith, Brian. (illus.) *Brian Wildsmith's Mother Goose: A Collection of Nursery Rhymes*. New York: Watts, 1964.

Books on Poetry

Belloc, Hilaire. *The Bad Child's Book of Beasts*. New York: Knopf, 1965.

Bennett, Jill. *Roger Was a Razor Fish*. New York: Lothrop, 1980.

Brooke, L. Leslie. *Johnny Crow's Party*. New York: Warne, 1907.

Ciardi, John. *I Met a Man*. Boston: Houghton Mifflin, 1961.

De Regniers, Beatrice S. *May I Bring a Friend*. New York: Atheneum, 1964.

Dickinson, Emily. *I'm Nobody! Who Are You? Poems of Emily Dickinson for Children*. Owing Mills, MD: Stemmer House, 1981.

Finlay, Ian H. *Going Barefoot*. New York: T. Y. Crowell, 1960.

Fujikawa, Gyo. (illus.) *A Child's Book of Poems*. New York: Grosset, 1981.

Fujikawa, Gyo. *Gyo Fujikawa's Come Follow Me to the Secret World of Elves, and Fairies and Gnomes and Trolls*. New York: Grosset, 1979.

Hillman, Priscilla. *A Merry Mouse Book of Favorite Poems*. New York: Doubleday, 1981.

Hopkins, Lee Bennett. *Elves, Fairies, and Gnomes*. New York: Knopf, 1980.

Lear, Edward. *The Owl and the Pussycat*. New York: Atheneum, 1977.

Lee, Dennis. (illus.) *Alligator Pie*. Boston: Houghton Mifflin, 1975.

Lee, Dennis. (illus.) *Garbage Delight*. Boston: Houghton Mifflin, 1977.

Milne, A. A. *Now We Are Six*. New York: Dutton, 1961.

Prelutsky, Jack. *The Queen of Eene*. New York: Greenwillow, 1978.

Sendak, Maurice. *Chicken Soup with Rice*. New York: Harper and Row, 1962.

Silverstein, Shel. *Giraffe and a Half*. New York: Harper and Row, 1964.

Silverstein, Shel. *Where the Sidewalk Ends*. New York: Harper and Row, 1974.

Stevenson, Robert Louis. *A Child's Garden of Verses*. New York: Western, 1951.

Tudor, Tasha. *First Poems of Childhood*. New York: Grosset, 1967.

Wallace, Daisy. (Ed.) *Giant Poems*. New York: Holiday, 1978.

Books on Songs

Beall, Pamela and Susan Nipp. *Wee Sing and Play: Musical Games and Rhymes for Children*. Los Angeles, CA: Price, Stern, Sloan, 1981.

Beall, Pamela and Susan Nipp. *Wee Sing: Children's Songs and Fingerplays*. Los Angeles, CA: Price, Stern, Sloan, 1979.

Bryan, Ashley. *Walk Together Children: Black American Spirituals*. New York: Atheneum, 1974.

Crane, Walter. *The Baby's Opera*. New York: Windmill, 1981.

Fowke, Edith. (compiler) *Sally Go Round the Sun: Three Hundred Children's Songs, Rhymes, and Games*. New York: Doubleday, 1970.

Ivimey, John W. *The Adventures of the Three Blind Mice*. New York: Scholastic, 1965.

John, Timothy. (Ed.) *The Great Song Book*. New York: Doubleday, 1978.

Poston, Elizabeth. *The Baby's Song Book*. New York: T. Y. Crowell, 1971.

Sendak, Maurice. *Maurice Sendak's Really Rosie: Starring the Nutshell Kids*. New York: Harper and Row, 1975.

Shoemaker, Kathryn. (illus.) *Children, Go Where I Send Thee*. Minneapolis, MN: Winston Press, 1969.

Thomas, Marlo. et al. *Free to Be . . . You and Me*. New York: McGraw, 1974.

Wilder, Alec. *Lullabies and Night Songs*. New York: Harper and Row, 1965.

Part IV

SOURCES OF MATERIALS

NANCY RENFRO STUDIOS

Puppet Characters

Mitt • Show • Media • Special Child

BOOKS In Paperback

Written Especially For
- Preschool and Elementary Teachers
- Librarians
- Youth Group Leaders
- Special Education Teachers
- Gifted Programs
- Art and Creative Dramatics

Puppetry In Early Childhood Education by Tamara Hunt and Nancy Renfro. Comprehensive resource for "Puppetization" of hundreds of new learning activites, Preschool through Grade 3. Easy-to-follow directions ranging from "Puppeteaching" to creative story and holiday activities with puppets.

Puppetry and the Art of Story Creation by Nancy Renfro. Excellent guide on "how-to" create a story with many simple puppet ideas for an integrated curriculum approach. Special section on puppetry for the disabled.

A Puppet Corner In Every Library by Nancy Renfro. Superb step-by-step guide for incorporating puppetry into the library for storytelling, loan-bags and setting up a puppet corner.

Puppetry and Creative Dramatics in Storytelling by Connie Champlin, illustrated by Nancy Renfro. Imaginative puppetry and creative dramatics activities for group participation based on children's stories.

Make Amazing Puppets by Nancy Renfro and Beverly Armstrong. Jammed packed with exciting ideas for making puppets from paper products and recycled junk.

Books, Puppets And The Mentally Retarded Student by John and Connie Champlin, illustrated by Carol A. Anderson. How to select and adapt books for telling stories; techniques for utilizing puppetry in programs. K-6.

Little Red Riding Hood (Script) by Athens Puppet Theatre. Charming, witty version of classical tale. Booklet includes patterns for making fabric puppets.

PUPPETRY WORKSHOPS
1002 Ways To Use Puppets Effectively

WRITE FOR FREE CATALOGUE:

1117 W. 9th Street, Austin, Tx 78703
(512) 472-2140

Organizations

PUPPETEERS OF AMERICA—National organization for the the betterment of puppetry, with membership from many parts of the world. Offers an annual Puppet Festival; a Puppetry Store for purchasing books and puppet items; a bi-monthly magazine; consultant services and affiliated guilds located around the country. A small membership fee is required. Write for information about your local puppet guild. Puppeteers of America, Gayle G. Schluter, Treasurer, #5 Cricklewood Path, Pasadena, CA 91107.

NATIONAL STORYTELLING RESOURCE CENTER—An organization specializing in exploring and upgrading the quality of storytelling techniques. Annual storytelling convention as well as a comprehensive resource center. National Storytelling Resource Center, P.O. Box 112, Jonesborough TN 37659.

ONTARIO PUPPETRY ASSOCIATION—A Canadian puppetry organization offering various activities and services. Kenneth McKay, Executive Secretary, 10 Skyview Crescent, Willowdale, Ontario M2J 1B8, Canada.

BRITISH PUPPET CENTRE—A British group offering various services. Write to: British Puppet Centre, Battersea Town Hall, Lavender Hill, London S.W.11, England.

Puppet Manufacturers

The following represents a wide assortment of puppet manufacturers across the country. Some of the companies sell wholesale and retail; others sell only wholesale requiring a minimal order ranging from $100 to $200. By writing for a free catalogue each company will forward their individual ordering policies and catalogue.

CLOTH CREATURES— A finely crafted line of adoring furry creatures with talking mouths. Of special interest is the Little People Lap Puppet (3 feet tall). Also makes custom puppets to order. Cloth Creatures, 281 E. Millan Street, Chula Vista, CA 92010

Child Guidance. This toy company puts out a line of the famed Sesame Street puppets in both hand and fingerpuppet types. Child Guidance. 41 Madison Ave. New York 10011

DAKIN & COMPANY— This well-known toy company has an extensive line of hand puppets and plush toys from an array of soft, cuddly fabrics, including most popular animals. Dakins, P.O. Box 7746, Rincon Annex, San Francisco CA 94120.

DOT DAWN— Sells a variety of puppet lines, retail, including Dakin, Furry Folks and a particularly lovable line of animals with super long arms for hugging. Dot Dawn, 324 County Line Road, Griffin GA 30223

DRAGONS ARE TOO SELDOM— Has a line of talking mouth hand puppets, some people, animals (Disco Duck, Abbey Deer and Lambie) and fantasy types. Dragons are too Seldom, 649 Main Street, Deadwood SD 57732.

FURRY FOLKS PUPPETS—Offers a selection of 23 cuddly furry wildlife creatures some of which have baby offsprings. Includes bears, seals, rabbits, squirrels and other woodland friends. Furry Folks Puppets, 1219 Park Avenue, Emeryville CA 94608.

HAPPY HOLLOW PUPPETS—Creates customized puppets, mascot puppets, and entire show kits to order as well as offering a standard line of popular fairy tale characters with cassettes and scenery sets. Happy Hollow Puppets, 324 Zorn Ave., Louisville, KY 40206.

L.K. HECHT CO., INC.—Specializes in a line of finger puppets. L.K. Hecht Company, Inc., 1140 Broadway, New York NY 10001.

LESWING PRESS—Kits for building reading, motor and speech skills. Includes a selection of hand and finger puppets for basic people, animals and fairy tales. Also carries Boris, Morris and Denny—large furry creatures. Leswing Press, P.O. Box 3577, San Rafael CA 94901.

LOLLY RUZOTARSKI—Features a "Dancing Bear" puppet kit with finger puppets and interchangable fairy tale scripts. Also carries soft sculpture body puppets and hand and rod puppets. Lolly Ruzotarski, 2019 N. Newhall Street, Milwaukee WI 53202.

MARY MEYER MFG. CO, INC.—Offers a large selection of stuffed toys and 36 hand puppet characters of basic people and animals. Included are community workers, hobo, indian, football player, owl and monkey. Mary Meyer Mfg. Co., Townshend, VT 05353.

NANCY RENFRO STUDIOS—Offers over 300 puppet characters! For use in storytelling, show production, library, special child and early childhood. All puppets are washable, durable and handcrafted. Includes almost every type of animal (gerbil, octopus, platypus, anteater, polar bear, shark, donkey are a few examples); Holiday and fairy tale characters; people puppets of varied flesh tones; show puppets with matching cassettes and scripts; and puppets designed for the special child. Nancy Renfro Studios 1117 W. 9th Street, Austin TX 78703.

PAKALUK PUPPETS—Stocks a colorful, well designed line of hand puppets featuring most popular animals (with cute talking sock mouths) and basic people (mexican, pirate, cowboy, fairy tale, etc.) Features large rod action puppets and a small sock puppet line that is especially appealing. Write to Pakaluk P.O. Box 129, Frericksbury TX 78624.

PLAYFUL PUPPETS, INC.—Carries a line of people puppets (in varied flesh tones) and numerous animal puppets (Booble Bird, Snider Spider and Thekla Turtle) with talking mouths. Playful Puppets, Inc. 4463 Charter Point Blvd. Jacksonville FL 32211.

POSSUM TROT—Markets an extensive line of cuddly, furry animal characters. Includes woodland creatures such as bunnies and opossums, Hee Haw characters, as well as a variety of other animals. Very appealing. Possum Trot, P.O. Box 249, McKee KY 40447.

POPPETS—Features a colorful doorway theater with a selection of 18 talking mouth, hand puppet characters.

252

Includes royalty, medical, clown, ant, elf, animals and people. Poppets, 1800 E. Olive Way, Seattle WA 98102

PUPPET PRODUCTION—Large scale talking mouth puppets with rod arms in basic people of varied flesh tones and animals. A professional type puppet for all uses they specialize in scripts and cassette media for puppetry ministry use. Puppet Productions, Inc., P.O. Box 82008, San Diego CA 92138.

REEVES INTERNATIONAL, INC.—Carries the famous German-made "Steiff" and "Kersa" brand puppets. Reeves International, Inc., 1107 Broadway, New York NY 10010.

RUSHTON—Stocks a wide range of stuffed toys and puppets made from soft, cuddly fur fabrics. Also carries a nice line of crocheted puppets and stuffed food characters. Write for local distributor: Rushton, 1275 Ellsworth Industrial Drive NW, Atlanta GA 30325.

SELF EXPRESSION—A puppetry educational media company that offers a wide variety of name brand puppets such as Furry Folks, Possum trot and others. Write to: Self Expression: 130 Boulevard, Mountain Lake NJ 07046.

Craft Suppliers

ZIMS—This mail order craft supply company sells retail all types of items, plastic eyes, glue, trims, pipe cleaners, etc. There is a four dollar charge (refundable upon first order of $20 or more) for a comprehensive book on all their items of excellent value to the ardent puppetmaker. Write to: Zim's P.O. Box 7620, Salt Lake City, UT 84107.

Stages and Equipment

PUPPET HARDWARE—Offers excellent stages to libraries, puppeteers and schools. Features portable and collapsible types as well as custom to individual needs. Constructed from steel piping. Puppet Hardware, 739 Ecton Road, Akron OH 44304.

GAYLORD BROS., INC.—Markets a lightweight, plastic corrugated small stage with window opening, ideal for a Puppet Corner or informal table-top performances. Order #L 104, Cost: $23.00. Write to: Gaylord Bros. Inc., Box 61, Syracuse NY 13201.

POPPETS—Features a colorful hanging doorway fabric stage. Poppets, 1800 E. Olive Way, Seattle WA 98102.

Recording

THE KING STREET RECORDING COMPANY—Offers custom recording, editing and duplication of tapes, cassettes, and 8-track cartridges. Poor recordings can be improved, and damaged recordings repaired. Com-

plete sound tracks with voices, music and sound effects can be created for plays, puppet shows and audio-visual presentations. Write or call: The King Street Recording Company, P.O. Box 402, Malvern PA 19355 (215) 647-4341.

Puppet Books

The following list of books is taken from an annotated list (condensed version) compiled by the Puppeteer's of America Bookstore. All items are quoted without postage and may be ordered from: The Puppetry Store, 14316 Sturtevant Road, Silver Spring, MD 20904.

ABC Puppetry, Vicki Rutter—A good reference book for the beginner. Information on making different types of puppets and stages. 77p. $5.95

Antique French Jumping Jacks, produced by Pellerin—11 easy-to assemble jumping jacks. They are printed on heavy stock and most of these colorful figures are modeled after the traditional characters in the Commedia dell' Arte. pap. $2.00

The Art of Making Puppets and Marionettes, Charlene Davis Roth—Covering finger puppets, hand puppets, ventriloquist's figures, and marionettes. Three short plays are also included. 198 p. pap. $6.95

The Art of the Puppet, Bil Baird—A record of puppets throughout the ages, covering all forms and types from all sections of the globe. 251 p. $19.95

Behind the White Screen, Sotiris Spatharis—Divided into two parts; his memoirs going back to the days before World War I and gives the main Karagiosis characters and schools of shadow puppetry. 150 p. $10.95

Bible Puppet Plays, Ewart A. & Lola Autry—Twelve puppet plays based on the lives of Old Testament characters. 133 p. pap. $2.95

Big Is Beautiful, Louise Glennie and Fran Dowie—Exciting ideas for "Giant Puppets," "body puppets" and other large puppets. 59 p. pap. $6.50

Books, Puppets and the Mentally Retarded Student, John and Connie Champlin—A unique book on cleverly integrating puppets and children's literature with the mentally retarded. 162 p. pap. $8.95

Bring on the Puppets, Helen Ferguson—Simple puppets for use in church or school teaching, including patterns. Six plays using various kinds of puppets, among them "The Christmas Story" and "The Story of Hannukkah." 31 p. pap. $3.25

Bunraku, Donald Keene—This large-size book has a text which "represents the most authoritative and penetrating study of Bunraku ever to appear in English." The sounds of Bunraku may be sampled by a record which is included along with the musical score for samisen and chanter. 287 p. $85.00

Bunraku, Donald Keene—This is a revised edition in paperback of the original hardbound work mentioned above. In addition to the text this edition has 22 black and white plates showing the puppets and puppet theater. 88 p. pap. $6.95

The Chinese Puppet Theatre, Sergei Obraztsov—An intimate and fascinating account of Obraztsov's visit to puppet theatres in China, and of his great interest in the puppeteers, the legends, and the staging of their shadow puppet plays. 55 p. Translated from the Russian by J.T. MacDermott $6.95

Creative Puppets in the Classroom, Mary Freericks with Joyce Segal—Shows how to bring spontaneity to the classroom through the use of puppets. Instructions are given for making imaginative puppets from inexpensive materials and it includes techniques for incorporating puppets into the curriculum. 144 p. pap. $5.95

Dictionary of Puppetry, A.R. Philpott—Technical, historical and biographical aspects of puppetry are covered in detail in this comprehensive handbook. 286 p. $11.95

Don't Just Stand There—Jiggle, Betty Jane Wylie—The 7 puppet plays in this book were written by a former Script Consultant for the P of A and they are all original, audience-tested, and written with humor. 223 p. pap. $9.95

The Dwiggins Marionettes, Dorothy Abbe—A comprehensive record of one man's experiments with the marionette puppet theatre. A large, beautiful book and a rich experience for the reader. 232 p. $29.95

Easy To Make Puppets, Frieda Gates—The appeal is to the very young would-be puppeteer. Clearly illustrated with many patterns for hand, hand and rod, simple marionettes, and shadow puppets. 47 p. $5.00

Easy To Make Puppets, Joyce Luckin—Over 20 puppets, mostly made of felt, are described. Both hand puppets and marionettes are shown, and one play is included. 47 p. $8.95

Easy To Make Puppets and How To Use Them: Early Childhood, Fran Rottman—Written for those who work with children 2 to 5 years of age, with emphasis on the use of puppets in the church, vacation Bible school, day camps, clubs, etc. Many patterns and illustrations. 96 p. pap. $3.95

Easy To Make Puppets and How To Use Them: Children & Youth, Fran Rottman—Emphasis is the same as in the book mentioned above, except with children of an older age group. 96 p. pap. $3.95

Eight Plays For Hand Puppets, edited by A.R. Philpott—Written by members of The Educational Puppetry Association in England. They are royalty-free and include such plays as "Punch and the Heartless Giant," "The Gingerbread Boy" and several original plays. 94 p. $7.95

Expert Puppet Technique, Eric Bramall and Christopher Somerville—A manual of production for puppeteers by two master puppet showmen, discussing scenic and puppet design, lighting, sound, movement, manipulation, writing plays and conducting rehearsals. 104 p. $7.95

Folding Paper Puppets, Shari Lewis and Lillian Oppenheimer—The techniques of Origami—the Japanese art of paperfolding, illustrated with clear step-by-step instructions. 90 p. pap. $2.95

Folk Puppet Plays For the Social Studies, Margaret Weeks Adair and Elizabeth Patapoff—Sixteen puppet plays suitable for schoolroom production have been adapted from American and other ethnic tales. 120 p. $12.50

Folk Tale Plays for Puppets, Lewis Mahlmann and David Cadwalader Jones—These 13 one-act plays are based on folk tales from countries around the world and include such favorites as Baba Yaga (Russia), Anansi and the Box of Stories (Africa), Uncle Remus Tales (United States), and Blue Willow (China). They are written to be performed with hand or rod puppets or marionettes. 142 p. $9.95

The Funcraft Book of Puppets, Violet Philpott and Mary Jean McNeil—Contains different ideas for "easy-to-make" puppets most of which could be made by an older child. Tips for staging, scenery, and sound effects are included. 45 p. pap. $2.95

Give Puppets a Hand, Violet Whittaker—A wide variety of scripts and includes basic instructions with illustrations and patterns, on how to get started in a puppet ministry. 104 p. pap. $4.95

Gustaf und sein Ensemble, Albrecht Roser—This book, by a world-renowned German puppeteer, contains both colored and black and white photographs of many of his puppets. Text is in German. Included also are instructions for making a scarf Marionette. 173 p. $16.00

History of the English Toy Theatre, George Speaight—Essential for those interested in the history of puppets, toys and English social life in the early 1800's. 224 p. $16.95

Holiday Plays For Puppets or People, Eleanor Boylan—Contains thirteen plays which include Aesop's fables, well-known fairy tales, original plays and Punch and Judy. 93 p. pap. $4.00

How To Do Punch and Judy, Sydney DeHempsey (Reprinted by Jay Marshall)—The complete Punch & Judy play, directions for making and using the characters. 106 p. pap. $4.00

Learning With Puppets, Hans J. Schmidt and Karl J. Schmidt—A guide to making and using puppets in the classroom. Stresses ways to enhance individual artistic expression and the acquisition of social and academic skills. 85 p. pap. $6.95

Learning With Puppets, David Currell—Technical directions are given for making all types of puppets. An excellent reference book for those past the stage of "easy-to-make," as well as those involved in education. 205 p. $15.95

The Magic of Puppetry: A Guide for Those Working with Young Children, Peggy Davison Jenkins—Aimed primarily at children 3 to 9 years old and has information on instant puppets, simple stages and manipulation. 142 p. pap. $5.95

Make Amazing Puppets, Nancy Renfro and Beverly Armstrong—Lots of very clever, easy-to-make puppets. All could be made by children and the clear drawings show the supplies needed, many different types and variations of these types. Some of the ideas given include trick puppets, puppets you can wear, cardboard marionettes and ways to stretch your imagination! 32 p.

254

pap. $3.95

Making Glove Puppets, Esmé McLaren—Many full size patterns (mostly animals). Includes full instructions on cutting and sewing the puppet, and on designing clothes and accessories. 218 p. $12.95

Making Puppets Come Alive, Larry Engler and Carol Fijan—A must for those learning manipulation with hand puppets. A method of learning and teaching hand puppetry, which has been called "The Stanislavsky of the hand puppet world." Good puppet theatrical technique, including voice use, improvisation, role characterization and other fundamental elements are covered. 191 p. $9.95

Les Marionettes Des Papier, Eric Merinat—Written in French, this amusing book is easy to understand. Simple patterns and drawings make up most of the book. A real challenge for adults and children. 95 p. pap. $4.00

Marionettes: How To Make and Work Them, Helen Fling—A complete book of marionette craft. One play is included. 185 p. pap. $3.00

Marionettes on Stage, Leonard Suib and Muriel Broadman—The book is divided into three major parts: "The New Marionette;" "Becoming a Puppeteer;" and "Puppet Theater Management." 243 p., 83 line drawings, 33 photos $16.95

Mime and Masks, Roberta Nobelman—Varieties of mime and techniques for making them work are offered along with ways to use masks. Five scenarios of mime and mask plays. 152 p. pap. $5.95

Modern Puppetry, A.R. Philpott—The making and operating of many kinds of puppets are covered with in-depth sections on characterization, shadow puppets, plasticine heads, rod puppets and marionettes. 128 p. $7.95

Monkey King: A Celestial Heritage—A catalog of an exhibit which was "An Introduction to Chinese Culture through the Performing Arts." The section on puppets contains many photographic examples of historical Chinese puppets with a description of each. 63 p. pap. $5.00

More Practical Puppet Plays, Irvy Gilbertson—Contains 17 puppet scripts to be used for children to teach everyday applications of Bible Scripture. 64 p. pap. $2.50

More Puppets With Pizazz, Joy Wilt and Gwen and John Hurn—50 ideas for rod, novelty and string puppets children can make and use. Includes patterns. 159 p. pap. $5.95

Needlework Puppets, Brenda Morton—A detailed pattern and instruction book for the making of some twenty hand puppets. 136 p. $6.95

Playing With Puppets, Liz Paludan—An excellent book for colorful fabric puppets. Primarily on the making and manipulation of hand puppets, it also includes many patterns, material on rod puppets, stages, scenery, and seven short plays. 144 p. $8.95

Plays For Puppet Performance, George Merten—Ten original scripts of puppet plays which can be performed with hand puppets or marionettes. 90 p. $9.95

Practical Puppet Plays, Irvy Gilbertson—17 short scripts for children ages 2–12 which include a Bible reference.

61 p. pap. $2.50

Punch and Judy, George Speaight—An excellent history as well as delightful reading. Chapters on Punch in America, as well as folk heroes of the European stage. 160 p. $14.95

The Puppet Book, Wall, White and Philpott—Discusses all forms of puppetry, all types of construction, plus chapters on plays and production. A couple of short hand puppet plays are included. 300 p. $9.95

Puppet Circus, Peter Fraser—Instructions for the traditional circus puppets, plus old toy puppets. 153 p. $7.95

The Puppet People, Pat Zabriskie—17 short skits in this book are all based on Bible truths and could be used for Sunday Schools or Vacation Bible Schools. 63 p. pap. $2.95

Puppet Shows That Reach and Teach Children, Joyce Reynolds—For teachers who want to present Bible truths using puppetry. Each volume includes 10 hand puppet stories, handcraft projects and a puppet theater pattern. pap.

    * Vol. 1 Parables of Jesus $2.95
    * Vol. 2 Life of Jesus $3.50
    * Vol. 3 Book of Acts $3.50

Puppet Stages and Props With Pizazz, Joy Wilt and Gwen and John Hurn—Very interesting ways to make simple stages and props for or with children. Lighting and simple puppet costumes are also explained. 140 p. pap. $5.95

The Puppet Theatre of Asia, J. Tilakasiri—Includes literary and critical estimates of the art, performances seen in villages and cities, and meetings and discussions with puppeteers, puppet makers, designers and directors. 166 p. $10.95

A Puppet Theatre of Japan, A.C. Scott—A "must" for the student of the Bunraku. It traces the history of Bunraku from its earliest days to the present. Includes a description and summary of ten popular Bunraku plays. 163 p. pap. $3.50

The Puppeteer's Library Guide, J. Frances Crothers—Vol. 1: The Historical Background—Puppetry and its Related Fields. The first volume of a projected six volume set, this unique reference work would be an asset to any library or the individual doing research in puppetry. Included in the vast amount of material are bibliographies of puppet literature, and material on organizations and publications devoted to puppetry. 474 p. $19.00

Puppetry and Creative Dramatics in Storytelling, Connie Champlin—Simple puppetry and creative dramatics are used to bring storytelling sessions to life. Ideas are given for group participation based on traditional and modern children's stories. Teachers, librarians or storytellers can use the suggestions for sound effects, music, action and pantomime with children from pre-school to 12 years old. 132 p. pap. $9.95

Puppetry and the Art of Story Creation, Nancy Renfro—This book is full of wonderful ideas for creating a story to be used with puppets. There are original and clever ideas for simple puppets along with a very complete list

255

of sources of material and information. The section on puppetry for the special child includes those who are physically disabled as well as those who are hearing and visually impaired. 166 p. pap. $9.95

Puppetry for School Children, David Currell—The sections include: Why do puppetry? Writing the script; Hand, Sock and Rod puppets; The Marionette; a Simple Stage and much more. 80 p. $5.95

Puppetry In Canada—An Art To Enchant, Kenneth B. McKay—An authoritative study of contemporary Canadian puppetry and it is illustrated with over 80 large, clear black and white photographs of the work of leading Canadian puppeteers. 168 p. $14.95

Puppetry In The Teaching of Foreign Language, Mary Nadjar Weinstein—Teaching and learning of foreign languages is a performing art. Theory is explained in the first section and the remainder of the book is devoted to "Three French Workshops on Stage," each of which contains a small play or dialogue. 38 p. $5.00

Puppetry, The Ultimate Disguise, George Latshaw—Many aspects of the puppet theatre are discussed, including design, voices and sound effects, characterization, stages and playwriting. Excellent for older students and college level puppetry. 158 p. $12.50

Puppets, Barbara Snook—Clear drawings and precise instructions give information on hand puppets, their costumes and stages. Marionettes are dealt with in even greater detail. 94 p. $5.95

Puppets and Therapy, edited by A.R. Philpott—Brings together innovative ideas and experiments for the use of puppets and puppetry with the physically handicapped and the emotionally and mentally impaired. 153 p. $5.95

Puppets For All Grades, Scott, May and Shaw—Various types of puppets constructed from simple materials. Very useful for teachers. Class projects made easy. 48 p. pap. $2.45

Puppets For Beginners, Moritz Jagendorf—Imaginative and colorful pictures help beginners create and use hand puppets and marionettes, make the stage and costumes. Recommended for age 7–12. 68 p. $7.95

Puppets For Dreaming and Scheming, Judy Sims, illustrated by Beverly Armstrong—Excellent for the teacher. What To Do with Puppets in the Classroom. A wide range of simple ideas are presented, as well as more specialized instructional and performing methods. 157 p. pap. $8.95

Puppets For the Classroom, Alison Vandergun—Puppets are designed to be quick and simple to make, and easy to teach. A loose folded sheet of patterns is included. 34 p. pap. $3.00

Puppets From Polyfoam: Sponge-Ees, Bruce Chessé and Beverly Armstrong—Special emphasis on construction, this book features guidelines for using polyfoam to construct quick and interesting hand puppets with glue or staple gun. Good for the young and the adult puppeteer. 37 p. pap. $3.95

Puppets Go To Church, Earl and Wilma Perry—Gives the "How-To's" of puppetry and then shares nineteen scripts which the authors have used with their handmade puppets and screens. 87 p. pap. $1.95

Puppets in Phonics and Reading, Charlotte Kohrs—The book's subtitle, "Nine ways to use puppets to build language skills and confidence" gives the purpose of the book. This is achieved through selected sounds, phrases and sentences incorporated into easy "I read/You read" dialogues, choral verse, and puppet plays. 83 p. pap. $3.50

Puppets With a Purpose, K.F. Hughes—Ideas, patterns and activities are given for many simple puppets made from easily found materials. Great ideas for those who work with children. 23 p. pap. $2.00

Puppets With Pizazz, Joy Witt and Gwen and John Hurn—52 Finger and Hand puppets children can make and use. 159 p. pap. $5.95

A Puppet Corner In Every Library, Nancy Renfro—Librarians everywhere are realizing that there is something quite extraordinary about puppets and that children's services can benefit from their use. A puppet on the hand of a sensitive person becomes an invaluable tool of communication, and on the hand of a child, an extension of his thoughts and feelings. Contains pictures, patterns, articles and resource list. 110 p. pap. $7.95

Puppet Making Through The Grades, Griseila Hopper—A book for young people, teachers, and others who work with children. Paper bags, boxes, socks, balloons, styrofoam and many other everyday items combine to form appealing puppets. 64 p. $6.95

Puppet Plays For Young Players, Lewis Mahlmann and David Cadwalader Jones—Twelve fast-paced scripts include original plays, adaptations, dramatizations, even spoofs on familiar fairy tales, legends and classics. 194 p. $9.95

Puppet Plays From Favorite Stories, Lewis Mahlmann and David Cadwalader Jones—A collection of 18 one-act, royalty-free puppet plays adapted from famous stories and fairy tales for production by young people. 204 p. $9.95

Puppet Scripts For Children's Church, Jessie P. Sullivan—In these scripts, Mortimer and Mathilda Puppet teach each other (and their audience) Bible verses, and apply Bible truths to the everyday situations children frequently encounter. 111 p. pap. $2.95

Puppet Theatre Handbook, Marjorie Batchelder—Covers practically every phase of puppet construction and production, bringing together contributions of technical knowledge from more than 50 outstanding puppeteers. Includes bibliography and materials supplement. 293 p. $9.95

The Puppet Theatre In America, Paul McPharlin, supplement by Marjorie McPharlin—An authentic and complete history of the growth of the puppet art in America. Many rare and unusual prints in the original text. 734 p. $13.95

Puppet Theatre In Performance, Nancy H. Cole—A valuable book for anyone interested in puppetry. In addition to giving a lively history of puppet theatre, it covers pertinent topics for adapting the essential theatre arts to the special needs of the puppet theatre. 272 p. $14.95

Putting It All Together In a Puppet Ministry, Fredda Marsh—This "how-to" manual tells how to present plays for children and organize a puppet ministry in your church. There are about 20 scripts based on Bible truths, each of which lasts 5 minutes. 144 p. pap. $6.95

Self-Supporting Scenery, James Hull Miller—Well-illustrated technical workbook with detailed information on the elements of stagecraft. Although not directly related to puppetry, this booklet might give you some imaginative staging ideas to use with puppets. 111 p. pap. $4.00

Shadow Images Of Asia, Bettie Erda—A selection of shadow puppets from The American Museum of Natural History are shown from China, India, Thailand, Malaysia, Java and Bali. 47 p. pap. $4.00

Shadow Plays, Edited by Betsy Stott—Directions are given for performing four authentic Asian shadow plays from China, India, Java and Thailand. Also included are directions for making shadow puppets and a simple shadow screen. 20 p. pap. $1.50

Shadow Puppetry For the Church School, Elain Carlson—Complete patterns and instructions for presenting four Bible stories with shadow puppets. Scripts are included for "The Birth of Jesus," "The Sower and the Seed," "The Good Samaritan," and "Jesus Beside the Sea." 24 oversize p. pap. $2.95

Shadow Puppetry on the Overhead Projector, Janibeth Johnson—A detailed, technical and somewhat complex description of this type of projection of shadow images that approach the quality of animated film. Many helpful tips on making shadow puppets and an invaluable list of equipment and materials. 20 p. $3.75

Shadow Puppets in Color, Louise Cochrane—For the beginner in shadow puppetry. Diagrams, patterns, and directions for staging and musical effects. Three shadow plays are included. A Chinese legend, a play from the Greek shadow theater, and a Hindu-Japanese legend. 48 p. $5.95

Shadow Puppets, Shadow Theatres and Shadow Films, Lotte Reiniger—The most complete book on shadow puppetry available. Describes the history of shadow theater, how to produce shadow shows and films, including animation, photography and synchronization of the sound track. 28 p. $10.00

Sir George's Book of Hand Puppetry, George Creegan—For the beginning puppeteer. Directions for making and manipulating hand puppets and rod puppets. Contains his adaptations of the play, "The Night It Rained Toys." 94 p. pap. $2.98

Space Age Puppets and Masks, M.C. Green and B.R.H. Targett—An up-to-date emphasis on puppet making for the older child. This book is useful for home or school as the puppets are made from easily found objects. $7.95

Tabletop Theaters and Plays, Louise Cochrane—Instructions are given for making model theaters of the past and present—an Elizabethan stage, an open stage, Punch and Judy, and the picture-frame design. Short scripts are given to use with the stages. $5.95

Teaching Bible Stories More Effectively With Puppets, Roland Sylwester—Step-by-step instructions for simple to more advanced hand puppets, shadow puppets, and marionettes, as well as twelve Bible story-based scripts with stage directions. 64 p. pap. $2.50

Traditional and Folk Puppets of the World, Michael R. Malkin—Among the many types of puppet theaters discussed are the shadow theater of China; the "temes nevinbur" of New Hebrides; the Bunraku of Japan; the Karagoz of Turkey and Punch and Judy in Europe and America. 224 p. $12.00

Ventriloquism, Darryl Hutton—For the beginning ventriloquist. "How to put on an act, use the power of suggestion, and make your own dummy." 128 p. $6.95

The Voices and Hands of Bunraku, Barbara Curtis Adachi—Deals with people of Bunraku—the narrators, the musicians, the puppeteers, and the unseen others, who carry on this highly developed puppet drama, a three hundred year old art. 148 p. $19.95

The Wonderful World of Puppets, Günter Bohmer—A beautiful book written by the Manager of the Puppet Collection of the City of Munich, Germany. An historical treasury of beautiful puppets, named, dated and described. 156 p. $9.95

Wood Spoon Puppets, Audrey Vincente Dean—Using wooden spoons for the construction of puppets. Detailed, well illustrated instructions are given for making twelve puppets, a simple stage, and two short plays. 92 p. $10.95

You Can Be a Puppeteer, Carolyn London—Describes various types of puppets for Christian education and how to make them. Several plays are included. 124 p. pap. $2.95

Pamphlets

Black Theatre, Coad Canada Puppets—This theatrical staging technique, relatively new to North America, is well explained and clearly diagrammed. 21 p. $3.00

Classroom Stages, Coad Canada Puppets—Detailed plans and explanation of five different stages. Most of the stages fold for storage. 22 p. $3.00

A Manual Of Hand Puppet Manipulation, Lettie Connell Schubert—So little has been written on this subject that not only beginners in hand puppetry, but even "experienced" puppeteers would benefit from the experiments and exercises suggested. 15 p. $3.00

Mouth Puppets, Bob Conrad—Actual size patterns for bird and animal puppets. 21 p. $4.50

Music For The Puppet Theater, Lewis Mahlmann and Leonard Suib—A list of many musical works and their composers is given in this reprint from "Marionettes Onstage." These are grouped by categories such as Love, Mystery, Animals, Humor, etc. Also included are the legal aspects of using music. 12 p. $2.50

Publicity For The Puppeteer, Sey Roman—While the emphasis of this manual is mainly on Guild publicity, it is valuable for any puppeteer interested in promotion. It includes information on writing news releases, on distributing publicity and on radio and television publicity. 35 p. $4.95

Puppet Theatre Management, Coad Canada Puppets—Outlines step by step the business operation involved in a successful puppet theater. 25 p. $3.00

Puppetry in the Classroom, Carol Sterling—This manual will help teachers use puppets for creative expression and curriculum development. 35 p. $1.00

Puppetry Workshop Manual, Conrad R. Woyce—Actual size patterns for making several types of hand puppets, animal puppets, mouth (or Muppet) -type puppets, rod puppets and marionettes. 28 p. patterns. $4.50

Puppets For Schools, Coad Canada Puppets—Provides teachers with instructions for making a wide range of functional puppets from materials that are reasonably easy to obtain and simple to handle. Includes diagrams and patterns. 20 p. $2.50

Rod Puppets, Coad Canada Puppets—Clear and precise diagrams and illustrations with tips on fabrics, paints, and other materials to make rod puppets. 11 p. $2.00

Script-Writing Workbook, Judy Brown—This workbook lets you write a puppet play for any type of puppet from your own imagination. A series of questions along with your own answers leads you from the first idea through style, characterization, action and dialogue. 25 p. $4.00

Shadow Puppet Know-How, Betty Polus—A pamphlet packed with information of the fundamentals of shadow puppet materials and techniques. Alternate methods of modern construction and control are explained, and variations are shown in the traditional methods of shadow puppetry—the Chinese, Japanese, and the Turkish. 27 p. $3.50

Start With A Balloon, R.C. (Nick) LeFeuvre—A step-by-step explanation of the method used in making puppet heads using a balloon as a base, each step clearly and fully illustrated. 12 p. $.65

Using Puppets in Schools, Coad Canada Puppets—The emphasis in this publication is on the effective use of hand puppets in a school situation rather than on puppet construction. Exercises to strengthen the puppeteers' hands, suggestions for voice, for characterization and for improvement of all phases of hand puppet manipulation. 16 p. $3.00

INDEX